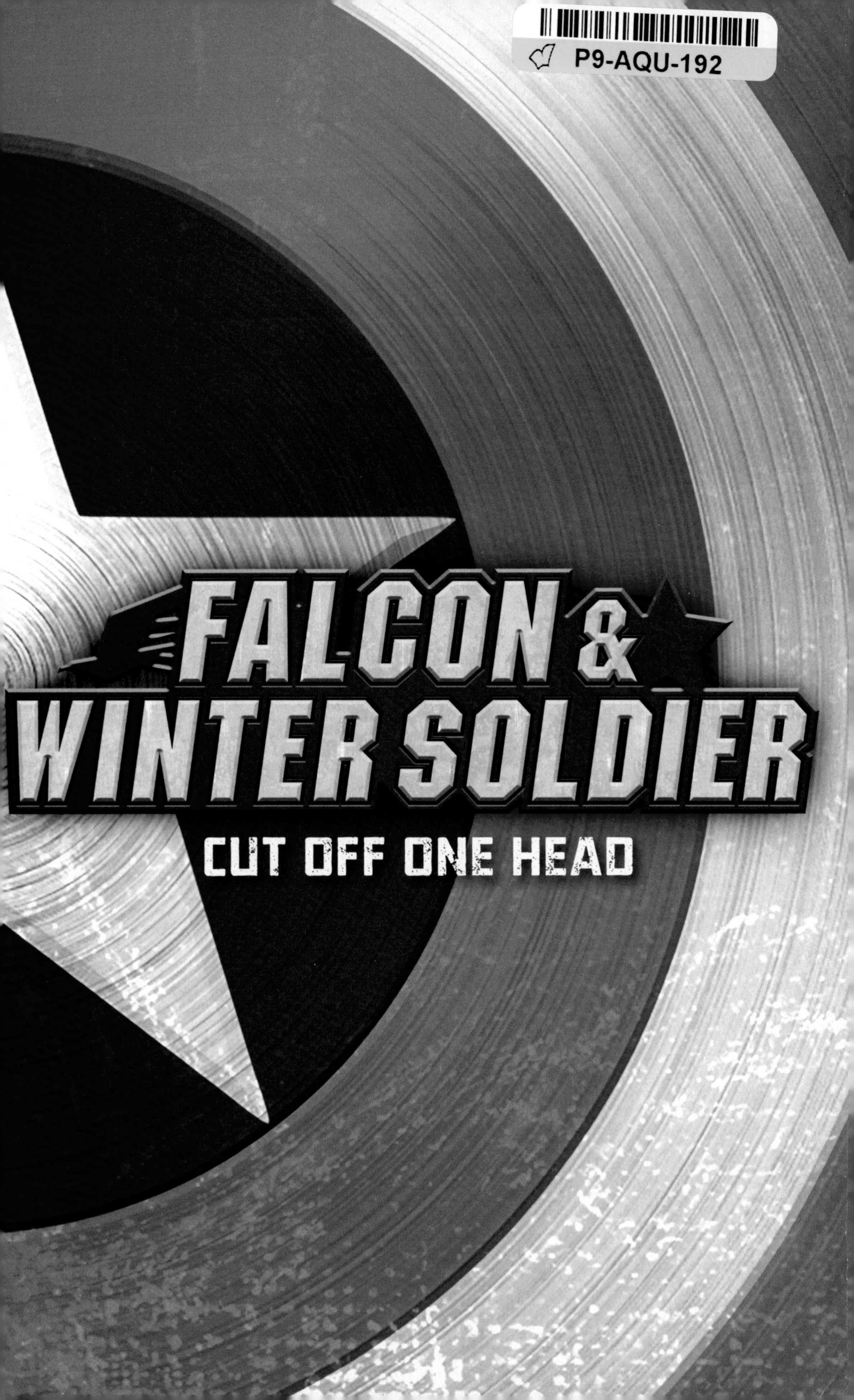
FALCON &
WINTER SOLDIER
CUT OFF ONE HEAD

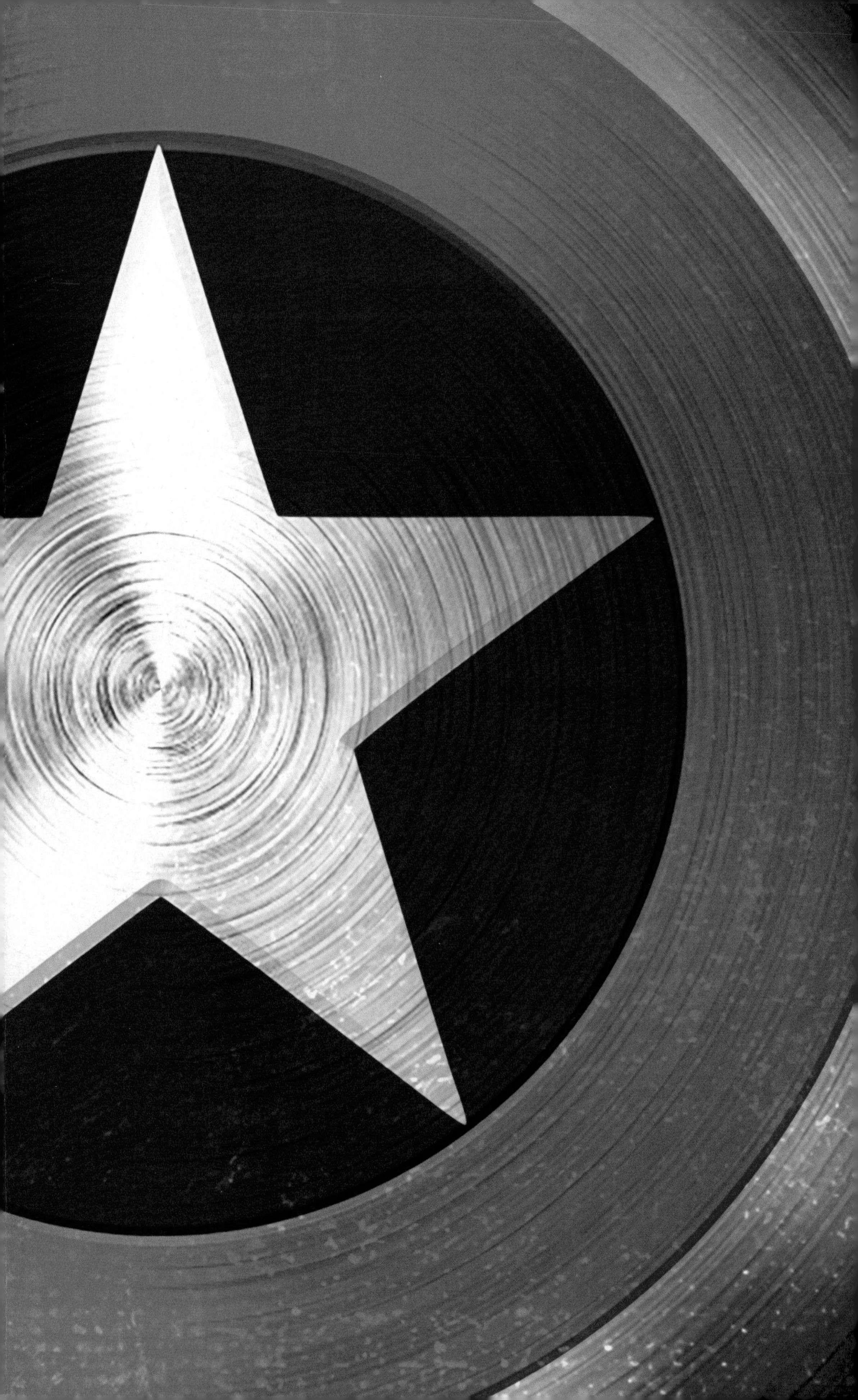

FALCON & ★ WINTER SOLDIER

CUT OFF ONE HEAD

DEREK LANDY
WRITER

FEDERICO VICENTINI
ARTIST

MATT MILLA
COLOR ARTIST

VC'S JOE CARAMAGNA
LETTERER

DAN MORA & DAVID CURIEL
COVER ART

SHANNON ANDREWS BALLESTEROS & MARTIN BIRO
ASSISTANT EDITORS

ALANNA SMITH
EDITOR

BUCKY BARNES CREATED BY **JOE SIMON & JACK KIRBY**

COLLECTION EDITOR: **JENNIFER GRÜNWALD**
ASSISTANT EDITOR: **DANIEL KIRCHHOFFER**
ASSISTANT MANAGING EDITOR: **MAIA LOY**
ASSISTANT MANAGING EDITOR: **LISA MONTALBANO**

VP PRODUCTION & SPECIAL PROJECTS: **JEFF YOUNGQUIST**
BOOK DESIGNER: **STACIE ZUCKER**
SVP PRINT, SALES & MARKETING: **DAVID GABRIEL**
EDITOR IN CHIEF: **C.B. CEBULSKI**

FALCON & WINTER SOLDIER: CUT OFF ONE HEAD. Contains material originally published in magazine form as FALCON & WINTER SOLDIER (2020) #1-5. Third printing 2021. ISBN 978-1-302-92309-9. Published by MARVEL WORLDWIDE, INC., a subsidiary of MARVEL ENTERTAINMENT, LLC. OFFICE OF PUBLICATION: 1290 Avenue of the Americas, New York, NY 10104. © 2020 MARVEL No similarity between any of the names, characters, persons, and/or institutions in this book with those of any living or dead person or institution is intended, and any such similarity which may exist is purely coincidental. **Printed in Canada.** KEVIN FEIGE, Chief Creative Officer; DAN BUCKLEY, President, Marvel Entertainment; JOE QUESADA, EVP & Creative Director; DAVID BOGART, Associate Publisher & SVP of Talent Affairs; TOM BREVOORT, VP, Executive Editor; NICK LOWE, Executive Editor, VP of Content, Digital Publishing; DAVID GABRIEL, VP of Print & Digital Publishing; JEFF YOUNGQUIST, VP of Production & Special Projects; ALEX MORALES, Director of Publishing Operations; DAN EDINGTON, Managing Editor; RICKEY PURDIN, Director of Talent Relations; JENNIFER GRUNWALD, Senior Editor, Special Projects; SUSAN CRESPI, Production Manager; STAN LEE, Chairman Emeritus. For information regarding advertising in Marvel Comics or on Marvel.com, please contact Vit DeBellis, Custom Solutions & Integrated Advertising

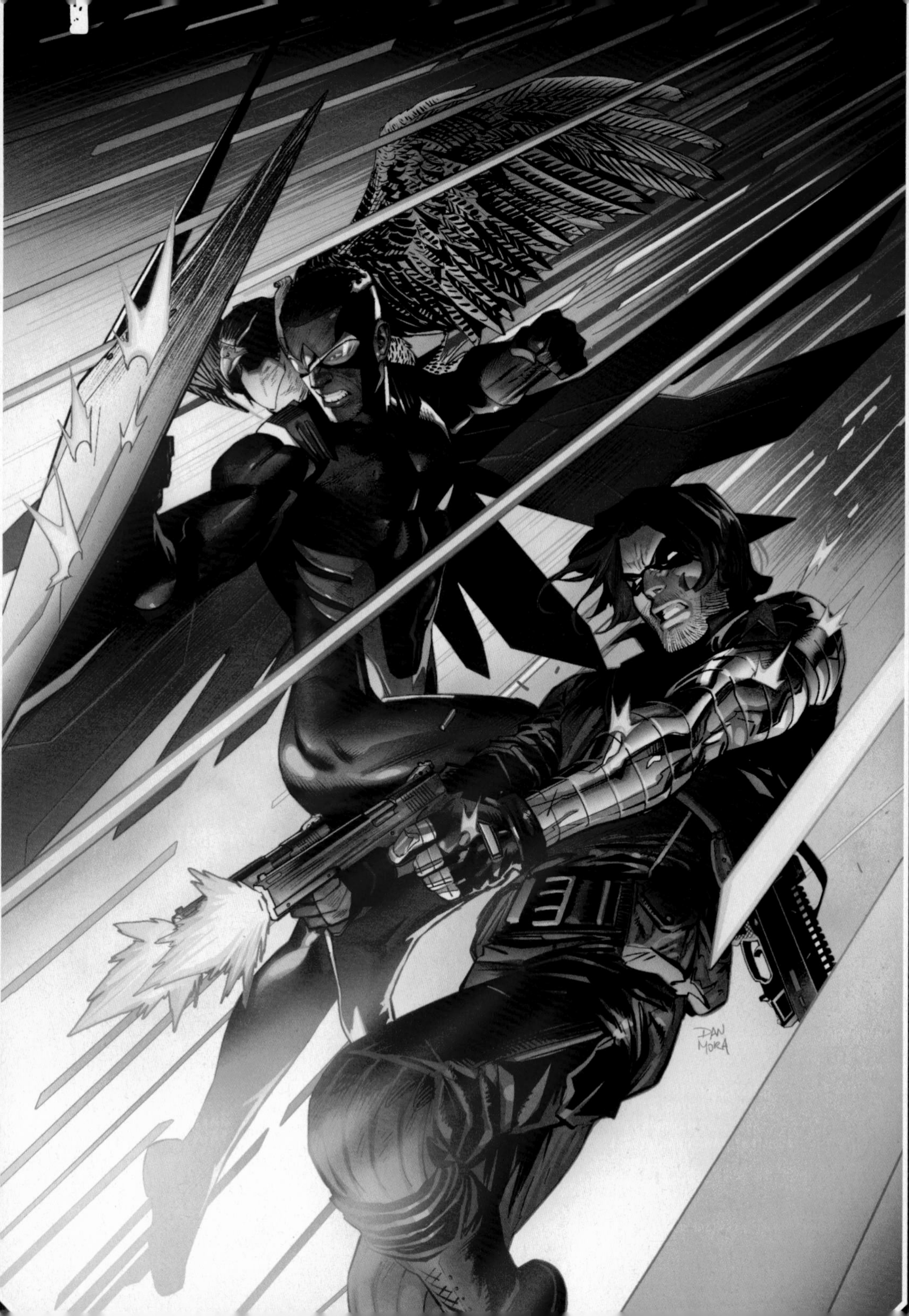
DAN
MORA

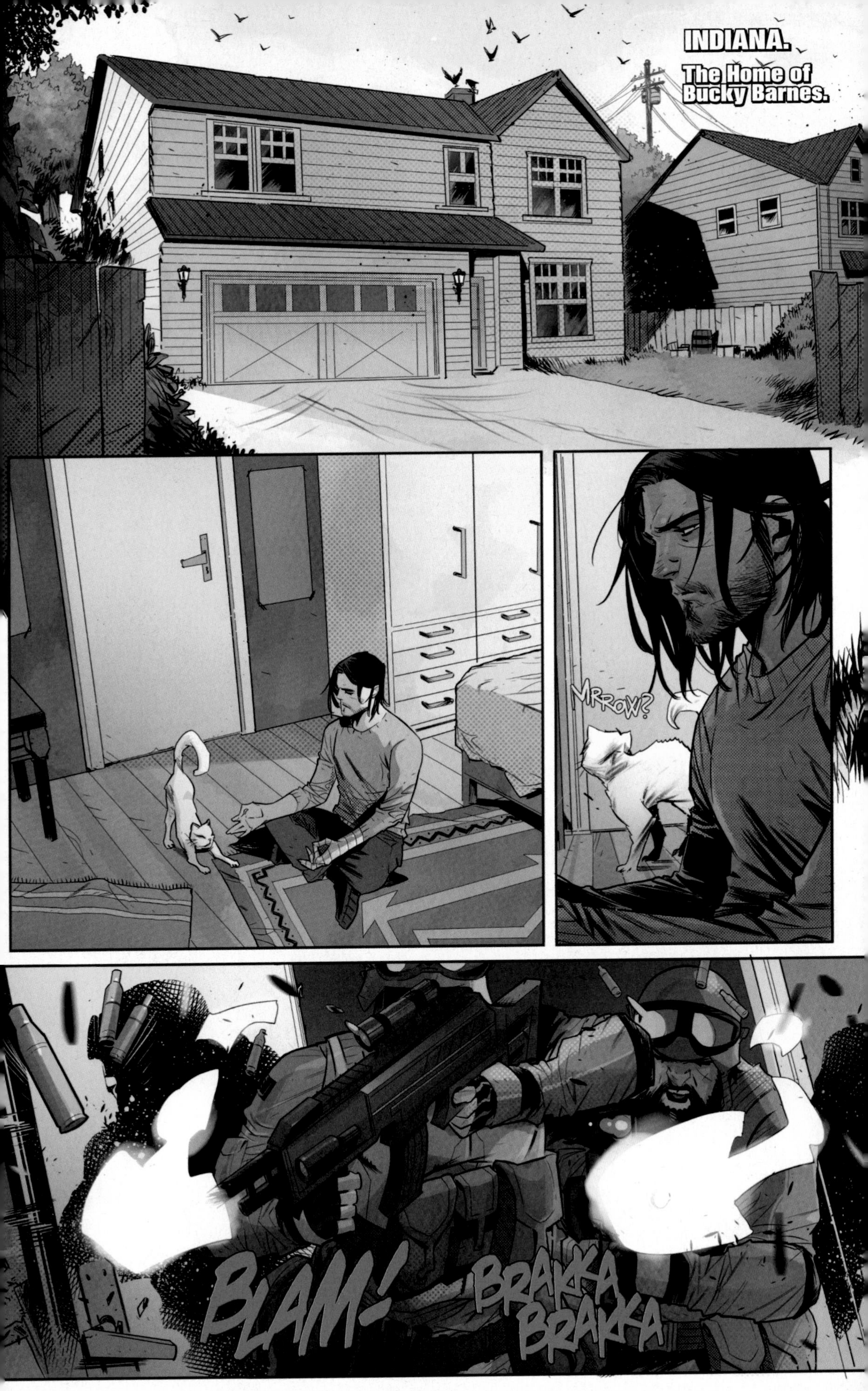
INDIANA.
The Home of Bucky Barnes.
MRROW?
BLAM-!
BRAKKA BRAKKA

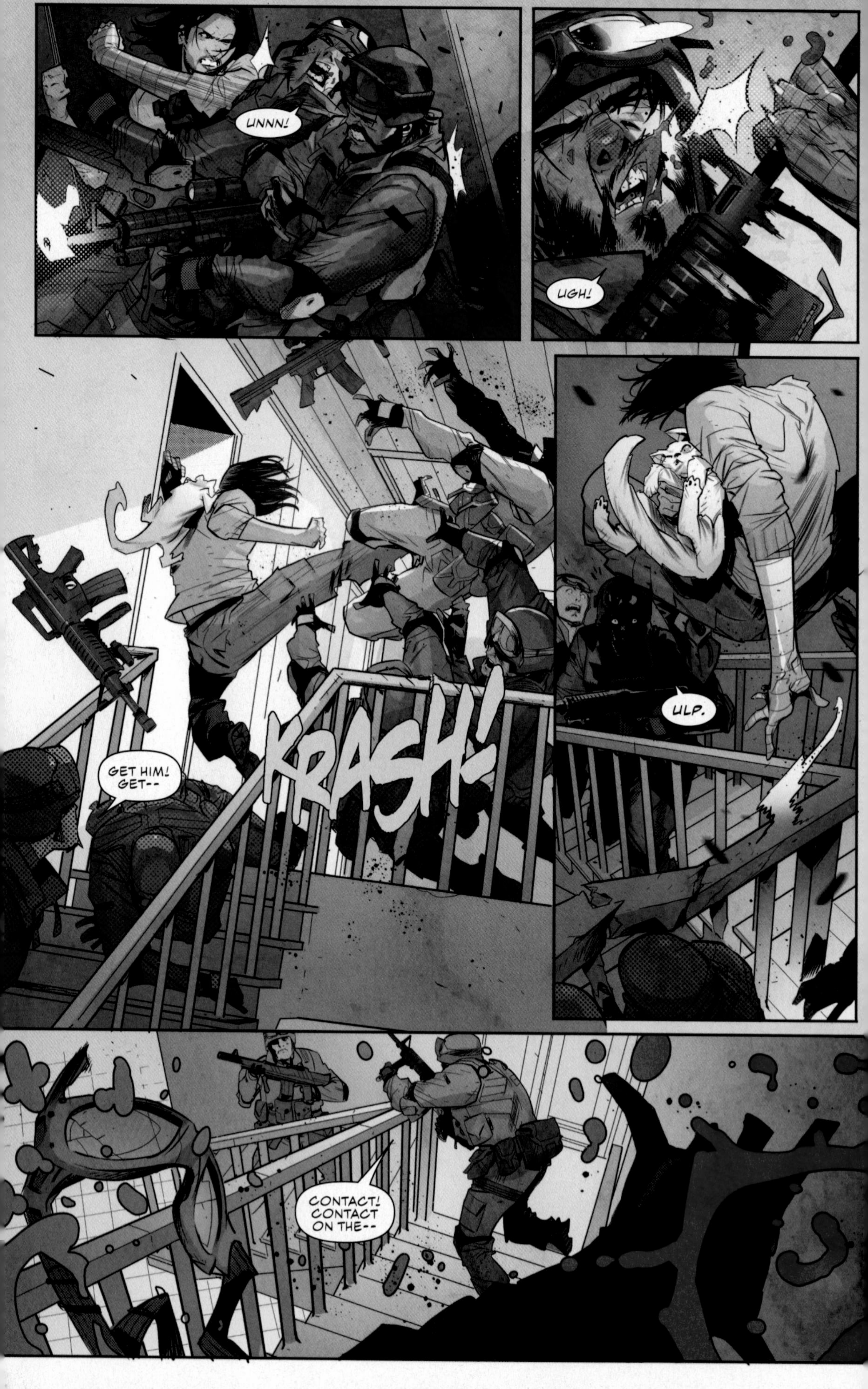
UNNN!
UGH!
GET HIM! GET--
KRASH!
ULP.
CONTACT! CONTACT ON THE--

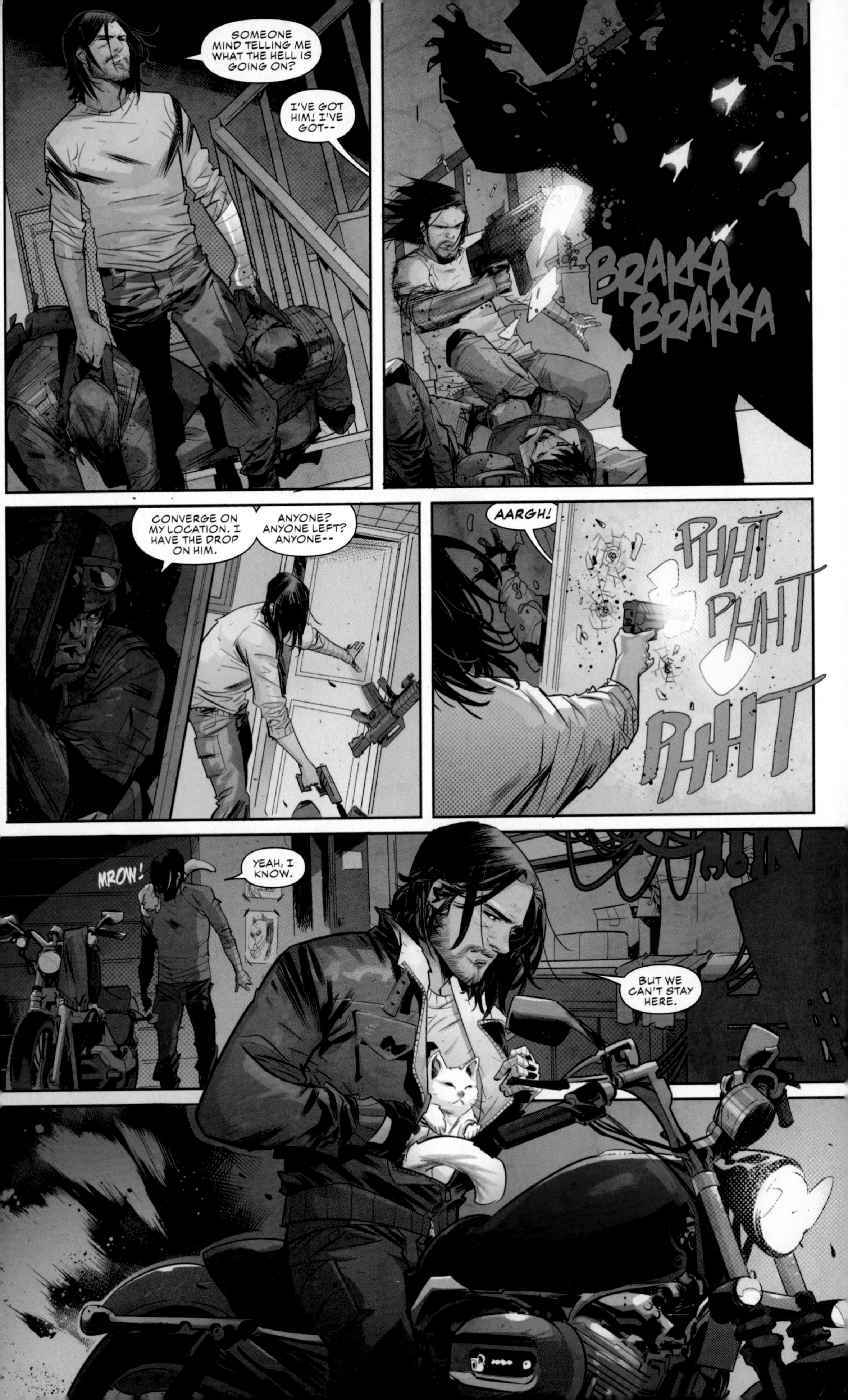
SOMEONE MIND TELLING ME WHAT THE HELL IS GOING ON?
I'VE GOT HIM! I'VE GOT--
BRAKKA BRAKKA
CONVERGE ON MY LOCATION. I HAVE THE DROP ON HIM.
ANYONE? ANYONE LEFT? ANYONE--
AARGH!
PHHT PHHT PHHT
MROW!
YEAH, I KNOW.
BUT WE CAN'T STAY HERE.

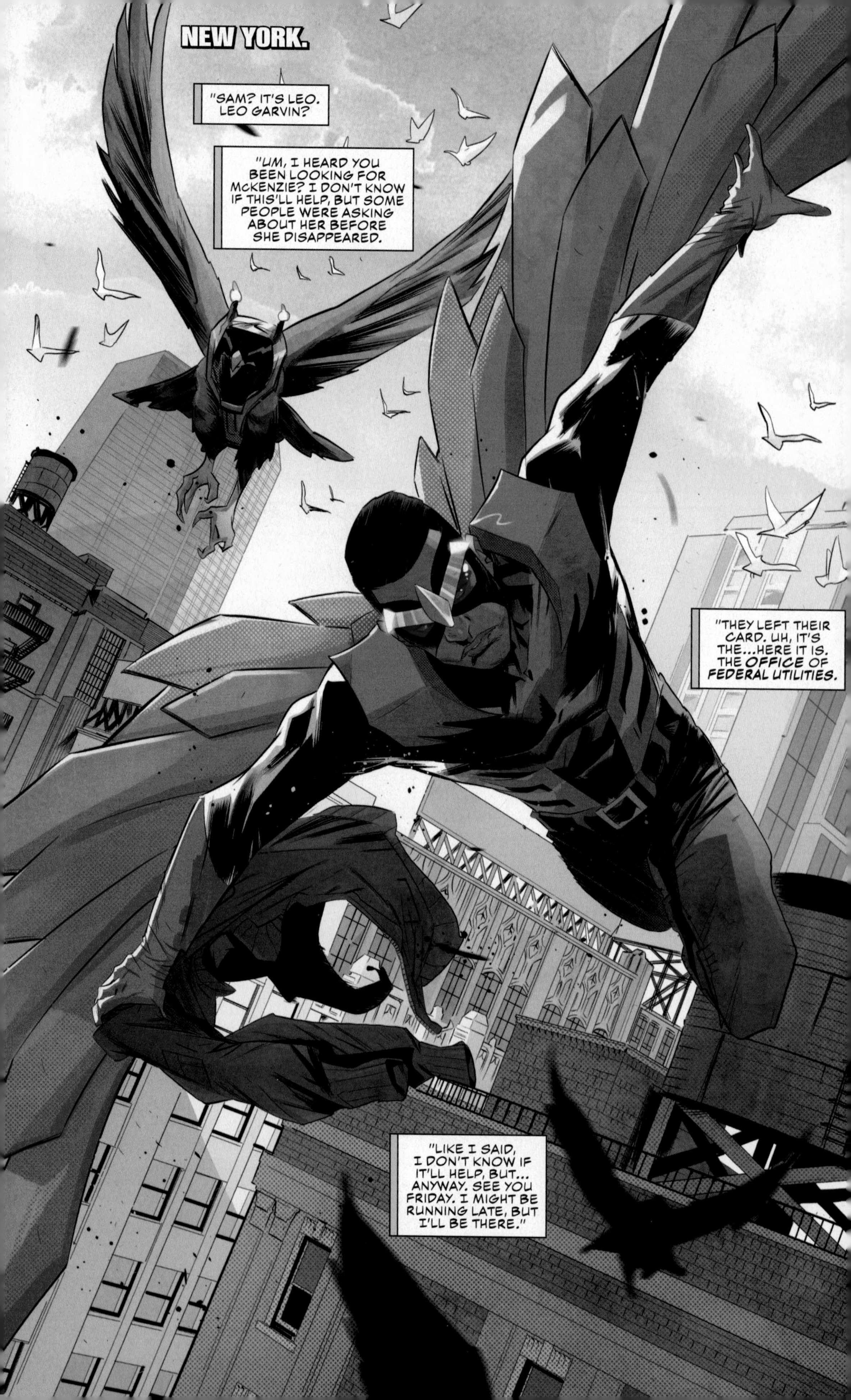
NEW YORK.
"SAM? IT'S LEO. LEO GARVIN?
"UM, I HEARD YOU BEEN LOOKING FOR McKENZIE? I DON'T KNOW IF THIS'LL HELP, BUT SOME PEOPLE WERE ASKING ABOUT HER BEFORE SHE DISAPPEARED.
"THEY LEFT THEIR CARD. UH, IT'S THE...HERE IT IS. THE OFFICE OF FEDERAL UTILITIES.
"LIKE I SAID, I DON'T KNOW IF IT'LL HELP, BUT... ANYWAY. SEE YOU FRIDAY. I MIGHT BE RUNNING LATE, BUT I'LL BE THERE."

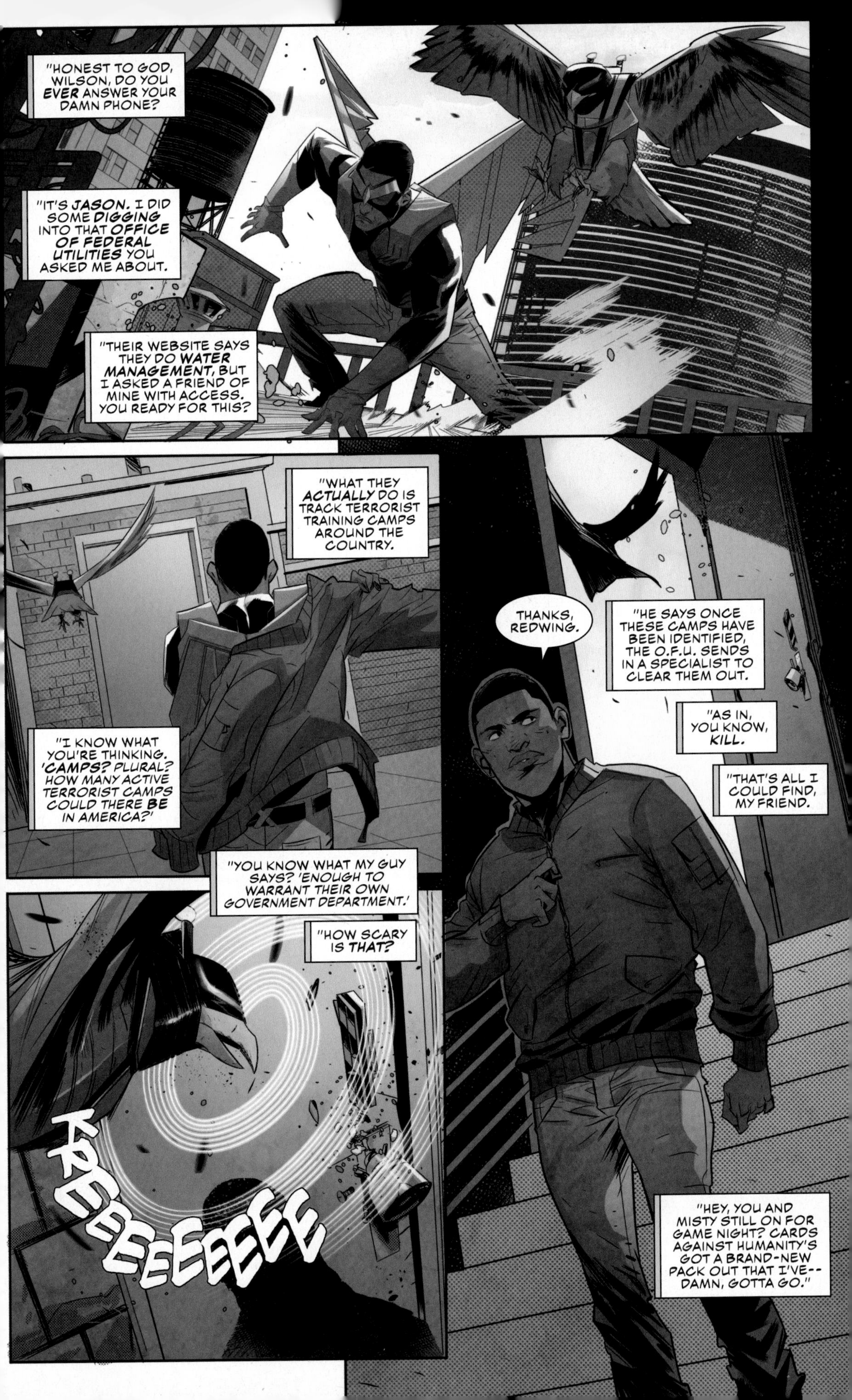
"HONEST TO GOD, WILSON, DO YOU EVER ANSWER YOUR DAMN PHONE?
"IT'S JASON. I DID SOME DIGGING INTO THAT OFFICE OF FEDERAL UTILITIES YOU ASKED ME ABOUT.
"THEIR WEBSITE SAYS THEY DO WATER MANAGEMENT, BUT I ASKED A FRIEND OF MINE WITH ACCESS. YOU READY FOR THIS?
"WHAT THEY ACTUALLY DO IS TRACK TERRORIST TRAINING CAMPS AROUND THE COUNTRY.
"I KNOW WHAT YOU'RE THINKING. 'CAMPS? PLURAL? HOW MANY ACTIVE TERRORIST CAMPS COULD THERE BE IN AMERICA?'
"YOU KNOW WHAT MY GUY SAYS? 'ENOUGH TO WARRANT THEIR OWN GOVERNMENT DEPARTMENT.'
"HOW SCARY IS THAT?
KREEEEEEEEE
THANKS, REDWING.
"HE SAYS ONCE THESE CAMPS HAVE BEEN IDENTIFIED, THE O.F.U. SENDS IN A SPECIALIST TO CLEAR THEM OUT.
"AS IN, YOU KNOW, KILL.
"THAT'S ALL I COULD FIND, MY FRIEND.
"HEY, YOU AND MISTY STILL ON FOR GAME NIGHT? CARDS AGAINST HUMANITY'S GOT A BRAND-NEW PACK OUT THAT I'VE-- DAMN, GOTTA GO."

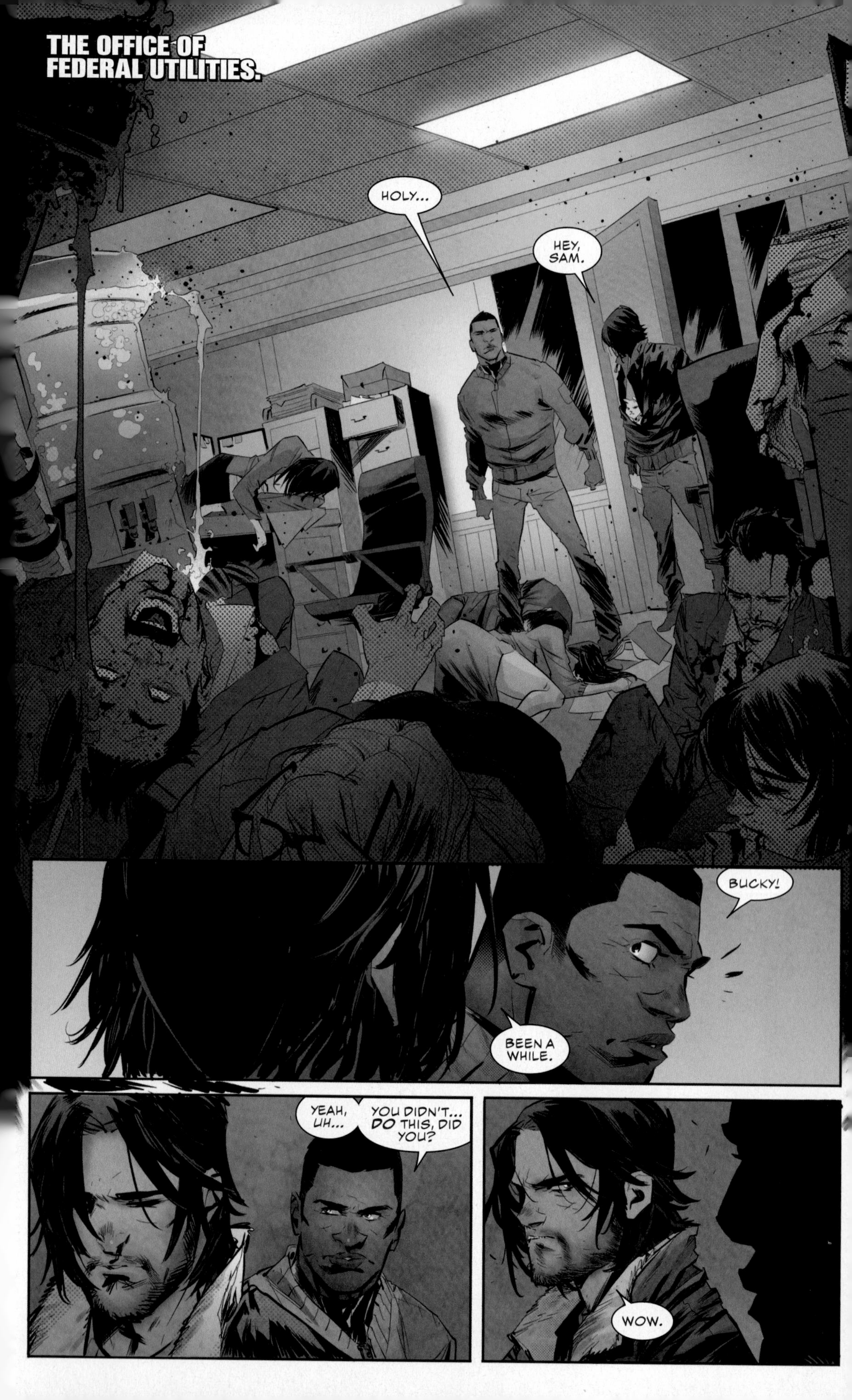
THE OFFICE OF FEDERAL UTILITIES.
HOLY...
HEY, SAM.
BUCKY!
BEEN A WHILE.
YEAH, UH...
YOU DIDN'T... DO THIS, DID YOU?
WOW.

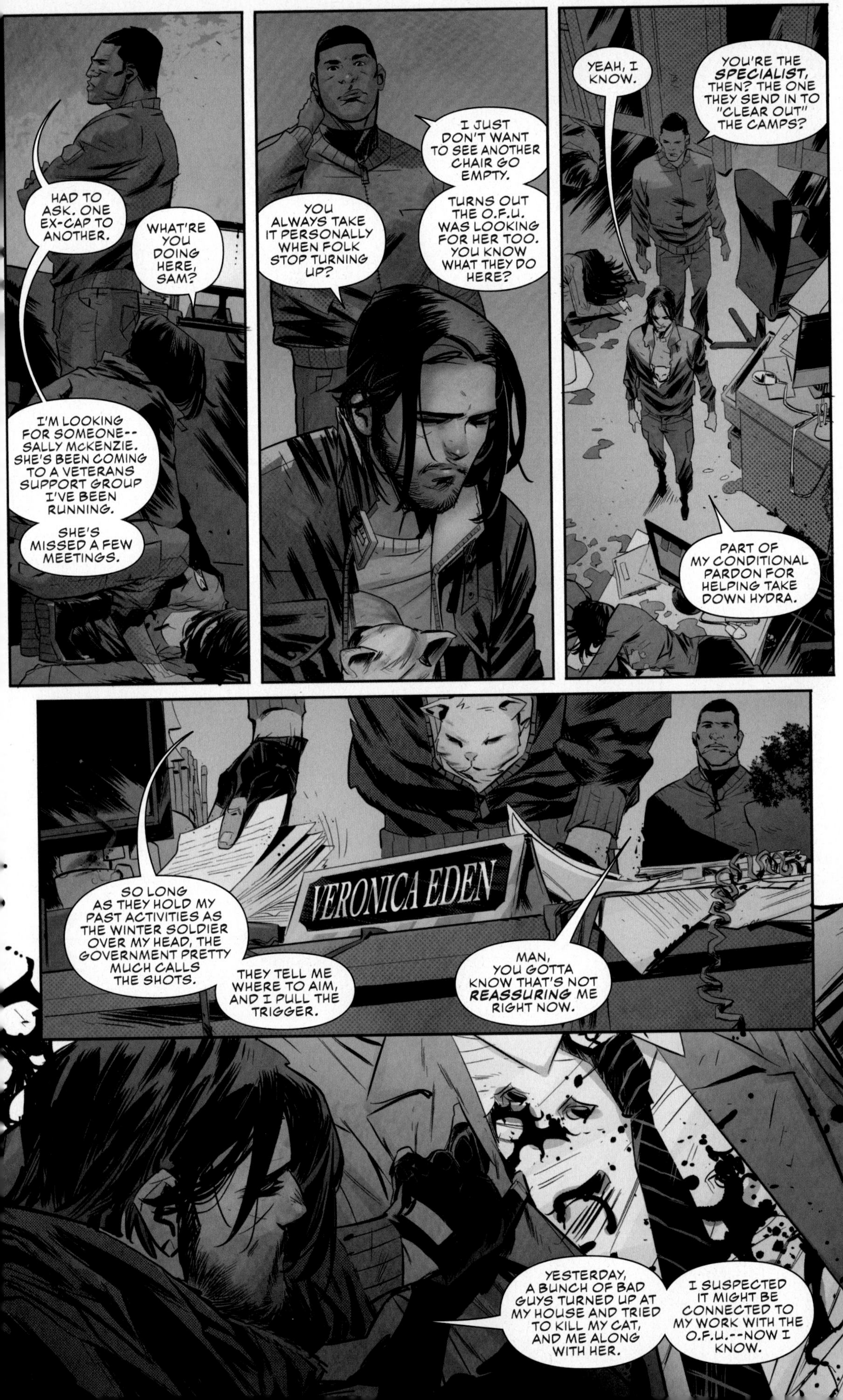

HAD TO ASK. ONE EX-CAP TO ANOTHER.
WHAT'RE YOU DOING HERE, SAM?
I'M LOOKING FOR SOMEONE--SALLY McKENZIE. SHE'S BEEN COMING TO A VETERANS SUPPORT GROUP I'VE BEEN RUNNING.
SHE'S MISSED A FEW MEETINGS.
YOU ALWAYS TAKE IT PERSONALLY WHEN FOLK STOP TURNING UP?
I JUST DON'T WANT TO SEE ANOTHER CHAIR GO EMPTY.
TURNS OUT THE O.F.U. WAS LOOKING FOR HER TOO. YOU KNOW WHAT THEY DO HERE?
YEAH, I KNOW.
YOU'RE THE SPECIALIST, THEN? THE ONE THEY SEND IN TO "CLEAR OUT" THE CAMPS?
PART OF MY CONDITIONAL PARDON FOR HELPING TAKE DOWN HYDRA.
VERONICA EDEN
SO LONG AS THEY HOLD MY PAST ACTIVITIES AS THE WINTER SOLDIER OVER MY HEAD, THE GOVERNMENT PRETTY MUCH CALLS THE SHOTS.
THEY TELL ME WHERE TO AIM, AND I PULL THE TRIGGER.
MAN, YOU GOTTA KNOW THAT'S NOT REASSURING ME RIGHT NOW.
YESTERDAY, A BUNCH OF BAD GUYS TURNED UP AT MY HOUSE AND TRIED TO KILL MY CAT, AND ME ALONG WITH HER.
I SUSPECTED IT MIGHT BE CONNECTED TO MY WORK WITH THE O.F.U.--NOW I KNOW.

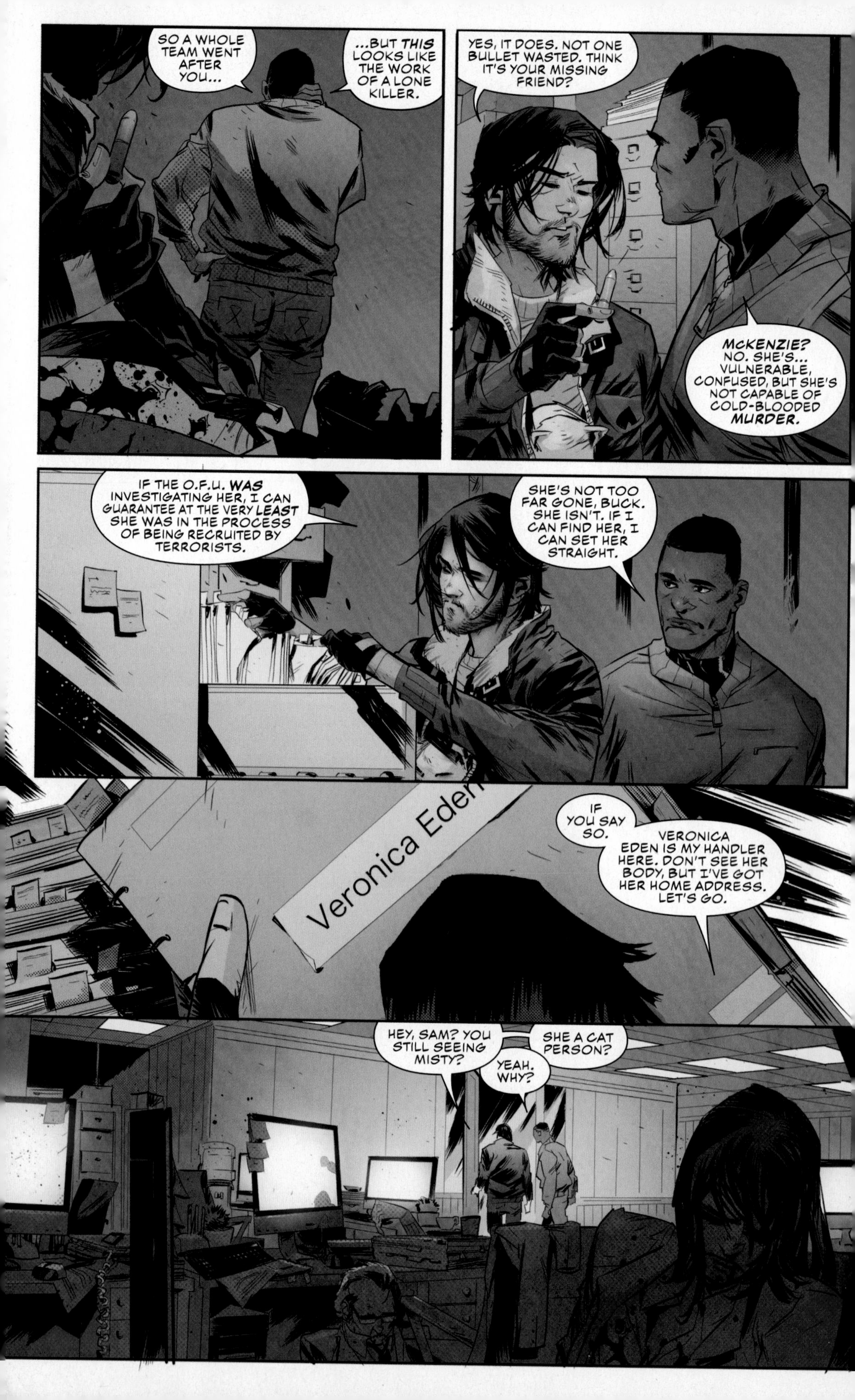
SO A WHOLE TEAM WENT AFTER YOU...
...BUT THIS LOOKS LIKE THE WORK OF A LONE KILLER.
YES, IT DOES. NOT ONE BULLET WASTED. THINK IT'S YOUR MISSING FRIEND?
MCKENZIE? NO. SHE'S... VULNERABLE, CONFUSED, BUT SHE'S NOT CAPABLE OF COLD-BLOODED MURDER.
IF THE O.F.U. WAS INVESTIGATING HER, I CAN GUARANTEE AT THE VERY LEAST SHE WAS IN THE PROCESS OF BEING RECRUITED BY TERRORISTS.
SHE'S NOT TOO FAR GONE, BUCK. SHE ISN'T. IF I CAN FIND HER, I CAN SET HER STRAIGHT.
Veronica Eden
IF YOU SAY SO.
VERONICA EDEN IS MY HANDLER HERE. DON'T SEE HER BODY, BUT I'VE GOT HER HOME ADDRESS. LET'S GO.
HEY, SAM? YOU STILL SEEING MISTY?
YEAH. WHY?
SHE A CAT PERSON?

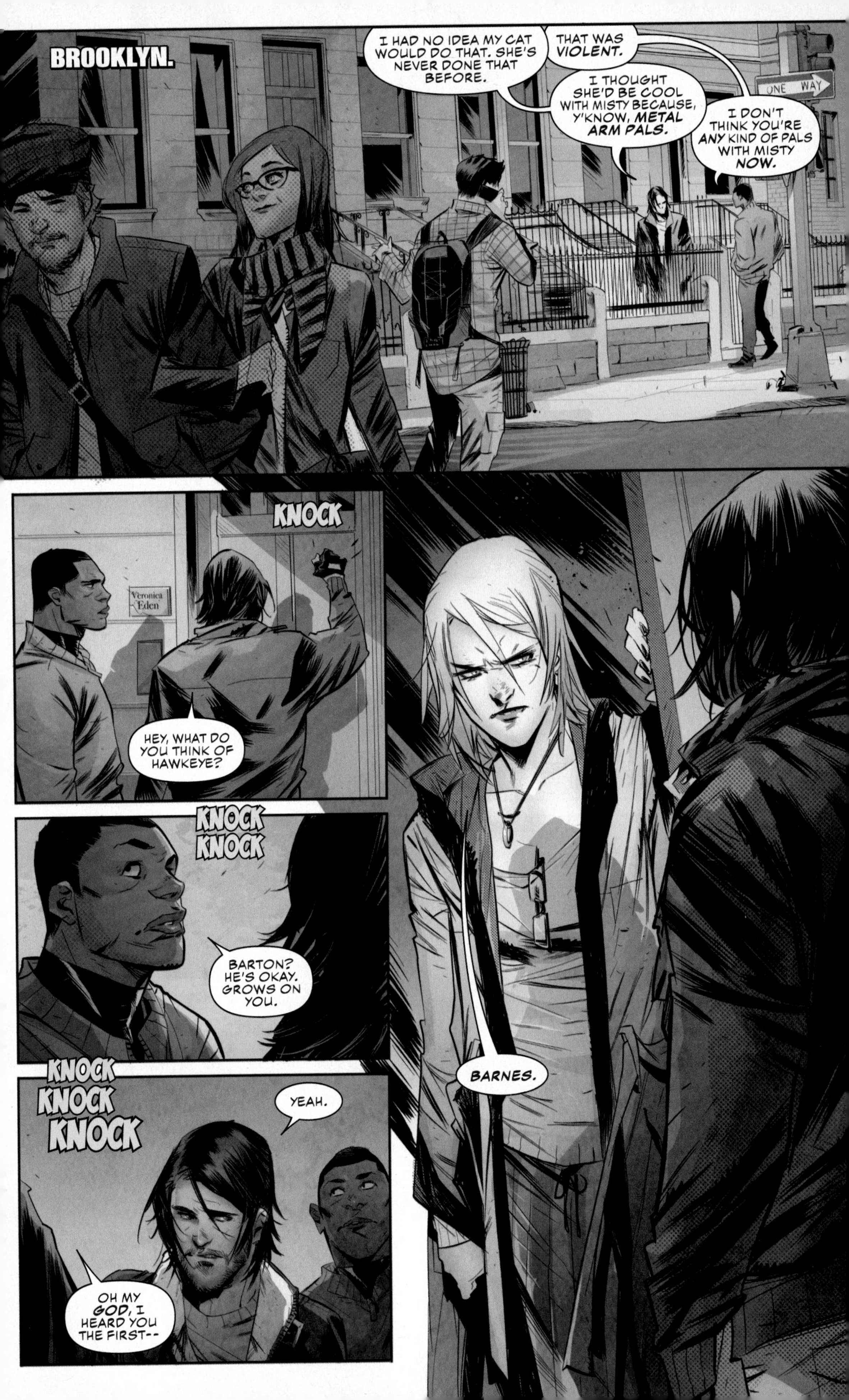
BROOKLYN.
I HAD NO IDEA MY CAT WOULD DO THAT. SHE'S NEVER DONE THAT BEFORE.
THAT WAS VIOLENT.
I THOUGHT SHE'D BE COOL WITH MISTY BECAUSE, Y'KNOW, METAL ARM PALS.
I DON'T THINK YOU'RE ANY KIND OF PALS WITH MISTY NOW.
ONE WAY
KNOCK
Veronica Eden
HEY, WHAT DO YOU THINK OF HAWKEYE?
KNOCK KNOCK
BARTON? HE'S OKAY. GROWS ON YOU.
KNOCK KNOCK KNOCK
YEAH.
OH MY GOD, I HEARD YOU THE FIRST--
BARNES.

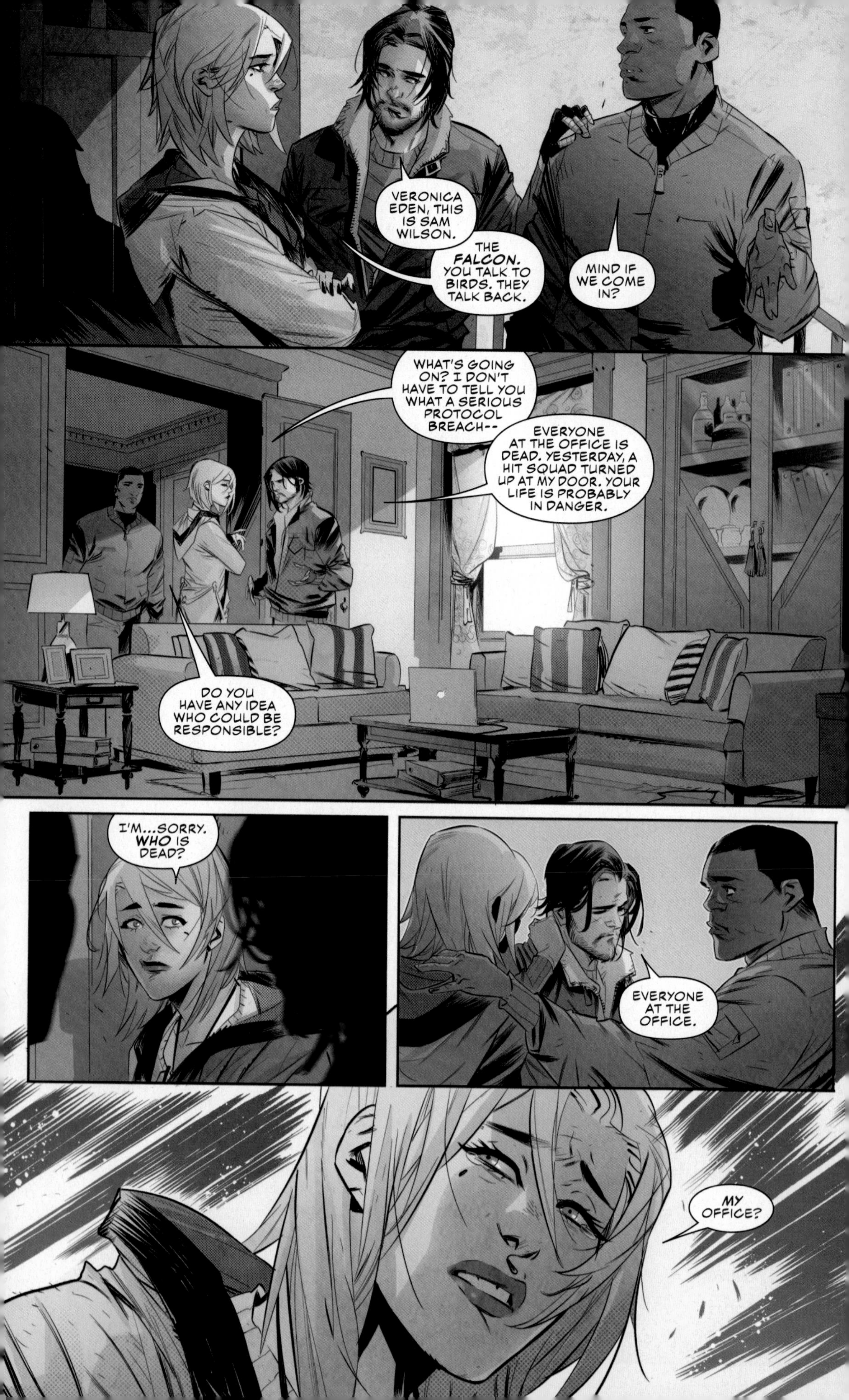
VERONICA EDEN, THIS IS SAM WILSON.
THE **FALCON.** YOU TALK TO BIRDS. THEY TALK BACK.
MIND IF WE COME IN?
WHAT'S GOING ON? I DON'T HAVE TO TELL YOU WHAT A SERIOUS PROTOCOL BREACH--
EVERYONE AT THE OFFICE IS DEAD. YESTERDAY, A HIT SQUAD TURNED UP AT MY DOOR. YOUR LIFE IS PROBABLY IN DANGER.
DO YOU HAVE ANY IDEA WHO COULD BE RESPONSIBLE?
I'M...SORRY. **WHO** IS DEAD?
EVERYONE AT THE OFFICE.
MY OFFICE?

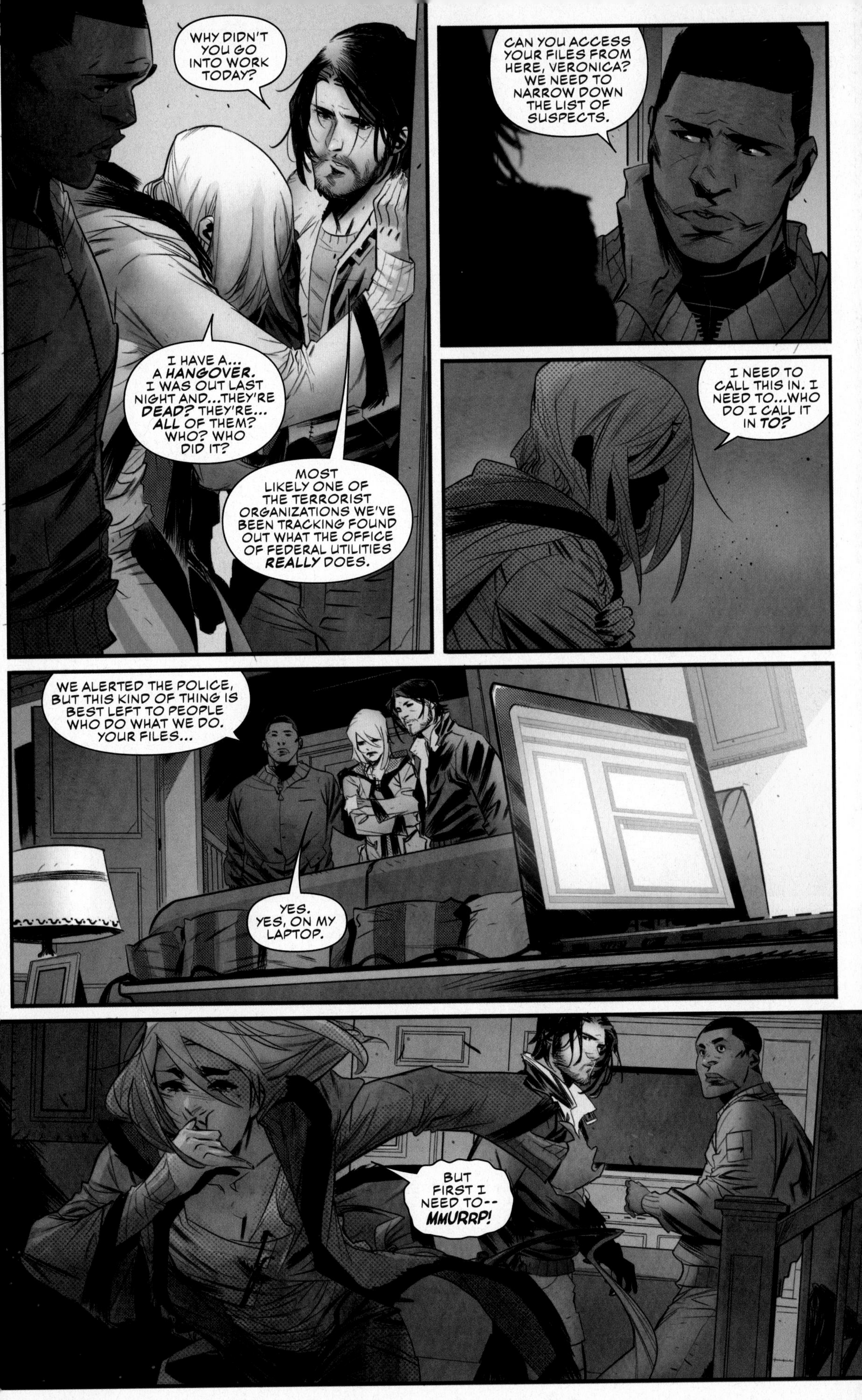
WHY DIDN'T YOU GO INTO WORK TODAY?
I HAVE A... A HANGOVER. I WAS OUT LAST NIGHT AND...THEY'RE DEAD? THEY'RE... ALL OF THEM? WHO? WHO DID IT?
MOST LIKELY ONE OF THE TERRORIST ORGANIZATIONS WE'VE BEEN TRACKING FOUND OUT WHAT THE OFFICE OF FEDERAL UTILITIES REALLY DOES.
CAN YOU ACCESS YOUR FILES FROM HERE, VERONICA? WE NEED TO NARROW DOWN THE LIST OF SUSPECTS.
I NEED TO CALL THIS IN. I NEED TO...WHO DO I CALL IT IN TO?
WE ALERTED THE POLICE, BUT THIS KIND OF THING IS BEST LEFT TO PEOPLE WHO DO WHAT WE DO. YOUR FILES...
YES. YES, ON MY LAPTOP.
BUT FIRST I NEED TO-- MMURRP!

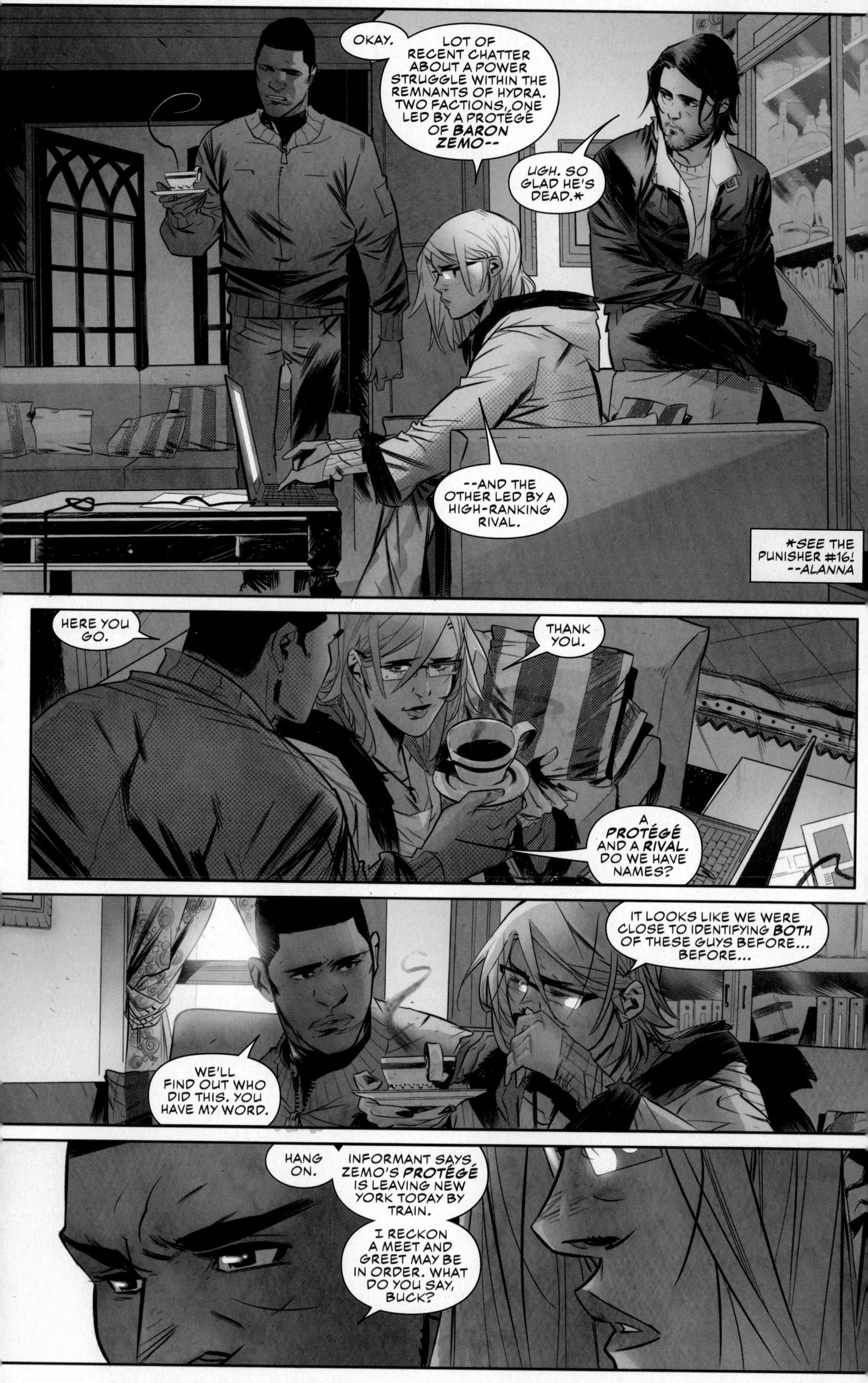
OKAY.
LOT OF RECENT CHATTER ABOUT A POWER STRUGGLE WITHIN THE REMNANTS OF HYDRA. TWO FACTIONS, ONE LED BY A PROTÉGÉ OF BARON ZEMO--
UGH. SO GLAD HE'S DEAD.*
--AND THE OTHER LED BY A HIGH-RANKING RIVAL.
*SEE THE PUNISHER #16! --ALANNA
HERE YOU GO.
THANK YOU.
A PROTÉGÉ AND A RIVAL. DO WE HAVE NAMES?
IT LOOKS LIKE WE WERE CLOSE TO IDENTIFYING BOTH OF THESE GUYS BEFORE... BEFORE...
WE'LL FIND OUT WHO DID THIS. YOU HAVE MY WORD.
HANG ON.
INFORMANT SAYS ZEMO'S PROTÉGÉ IS LEAVING NEW YORK TODAY BY TRAIN.
I RECKON A MEET AND GREET MAY BE IN ORDER. WHAT DO YOU SAY, BUCK?

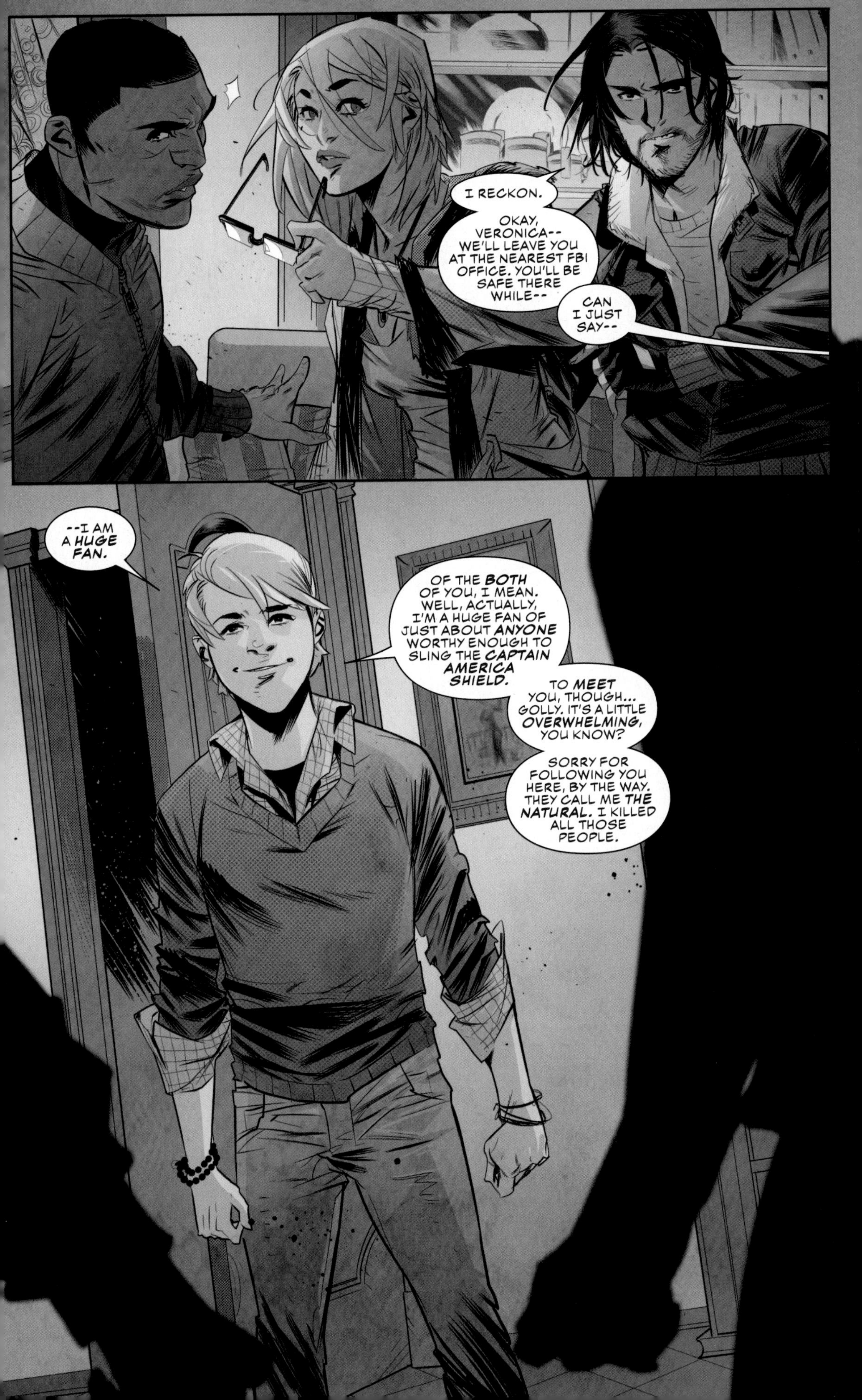
I RECKON.
OKAY, VERONICA-- WE'LL LEAVE YOU AT THE NEAREST FBI OFFICE. YOU'LL BE SAFE THERE WHILE--
CAN I JUST SAY--
--I AM A **HUGE FAN.**
OF THE **BOTH** OF YOU, I MEAN. WELL, ACTUALLY, I'M A HUGE FAN OF JUST ABOUT **ANYONE** WORTHY ENOUGH TO SLING THE **CAPTAIN AMERICA SHIELD.**
TO **MEET** YOU, THOUGH... GOLLY. IT'S A LITTLE **OVERWHELMING,** YOU KNOW?
SORRY FOR FOLLOWING YOU HERE, BY THE WAY. THEY CALL ME **THE NATURAL.** I KILLED ALL THOSE PEOPLE.

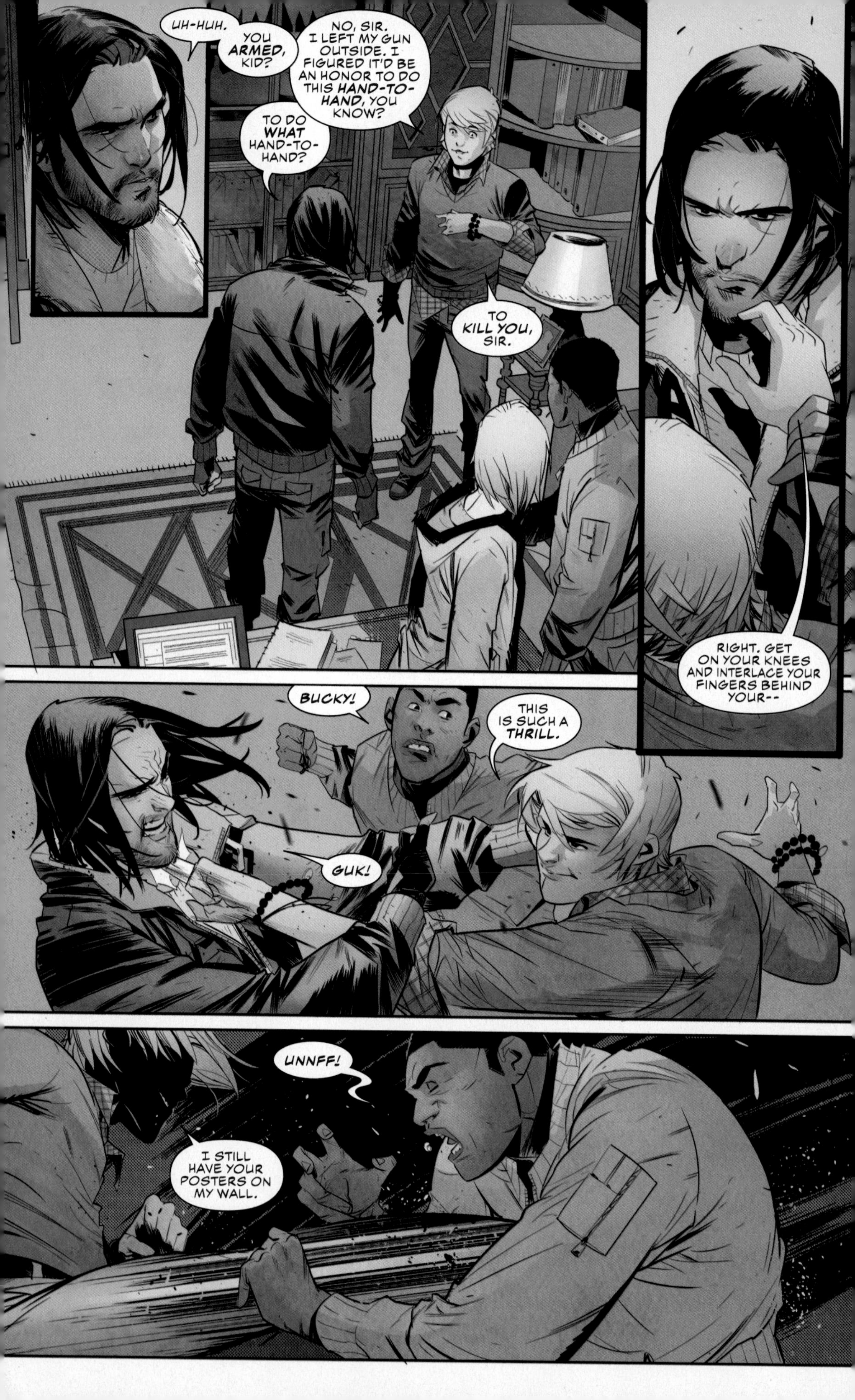
UH-HUH.
YOU ARMED, KID?
NO, SIR. I LEFT MY GUN OUTSIDE. I FIGURED IT'D BE AN HONOR TO DO THIS HAND-TO-HAND, YOU KNOW?
TO DO WHAT HAND-TO-HAND?
TO KILL YOU, SIR.
RIGHT. GET ON YOUR KNEES AND INTERLACE YOUR FINGERS BEHIND YOUR--
BUCKY!
THIS IS SUCH A THRILL.
GUK!
UNNFF!
I STILL HAVE YOUR POSTERS ON MY WALL.

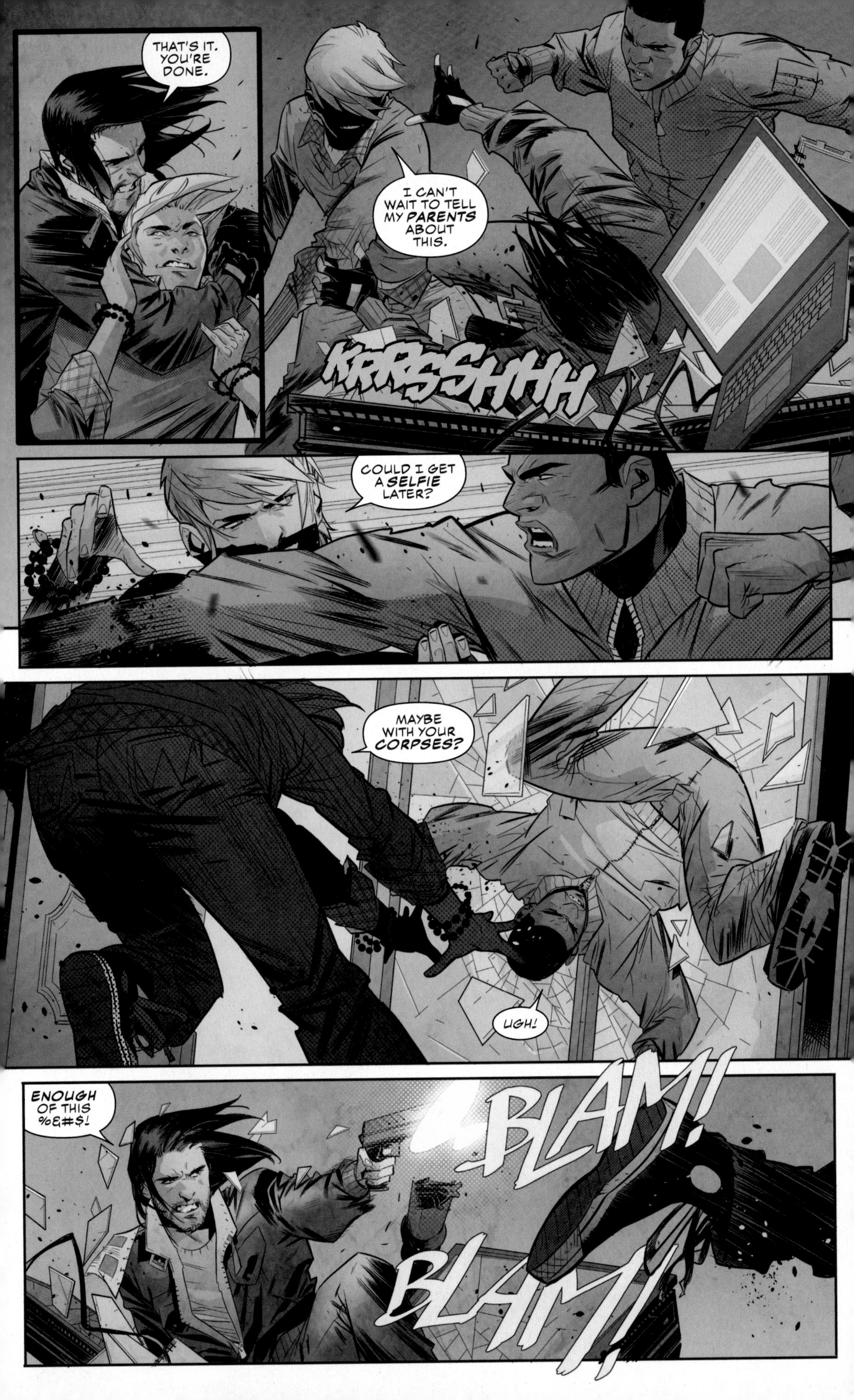

THAT'S IT. YOU'RE DONE.
I CAN'T WAIT TO TELL MY PARENTS ABOUT THIS.
KRRSHHH
COULD I GET A SELFIE LATER?
MAYBE WITH YOUR CORPSES?
UGH!
ENOUGH OF THIS %&#$!
BLAM!
BLAM!

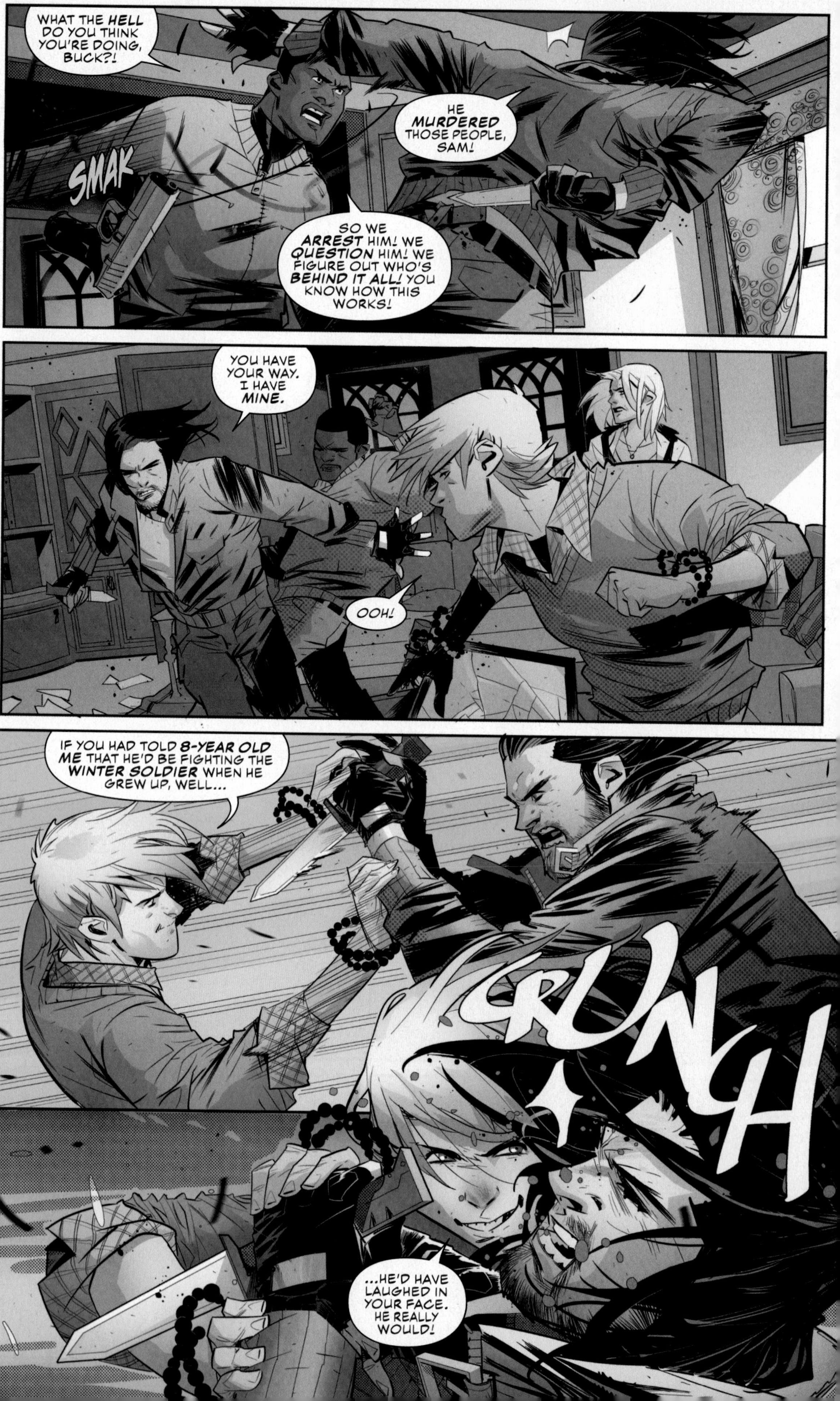
WHAT THE HELL DO YOU THINK YOU'RE DOING, BUCK?!
HE MURDERED THOSE PEOPLE, SAM!
SMAK
SO WE ARREST HIM! WE QUESTION HIM! WE FIGURE OUT WHO'S BEHIND IT ALL! YOU KNOW HOW THIS WORKS!
YOU HAVE YOUR WAY. I HAVE MINE.
OOH!
IF YOU HAD TOLD 8-YEAR OLD ME THAT HE'D BE FIGHTING THE WINTER SOLDIER WHEN HE GREW UP, WELL...
CRUNCH
...HE'D HAVE LAUGHED IN YOUR FACE. HE REALLY WOULD!

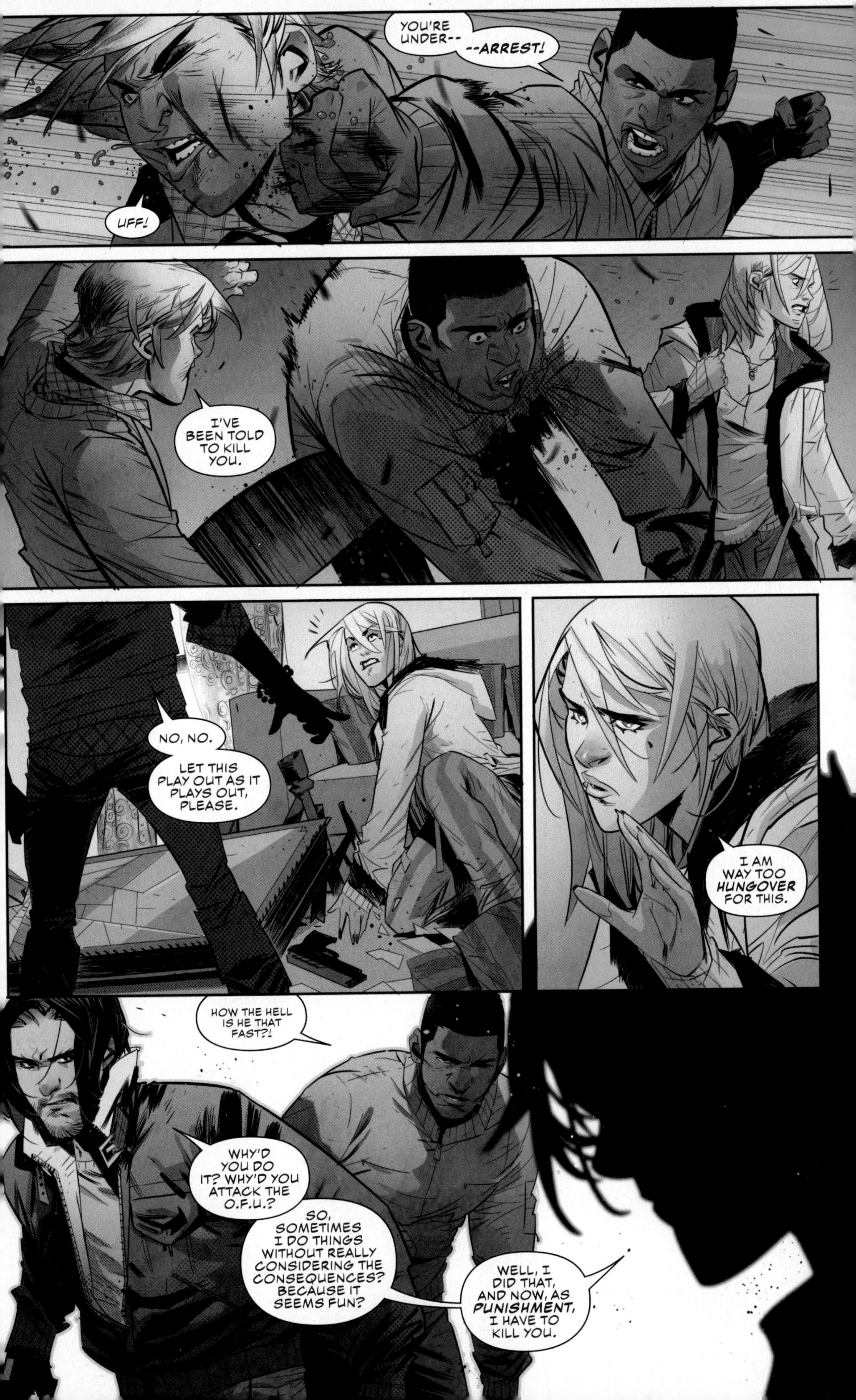
YOU'RE UNDER--
--ARREST!
UFF!
I'VE BEEN TOLD TO KILL YOU.
NO, NO.
LET THIS PLAY OUT AS IT PLAYS OUT, PLEASE.
I AM WAY TOO HUNGOVER FOR THIS.
HOW THE HELL IS HE THAT FAST?!
WHY'D YOU DO IT? WHY'D YOU ATTACK THE O.F.U.?
SO, SOMETIMES I DO THINGS WITHOUT REALLY CONSIDERING THE CONSEQUENCES? BECAUSE IT SEEMS FUN?
WELL, I DID THAT, AND NOW, AS PUNISHMENT, I HAVE TO KILL YOU.

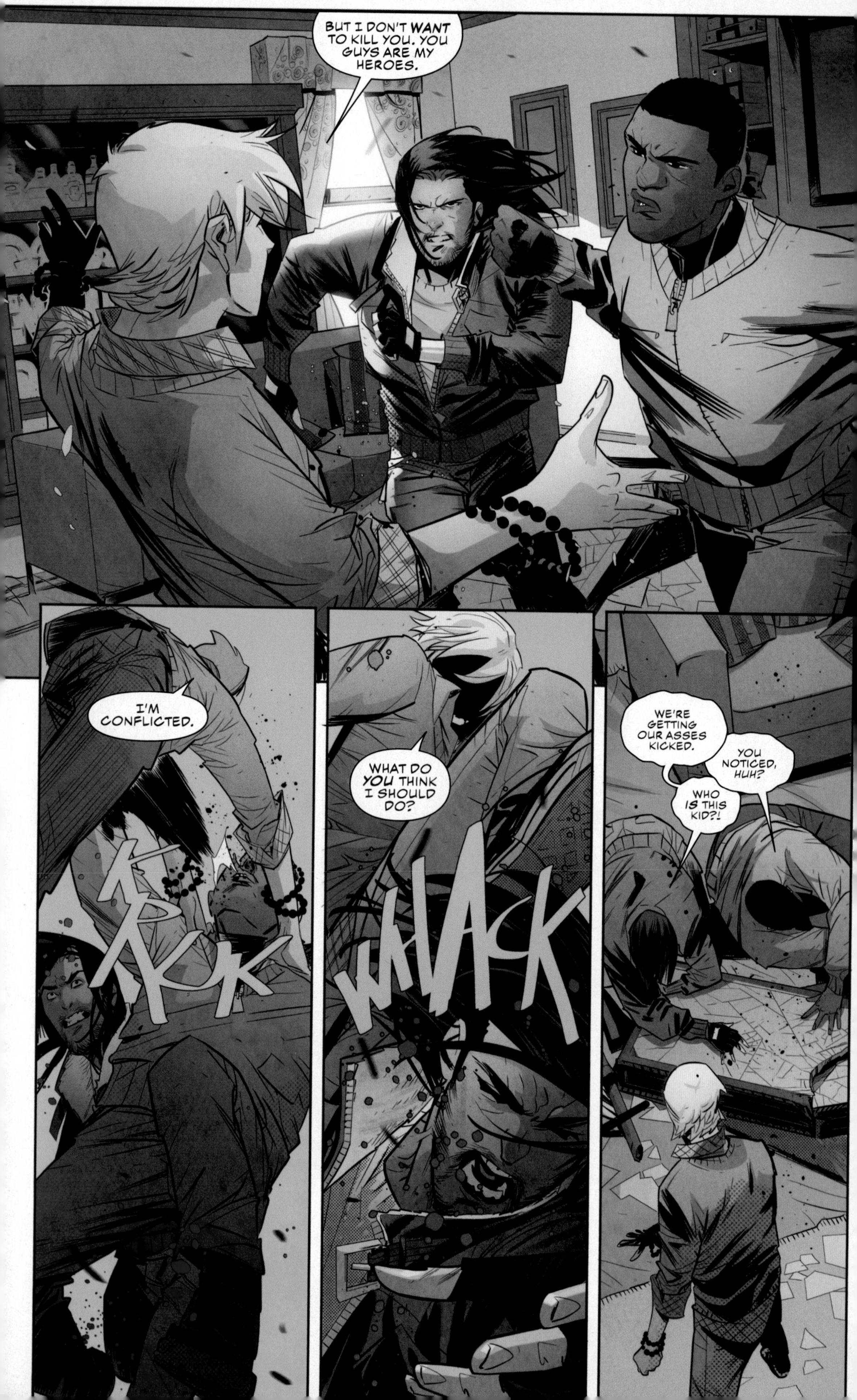
BUT I DON'T WANT TO KILL YOU. YOU GUYS ARE MY HEROES.
I'M CONFLICTED.
KRAKK
WHAT DO YOU THINK I SHOULD DO?
WHACK
WE'RE GETTING OUR ASSES KICKED.
YOU NOTICED, HUH?
WHO IS THIS KID?!

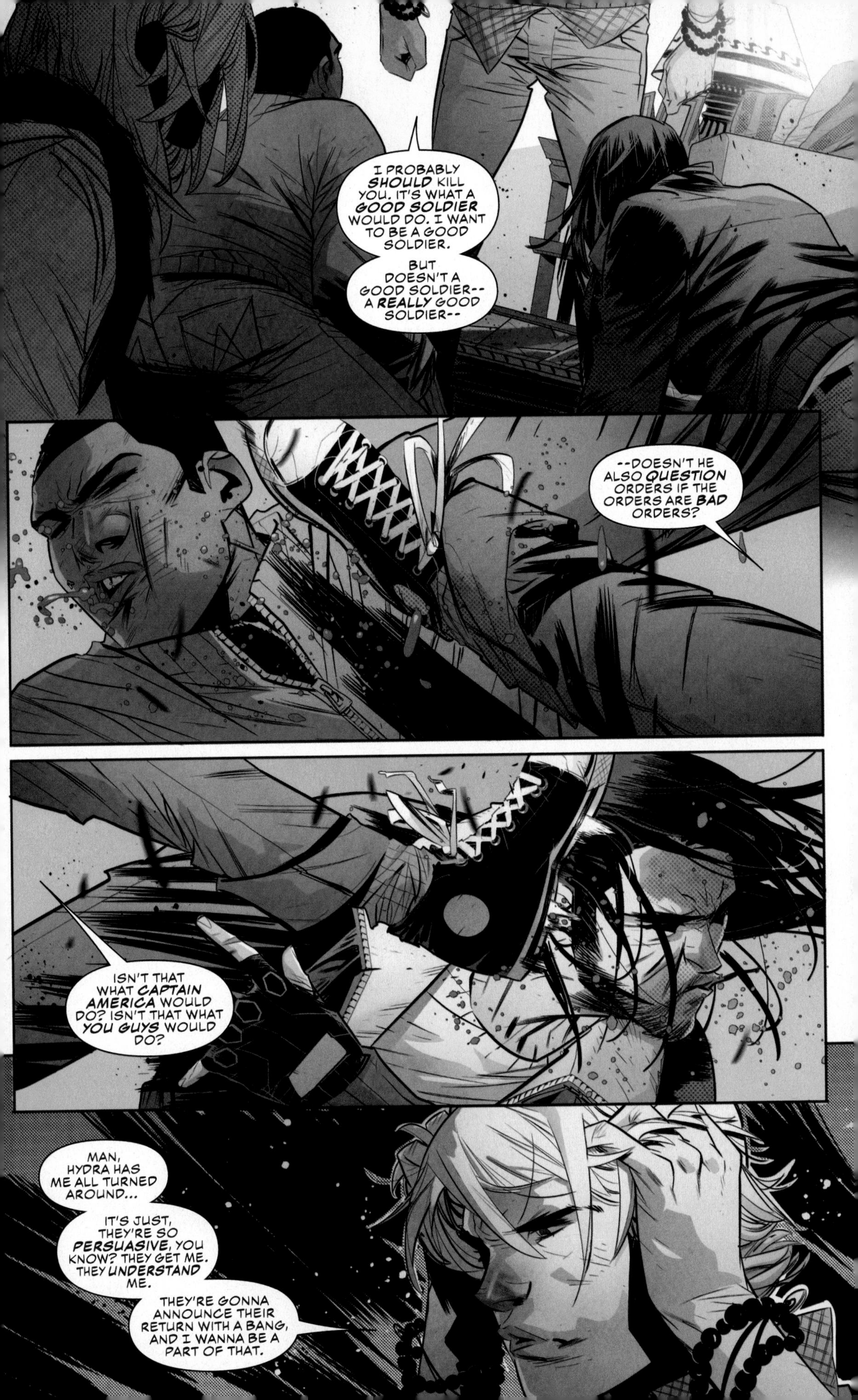

I PROBABLY SHOULD KILL YOU. IT'S WHAT A GOOD SOLDIER WOULD DO. I WANT TO BE A GOOD SOLDIER.
BUT DOESN'T A GOOD SOLDIER-- A REALLY GOOD SOLDIER--
--DOESN'T HE ALSO QUESTION ORDERS IF THE ORDERS ARE BAD ORDERS?
ISN'T THAT WHAT CAPTAIN AMERICA WOULD DO? ISN'T THAT WHAT YOU GUYS WOULD DO?
MAN, HYDRA HAS ME ALL TURNED AROUND...
IT'S JUST, THEY'RE SO PERSUASIVE, YOU KNOW? THEY GET ME. THEY UNDERSTAND ME.
THEY'RE GONNA ANNOUNCE THEIR RETURN WITH A BANG, AND I WANNA BE A PART OF THAT.

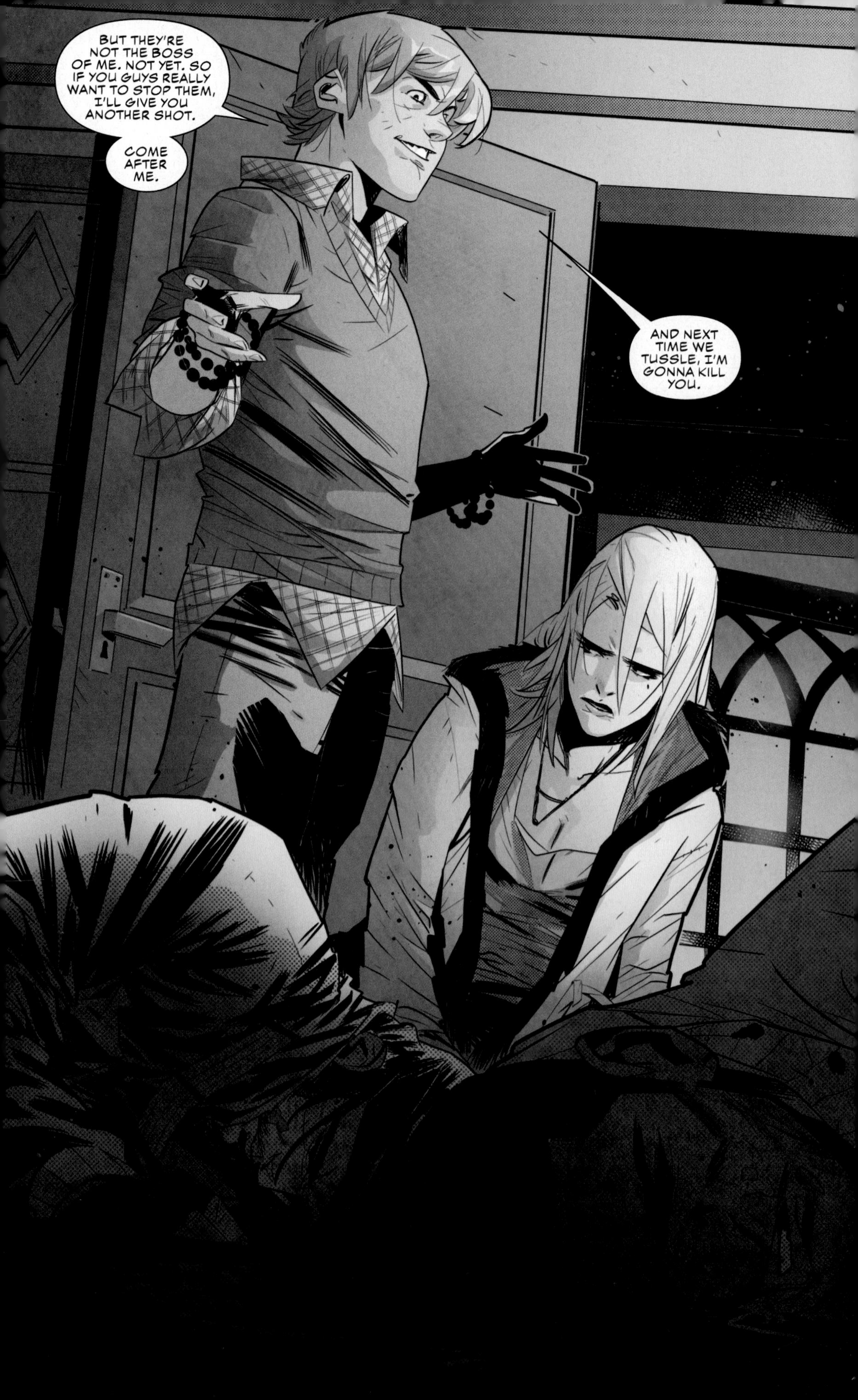
BUT THEY'RE NOT THE BOSS OF ME. NOT YET. SO IF YOU GUYS REALLY WANT TO STOP THEM, I'LL GIVE YOU ANOTHER SHOT.
COME AFTER ME.
AND NEXT TIME WE TUSSLE, I'M GONNA KILL YOU.

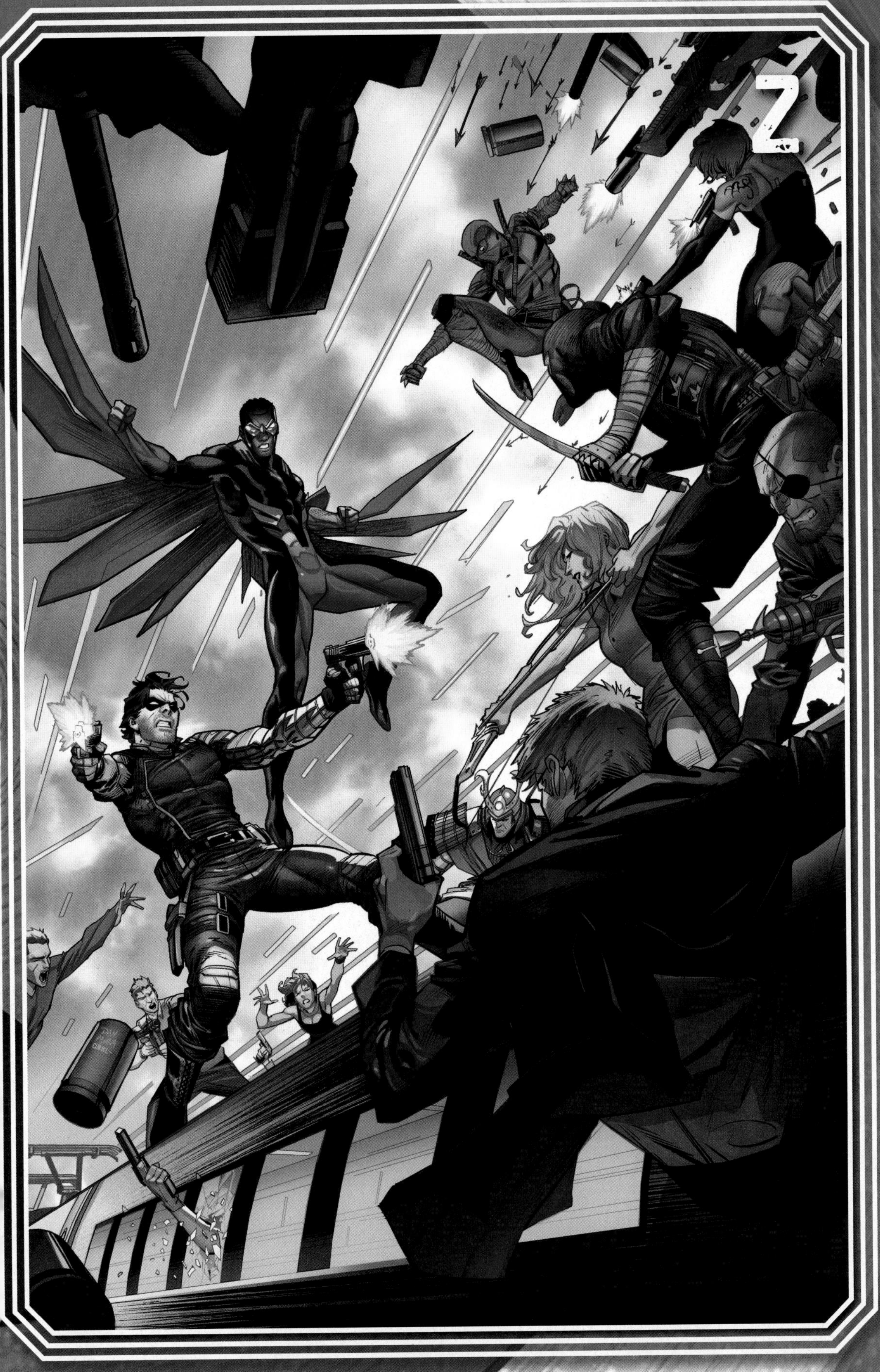
Z

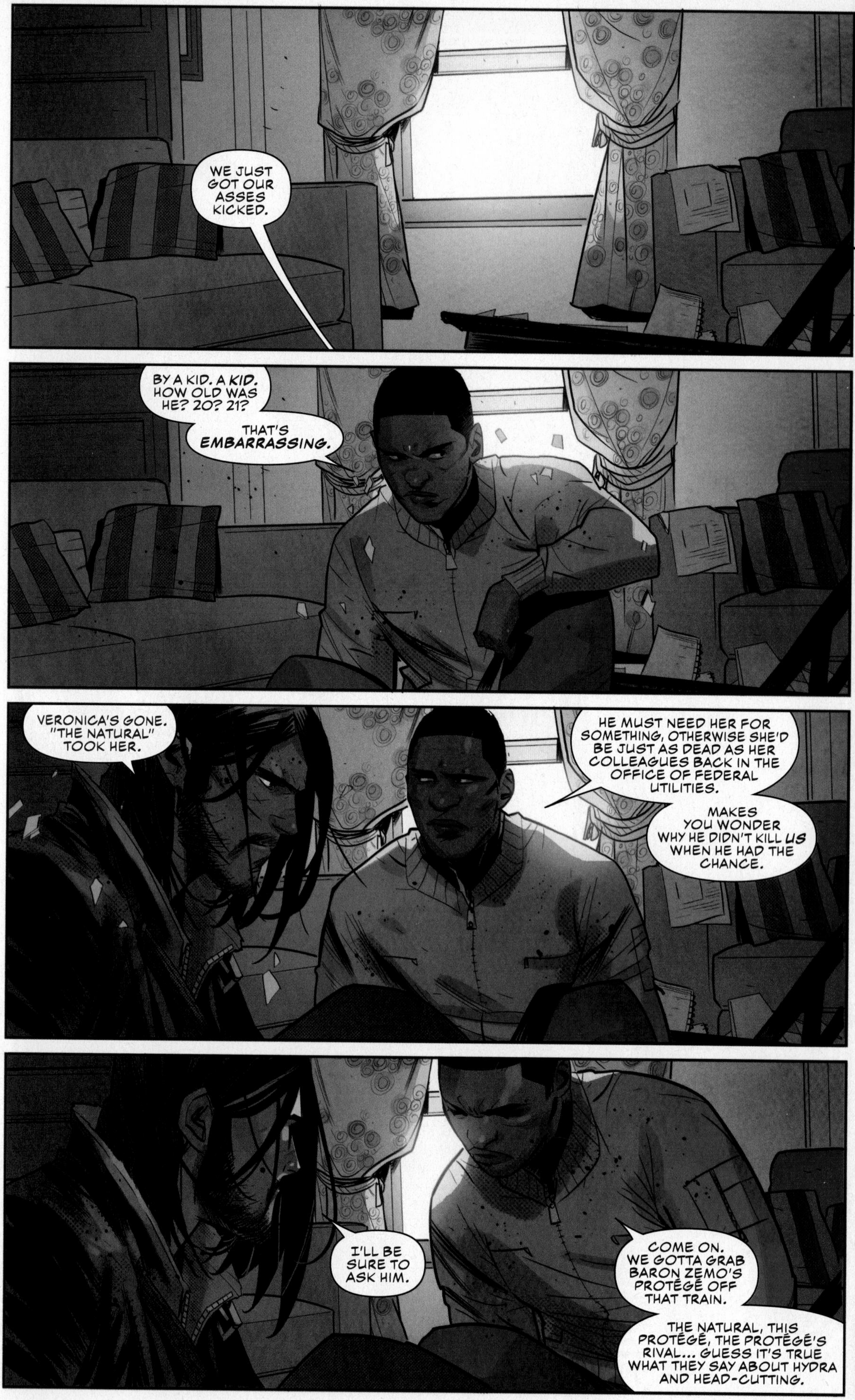
WE JUST GOT OUR ASSES KICKED.
BY A KID. A KID. HOW OLD WAS HE? 20? 21?
THAT'S EMBARRASSING.
VERONICA'S GONE. "THE NATURAL" TOOK HER.
HE MUST NEED HER FOR SOMETHING, OTHERWISE SHE'D BE JUST AS DEAD AS HER COLLEAGUES BACK IN THE OFFICE OF FEDERAL UTILITIES.
MAKES YOU WONDER WHY HE DIDN'T KILL US WHEN HE HAD THE CHANCE.
I'LL BE SURE TO ASK HIM.
COME ON. WE GOTTA GRAB BARON ZEMO'S PROTÉGÉ OFF THAT TRAIN.
THE NATURAL, THIS PROTÉGÉ, THE PROTÉGÉ'S RIVAL... GUESS IT'S TRUE WHAT THEY SAY ABOUT HYDRA AND HEAD-CUTTING.

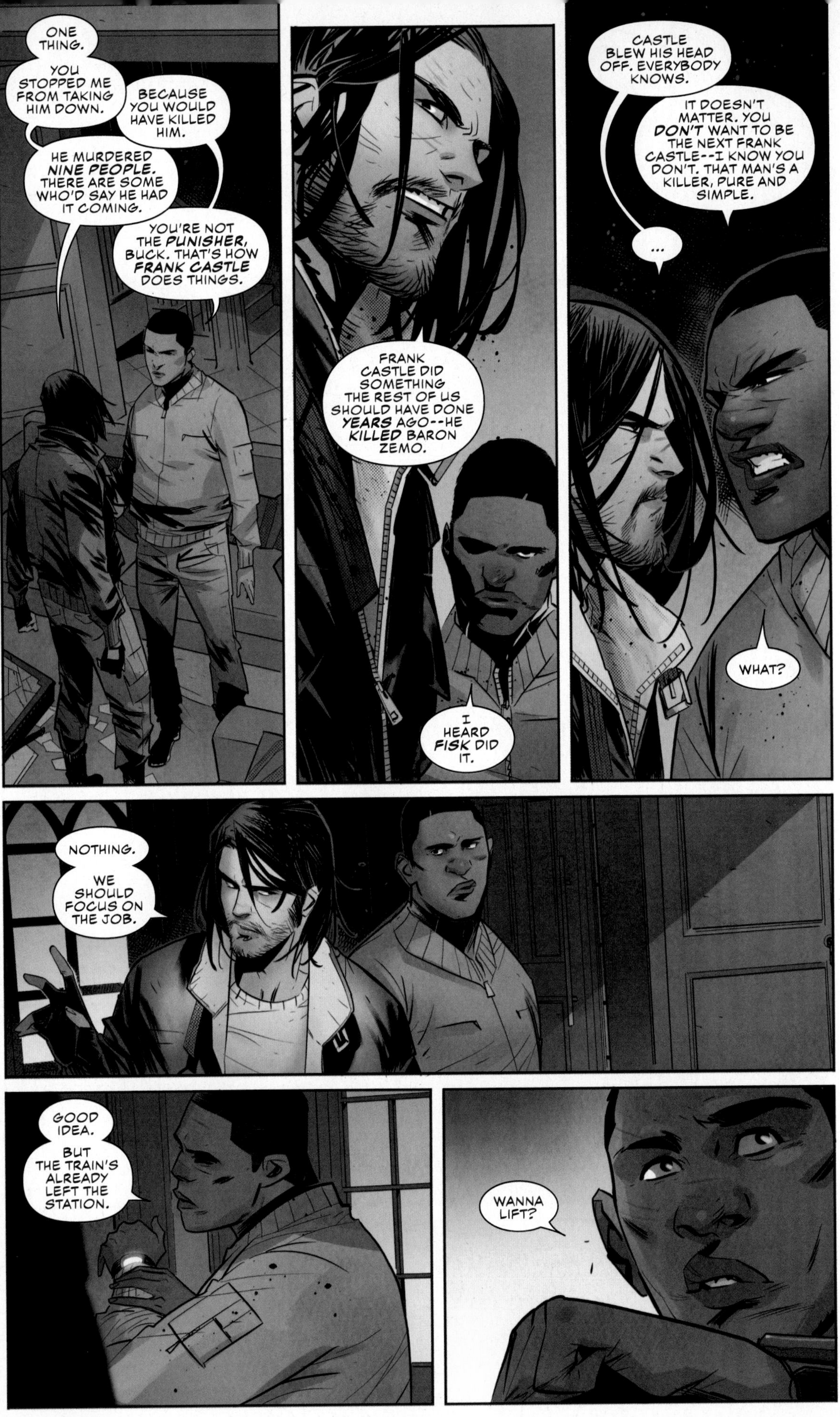

ONE THING.
YOU STOPPED ME FROM TAKING HIM DOWN.
BECAUSE YOU WOULD HAVE KILLED HIM.
HE MURDERED NINE PEOPLE. THERE ARE SOME WHO'D SAY HE HAD IT COMING.
YOU'RE NOT THE PUNISHER, BUCK. THAT'S HOW FRANK CASTLE DOES THINGS.
FRANK CASTLE DID SOMETHING THE REST OF US SHOULD HAVE DONE YEARS AGO--HE KILLED BARON ZEMO.
I HEARD FISK DID IT.
CASTLE BLEW HIS HEAD OFF. EVERYBODY KNOWS.
IT DOESN'T MATTER. YOU DON'T WANT TO BE THE NEXT FRANK CASTLE--I KNOW YOU DON'T. THAT MAN'S A KILLER, PURE AND SIMPLE.
...
WHAT?
NOTHING.
WE SHOULD FOCUS ON THE JOB.
GOOD IDEA.
BUT THE TRAIN'S ALREADY LEFT THE STATION.
WANNA LIFT?

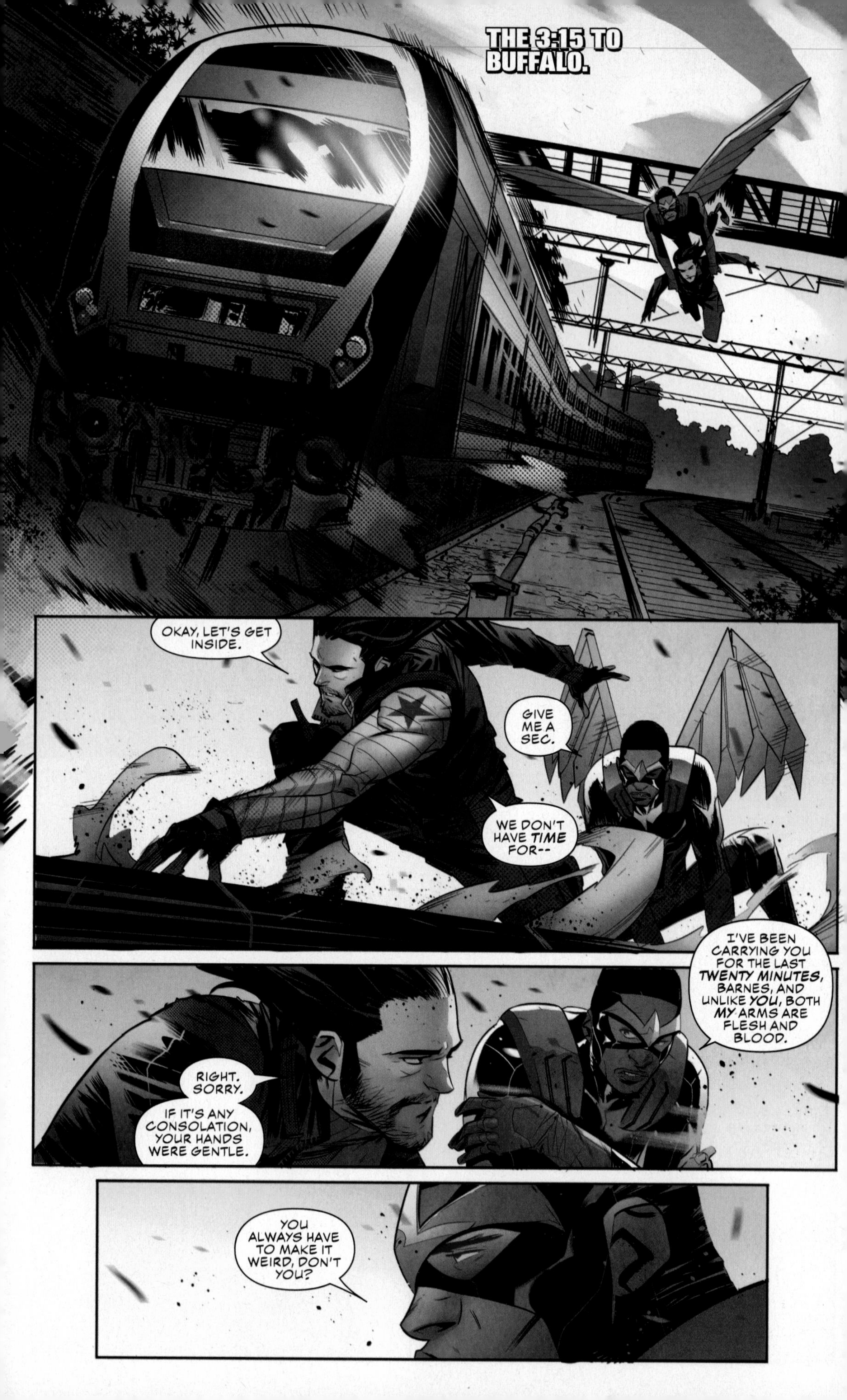
THE 3:15 TO BUFFALO.
OKAY, LET'S GET INSIDE.
GIVE ME A SEC.
WE DON'T HAVE TIME FOR--
I'VE BEEN CARRYING YOU FOR THE LAST TWENTY MINUTES, BARNES, AND UNLIKE YOU, BOTH MY ARMS ARE FLESH AND BLOOD.
RIGHT. SORRY.
IF IT'S ANY CONSOLATION, YOUR HANDS WERE GENTLE.
YOU ALWAYS HAVE TO MAKE IT WEIRD, DON'T YOU?

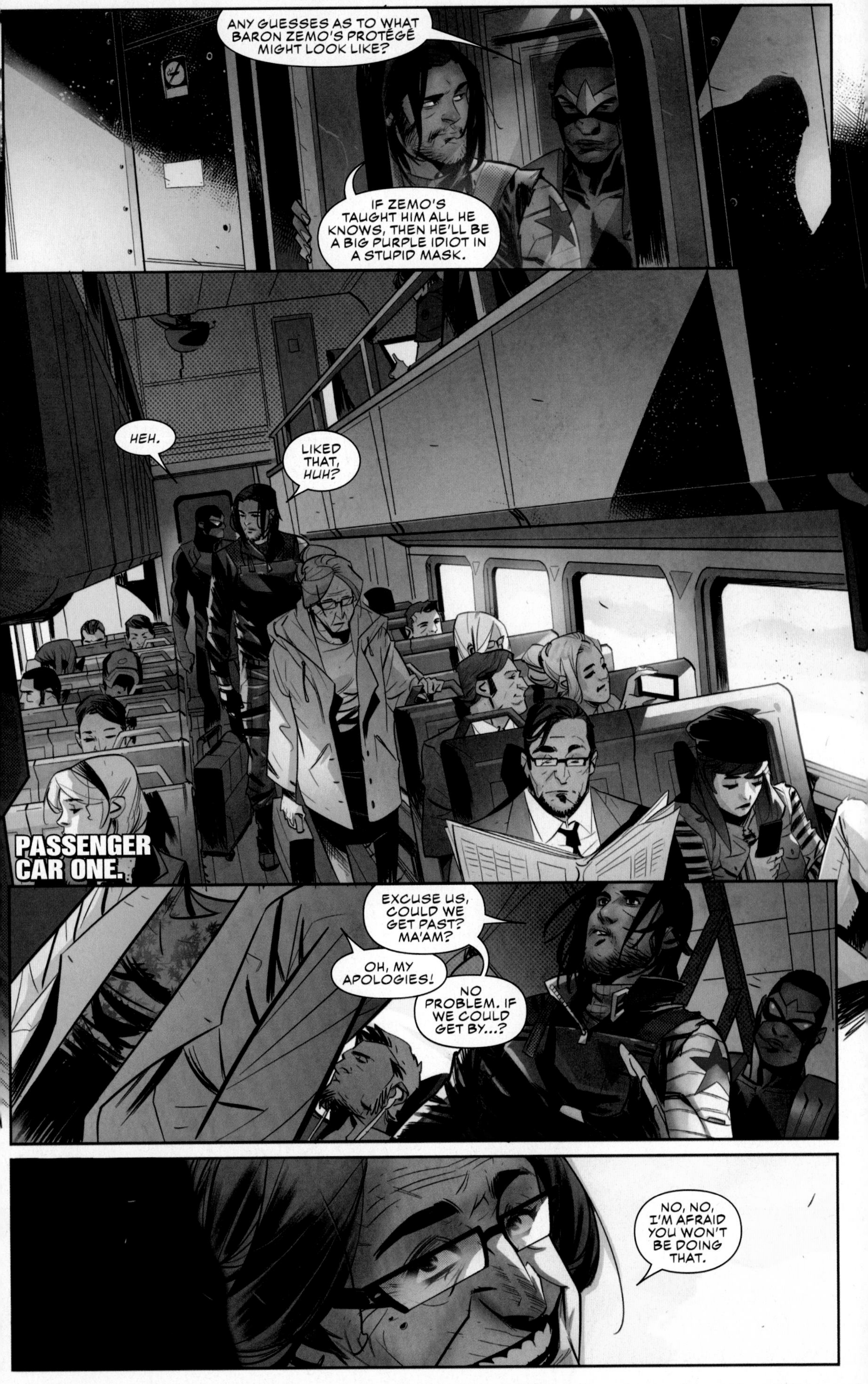
ANY GUESSES AS TO WHAT BARON ZEMO'S PROTÉGÉ MIGHT LOOK LIKE?
IF ZEMO'S TAUGHT HIM ALL HE KNOWS, THEN HE'LL BE A BIG PURPLE IDIOT IN A STUPID MASK.
HEH.
LIKED THAT, HUH?
PASSENGER CAR ONE.
EXCUSE US, COULD WE GET PAST? MA'AM?
OH, MY APOLOGIES!
NO PROBLEM. IF WE COULD GET BY...?
NO, NO, I'M AFRAID YOU WON'T BE DOING THAT.

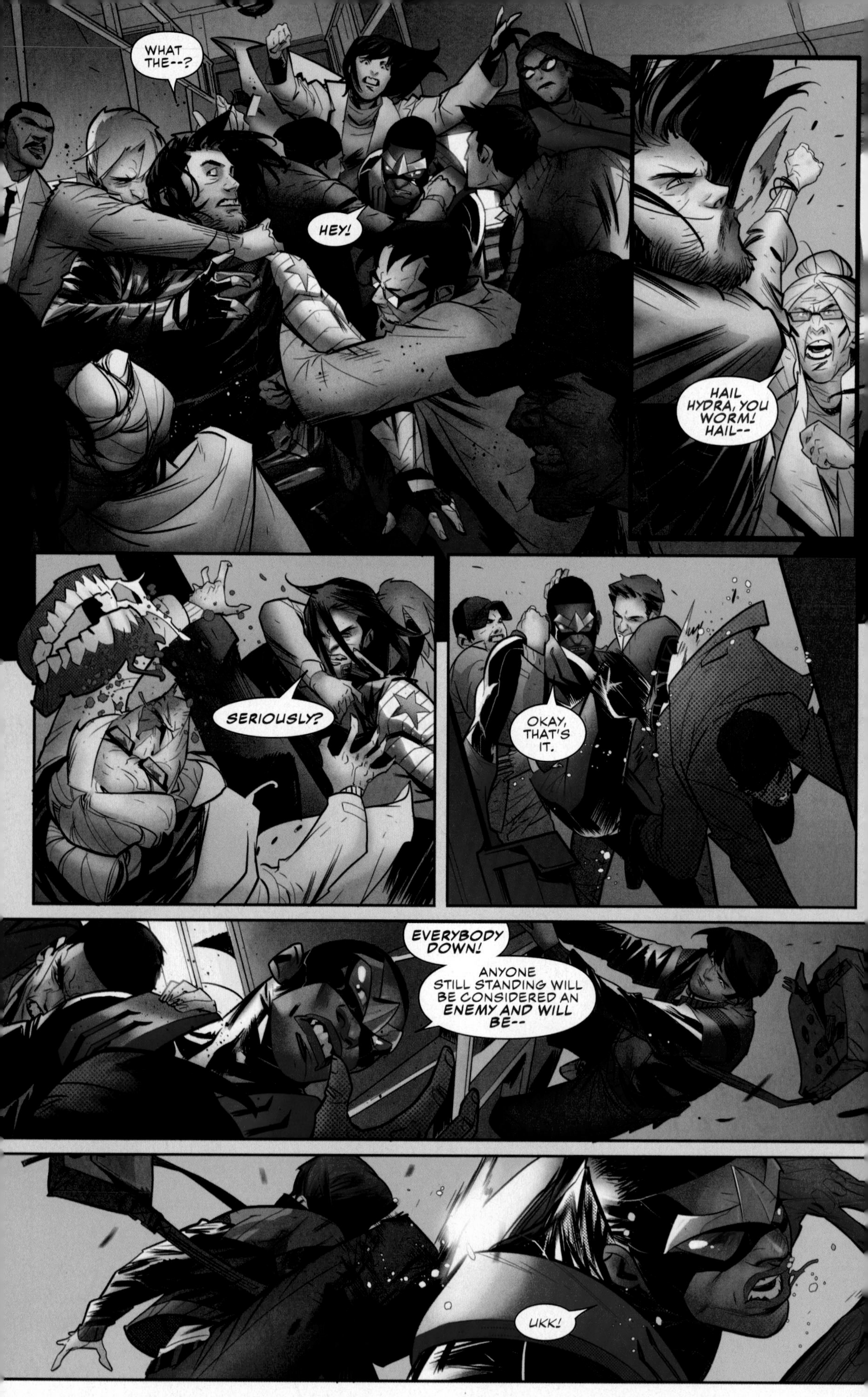
WHAT THE--?
HEY!
HAIL HYDRA, YOU WORM! HAIL--
SERIOUSLY?
OKAY, THAT'S IT.
EVERYBODY DOWN!
ANYONE STILL STANDING WILL BE CONSIDERED AN ENEMY AND WILL BE--
UKK!

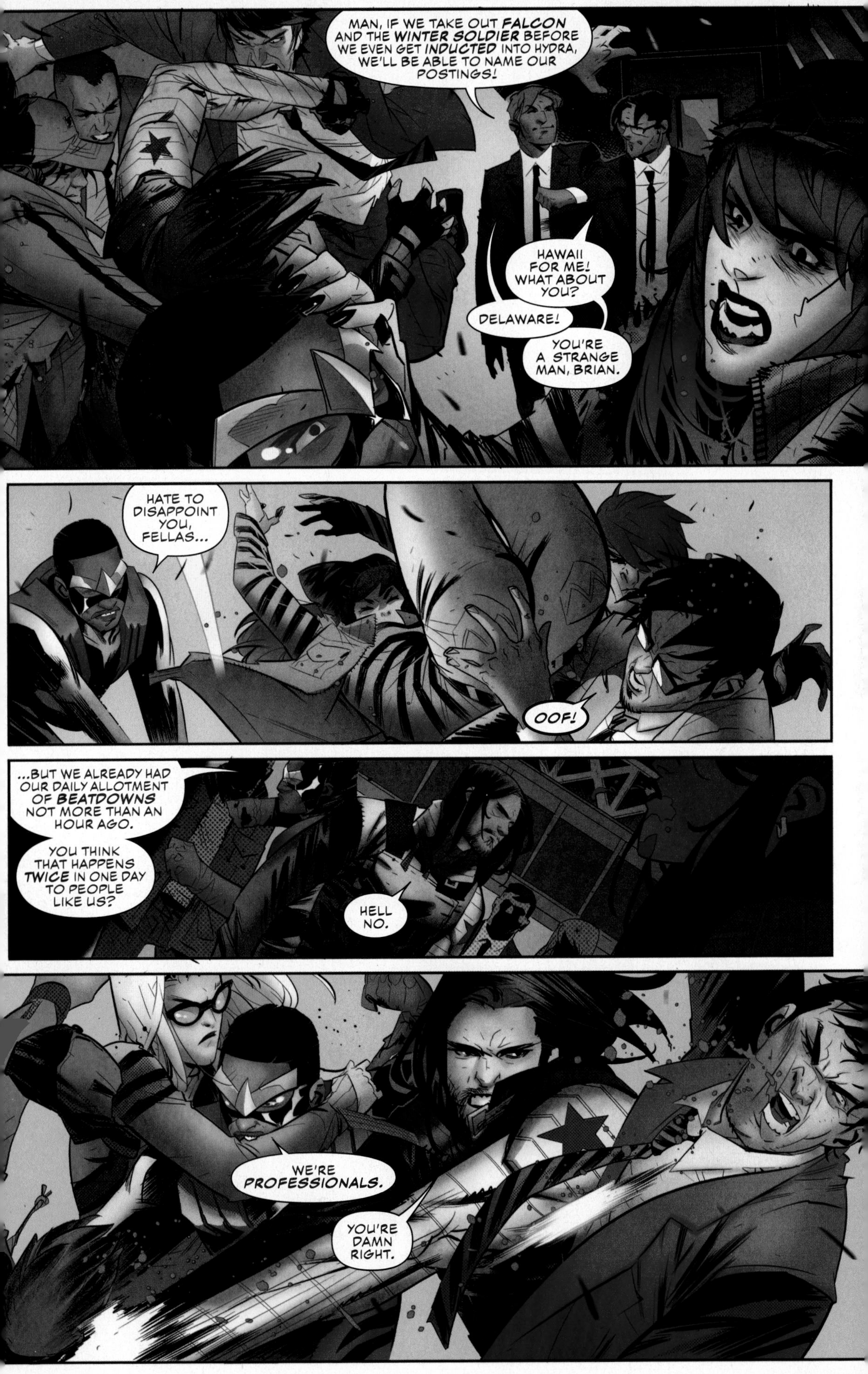
MAN, IF WE TAKE OUT FALCON AND THE WINTER SOLDIER BEFORE WE EVEN GET INDUCTED INTO HYDRA, WE'LL BE ABLE TO NAME OUR POSTINGS!
HAWAII FOR ME! WHAT ABOUT YOU?
DELAWARE!
YOU'RE A STRANGE MAN, BRIAN.
HATE TO DISAPPOINT YOU, FELLAS...
OOF!
...BUT WE ALREADY HAD OUR DAILY ALLOTMENT OF BEATDOWNS NOT MORE THAN AN HOUR AGO.
YOU THINK THAT HAPPENS TWICE IN ONE DAY TO PEOPLE LIKE US?
HELL NO.
WE'RE PROFESSIONALS.
YOU'RE DAMN RIGHT.

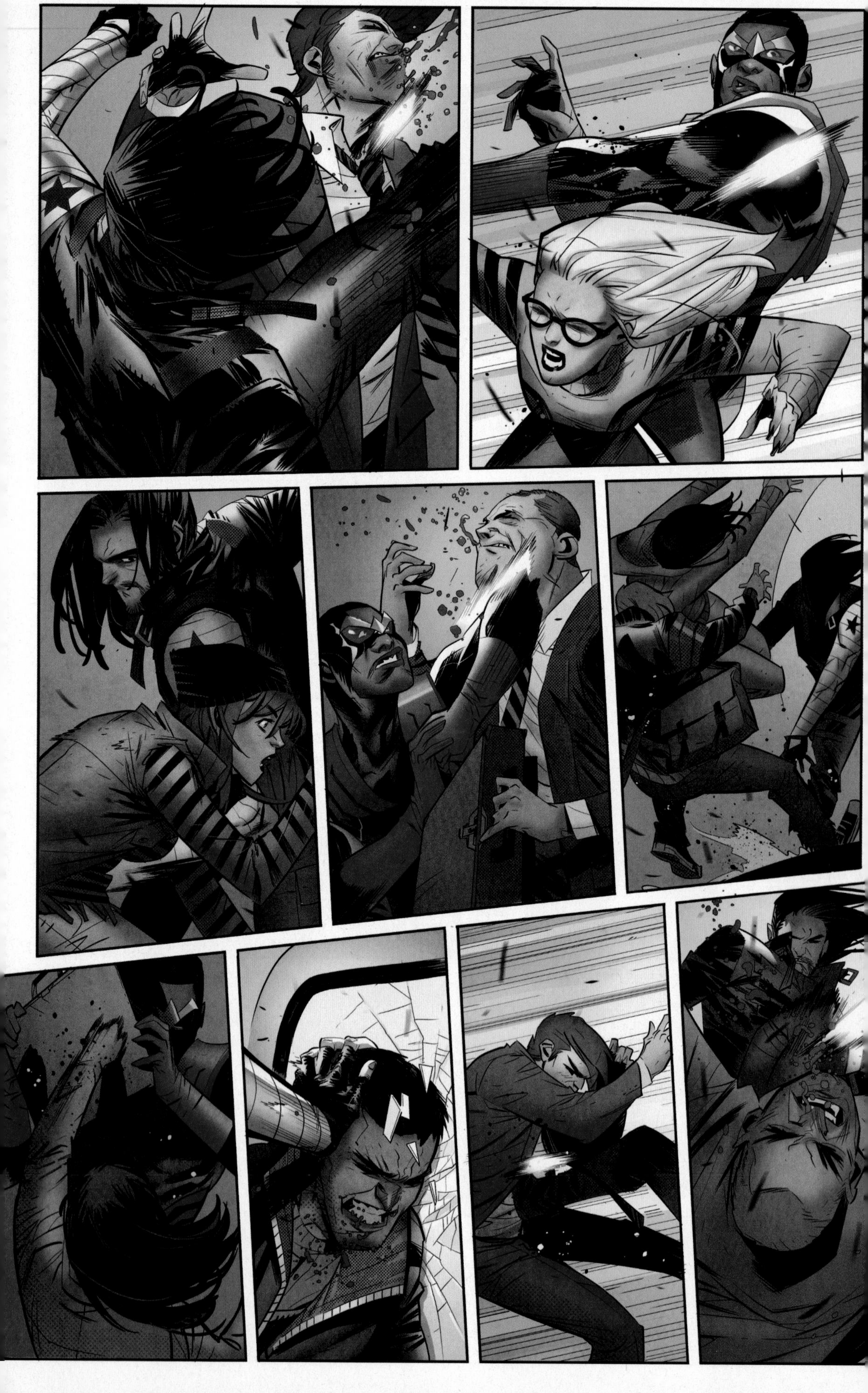

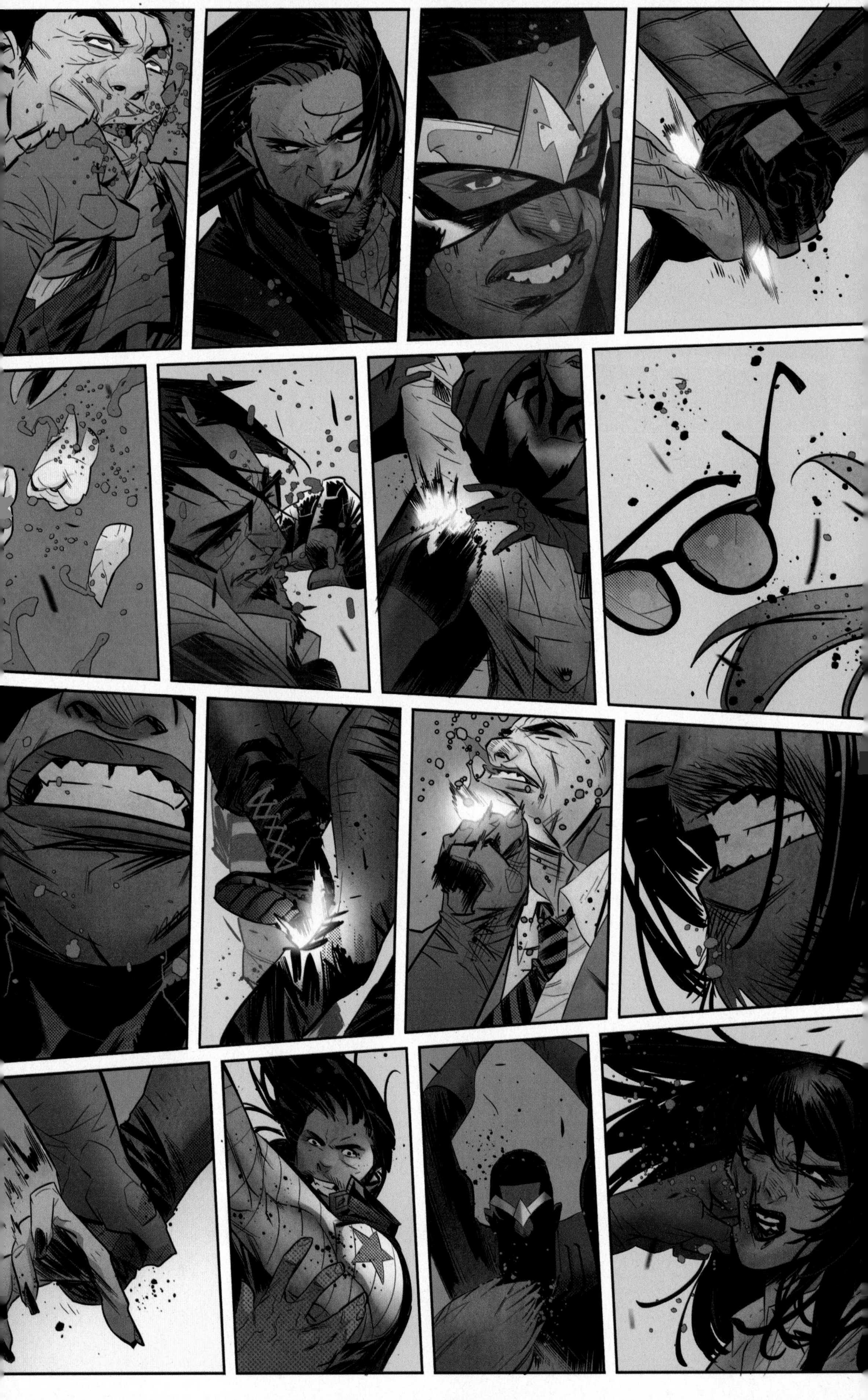

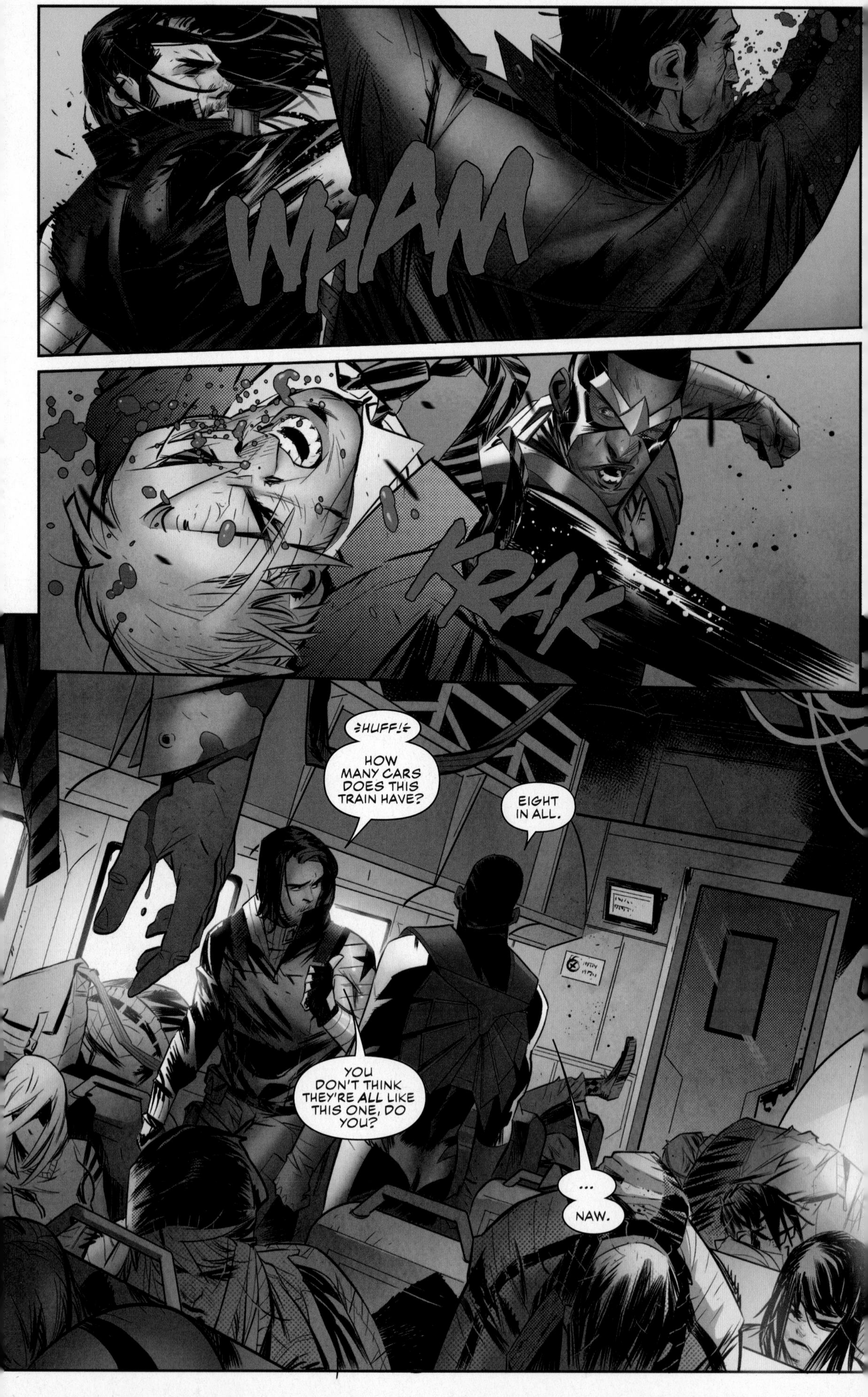
WHAM
KRAK
HUFF!
HOW MANY CARS DOES THIS TRAIN HAVE?
EIGHT IN ALL.
YOU DON'T THINK THEY'RE ALL LIKE THIS ONE, DO YOU?
...
NAW.

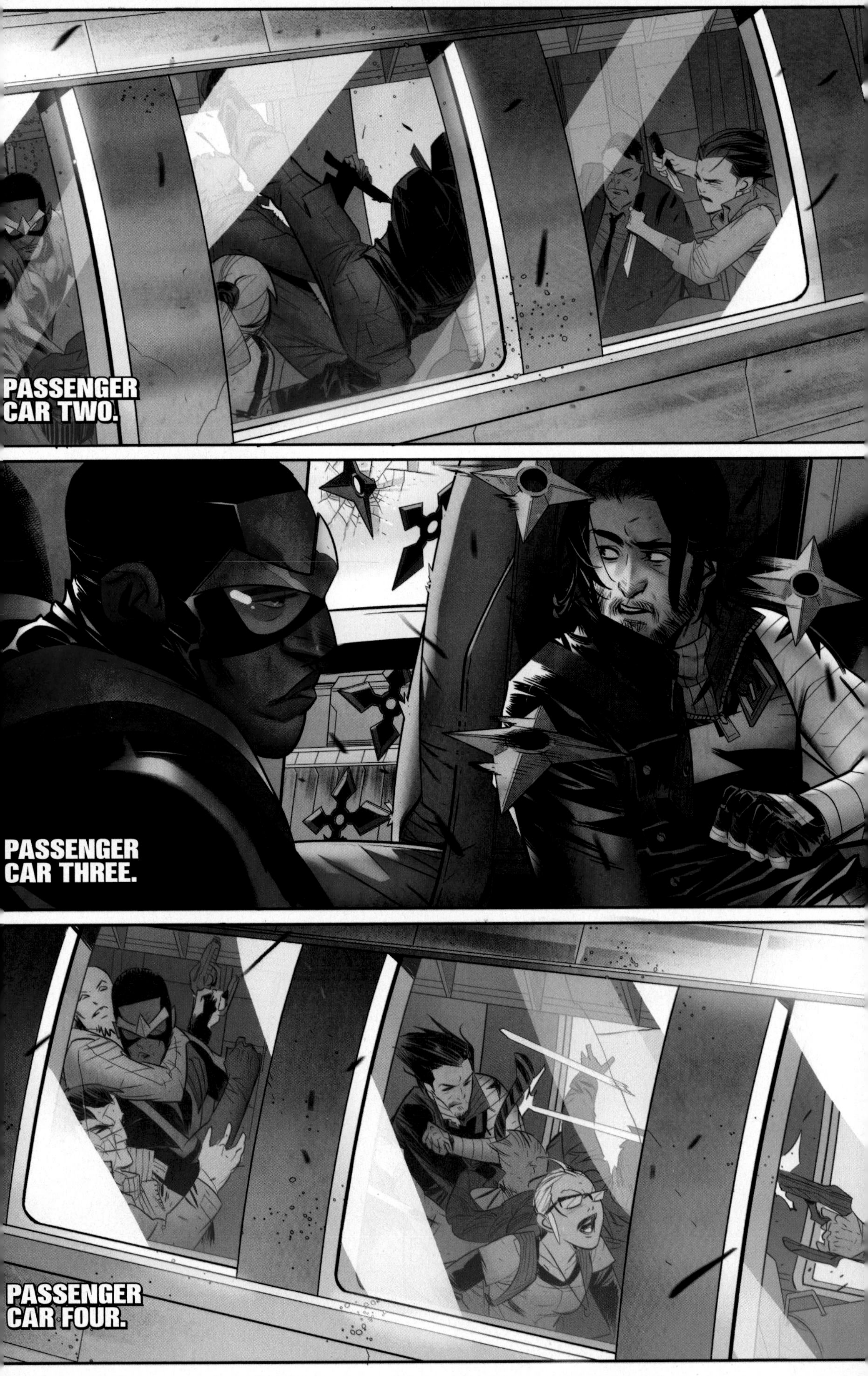
PASSENGER CAR TWO.
PASSENGER CAR THREE.
PASSENGER CAR FOUR.

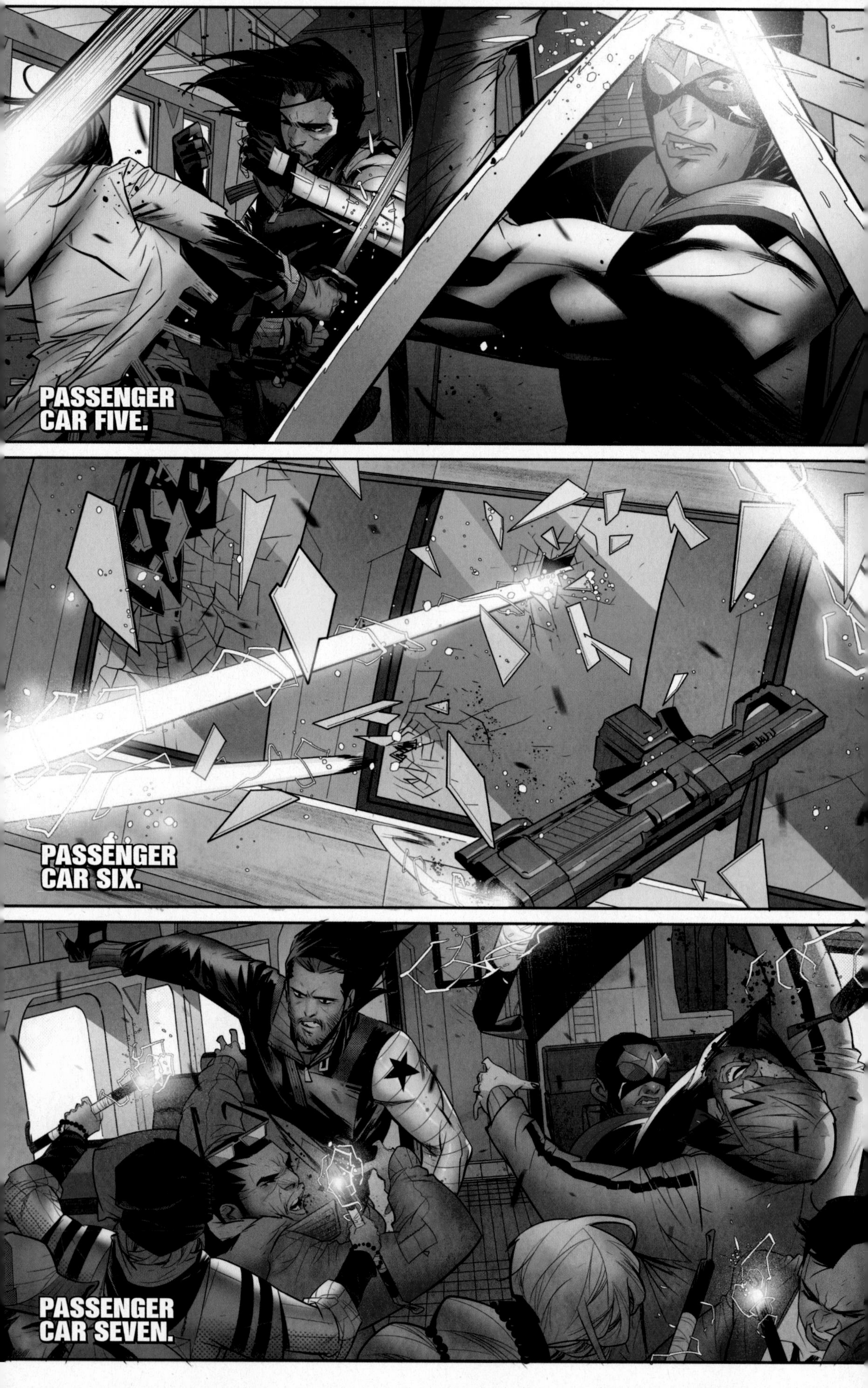
PASSENGER CAR FIVE.
PASSENGER CAR SIX.
PASSENGER CAR SEVEN.

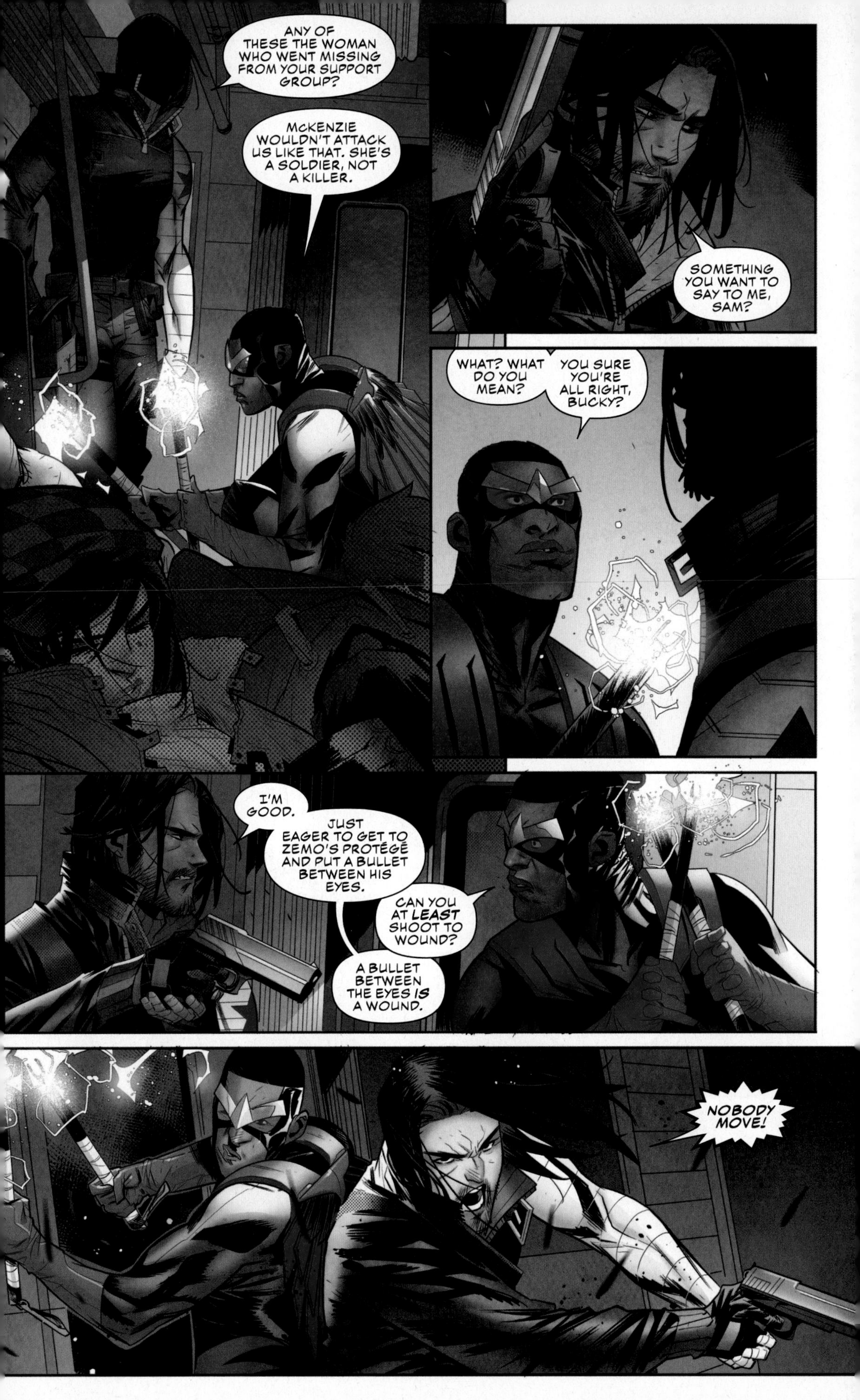
ANY OF THESE THE WOMAN WHO WENT MISSING FROM YOUR SUPPORT GROUP?
McKENZIE WOULDN'T ATTACK US LIKE THAT. SHE'S A SOLDIER, NOT A KILLER.
SOMETHING YOU WANT TO SAY TO ME, SAM?
WHAT? WHAT DO YOU MEAN?
YOU SURE YOU'RE ALL RIGHT, BUCKY?
I'M GOOD.
JUST EAGER TO GET TO ZEMO'S PROTÉGÉ AND PUT A BULLET BETWEEN HIS EYES.
CAN YOU AT LEAST SHOOT TO WOUND?
A BULLET BETWEEN THE EYES IS A WOUND.
NOBODY MOVE!

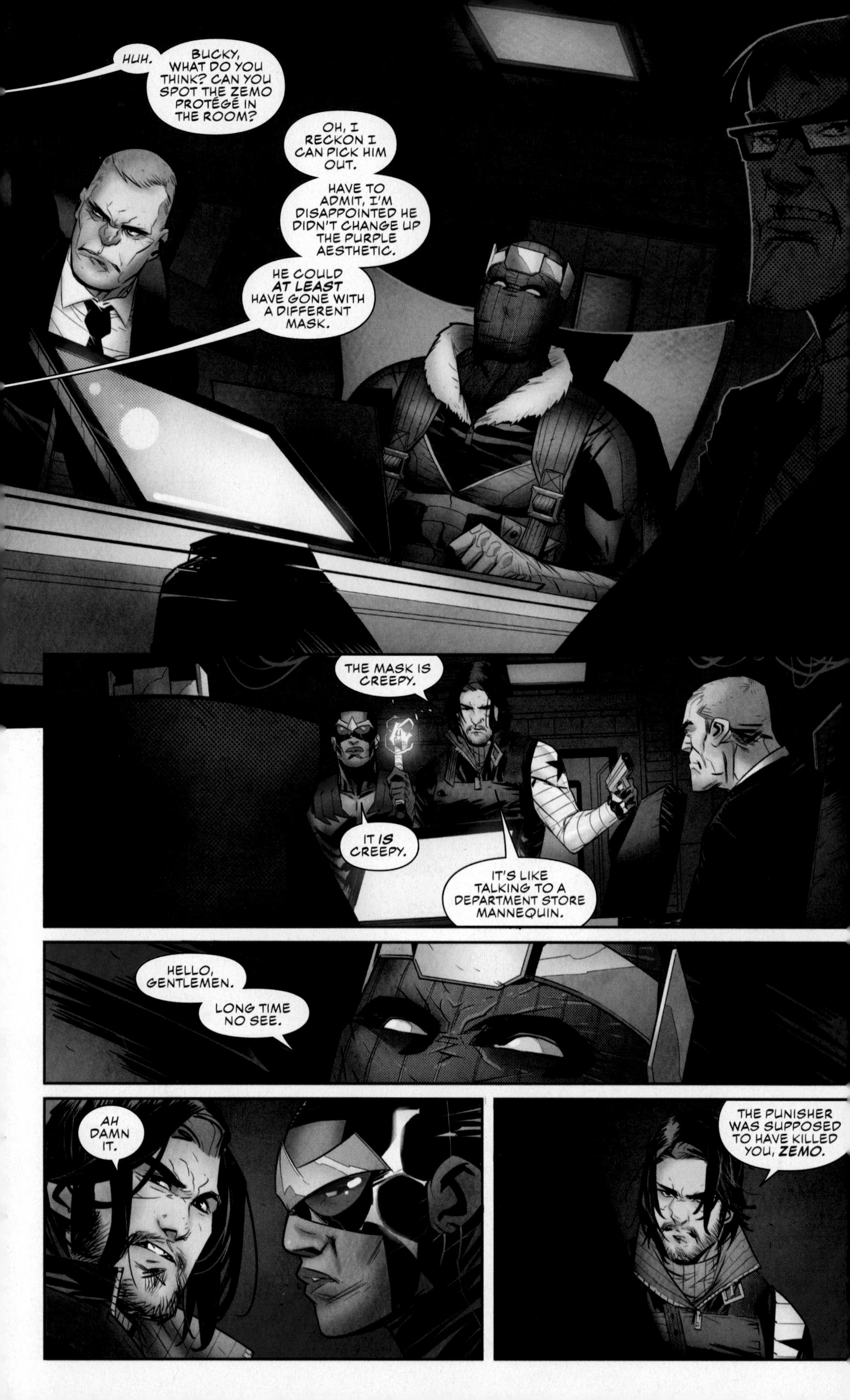
HUH.
BUCKY, WHAT DO YOU THINK? CAN YOU SPOT THE ZEMO PROTÉGÉ IN THE ROOM?
OH, I RECKON I CAN PICK HIM OUT.
HAVE TO ADMIT, I'M DISAPPOINTED HE DIDN'T CHANGE UP THE PURPLE AESTHETIC.
HE COULD **AT LEAST** HAVE GONE WITH A DIFFERENT MASK.
THE MASK IS CREEPY.
IT *IS* CREEPY.
IT'S LIKE TALKING TO A DEPARTMENT STORE MANNEQUIN.
HELLO, GENTLEMEN.
LONG TIME NO SEE.
AH DAMN IT.
THE PUNISHER WAS SUPPOSED TO HAVE KILLED YOU, **ZEMO**.

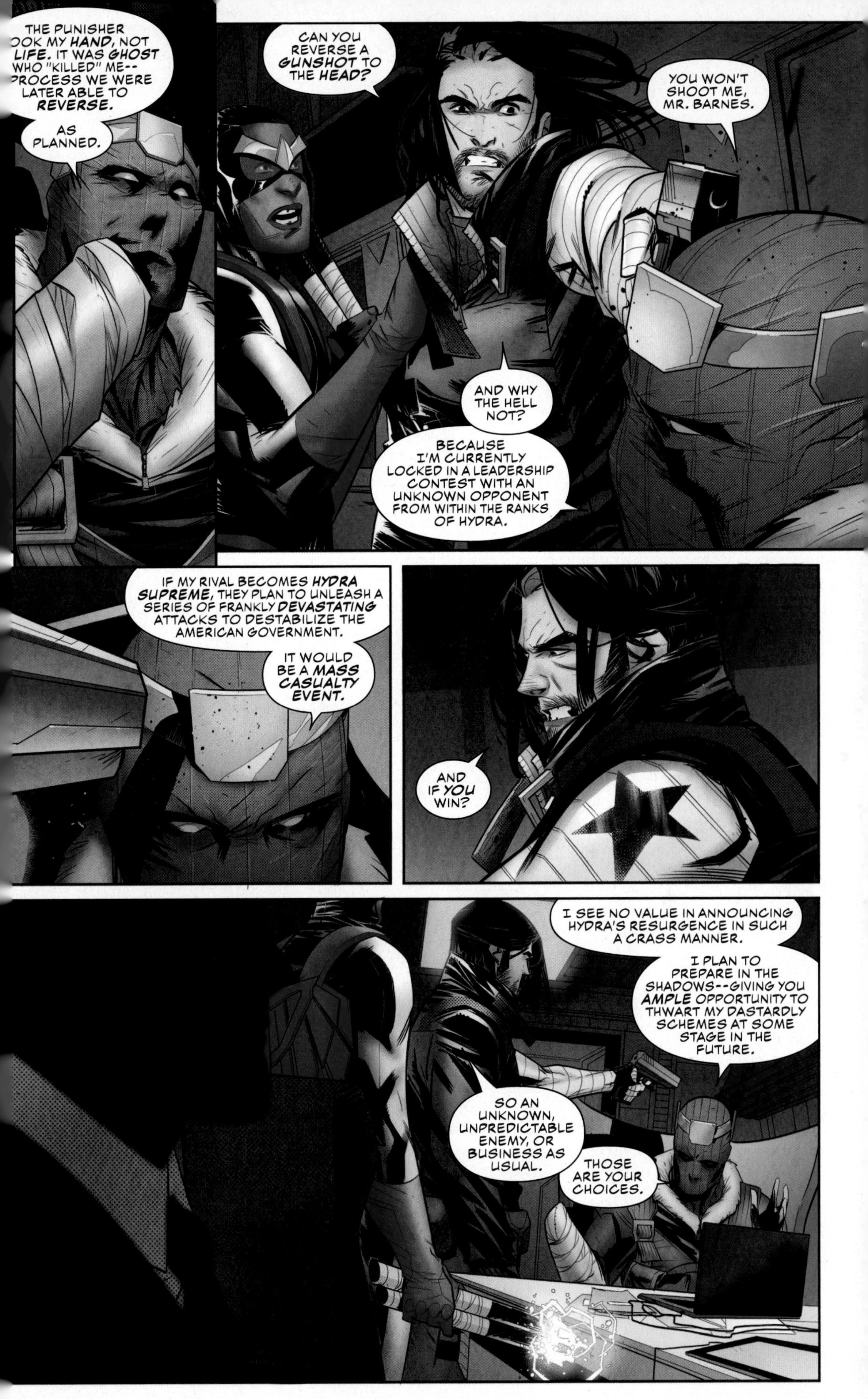
THE PUNISHER TOOK MY HAND, NOT MY LIFE. IT WAS GHOST WHO "KILLED" ME--A PROCESS WE WERE LATER ABLE TO REVERSE.
AS PLANNED.
CAN YOU REVERSE A GUNSHOT TO THE HEAD?
YOU WON'T SHOOT ME, MR. BARNES.
AND WHY THE HELL NOT?
BECAUSE I'M CURRENTLY LOCKED IN A LEADERSHIP CONTEST WITH AN UNKNOWN OPPONENT FROM WITHIN THE RANKS OF HYDRA.
IF MY RIVAL BECOMES HYDRA SUPREME, THEY PLAN TO UNLEASH A SERIES OF FRANKLY DEVASTATING ATTACKS TO DESTABILIZE THE AMERICAN GOVERNMENT.
IT WOULD BE A MASS CASUALTY EVENT.
AND IF YOU WIN?
I SEE NO VALUE IN ANNOUNCING HYDRA'S RESURGENCE IN SUCH A CRASS MANNER.
I PLAN TO PREPARE IN THE SHADOWS--GIVING YOU AMPLE OPPORTUNITY TO THWART MY DASTARDLY SCHEMES AT SOME STAGE IN THE FUTURE.
SO AN UNKNOWN, UNPREDICTABLE ENEMY, OR BUSINESS AS USUAL.
THOSE ARE YOUR CHOICES.

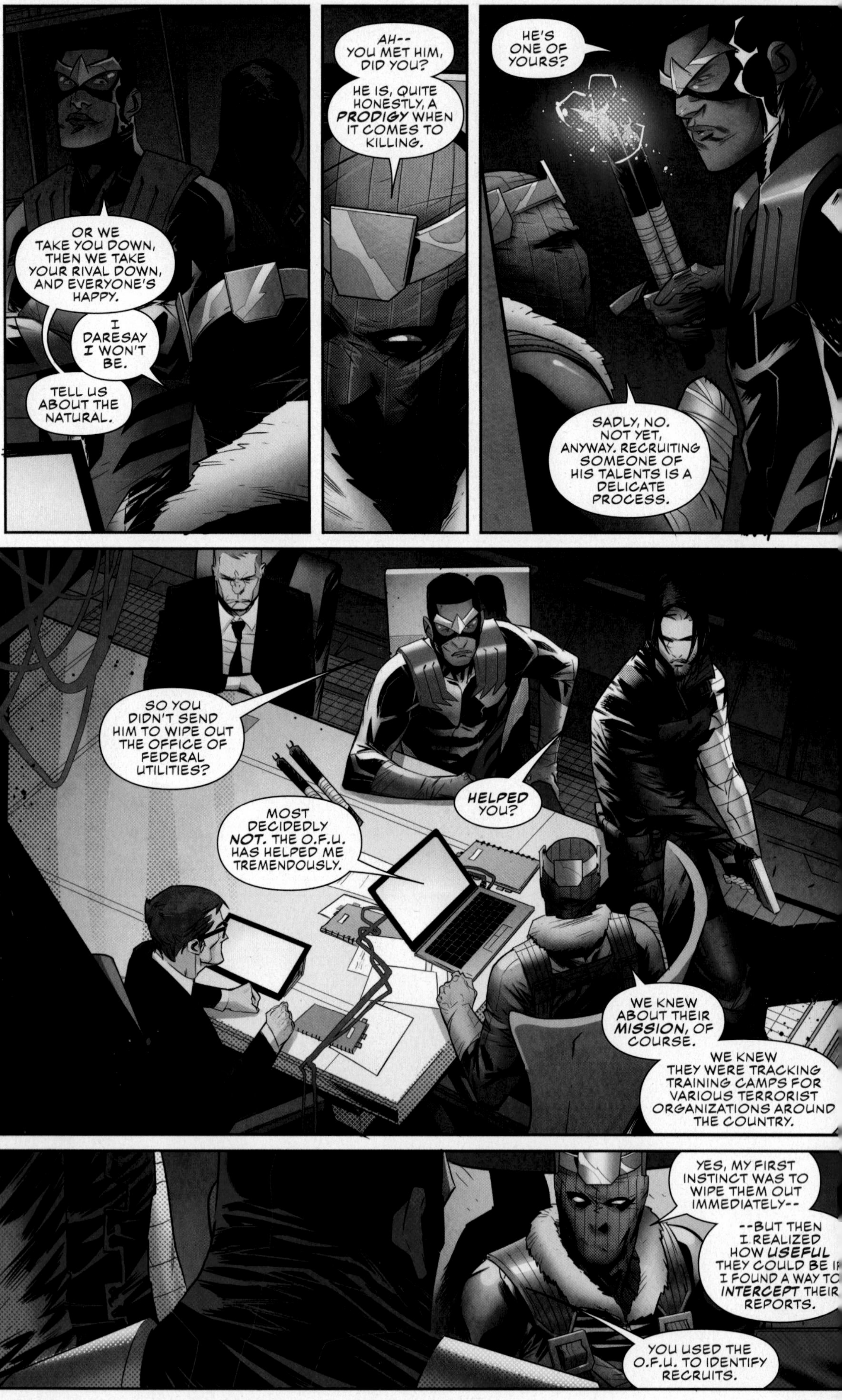

OR WE TAKE YOU DOWN, THEN WE TAKE YOUR RIVAL DOWN, AND EVERYONE'S HAPPY.
I DARESAY I WON'T BE.
TELL US ABOUT THE NATURAL.
AH-- YOU MET HIM, DID YOU?
HE IS, QUITE HONESTLY, A PRODIGY WHEN IT COMES TO KILLING.
HE'S ONE OF YOURS?
SADLY, NO. NOT YET, ANYWAY. RECRUITING SOMEONE OF HIS TALENTS IS A DELICATE PROCESS.
SO YOU DIDN'T SEND HIM TO WIPE OUT THE OFFICE OF FEDERAL UTILITIES?
MOST DECIDEDLY NOT. THE O.F.U. HAS HELPED ME TREMENDOUSLY.
HELPED YOU?
WE KNEW ABOUT THEIR MISSION, OF COURSE.
WE KNEW THEY WERE TRACKING TRAINING CAMPS FOR VARIOUS TERRORIST ORGANIZATIONS AROUND THE COUNTRY.
YES, MY FIRST INSTINCT WAS TO WIPE THEM OUT IMMEDIATELY--
--BUT THEN I REALIZED HOW USEFUL THEY COULD BE IF I FOUND A WAY TO INTERCEPT THEIR REPORTS.
YOU USED THE O.F.U. TO IDENTIFY RECRUITS.

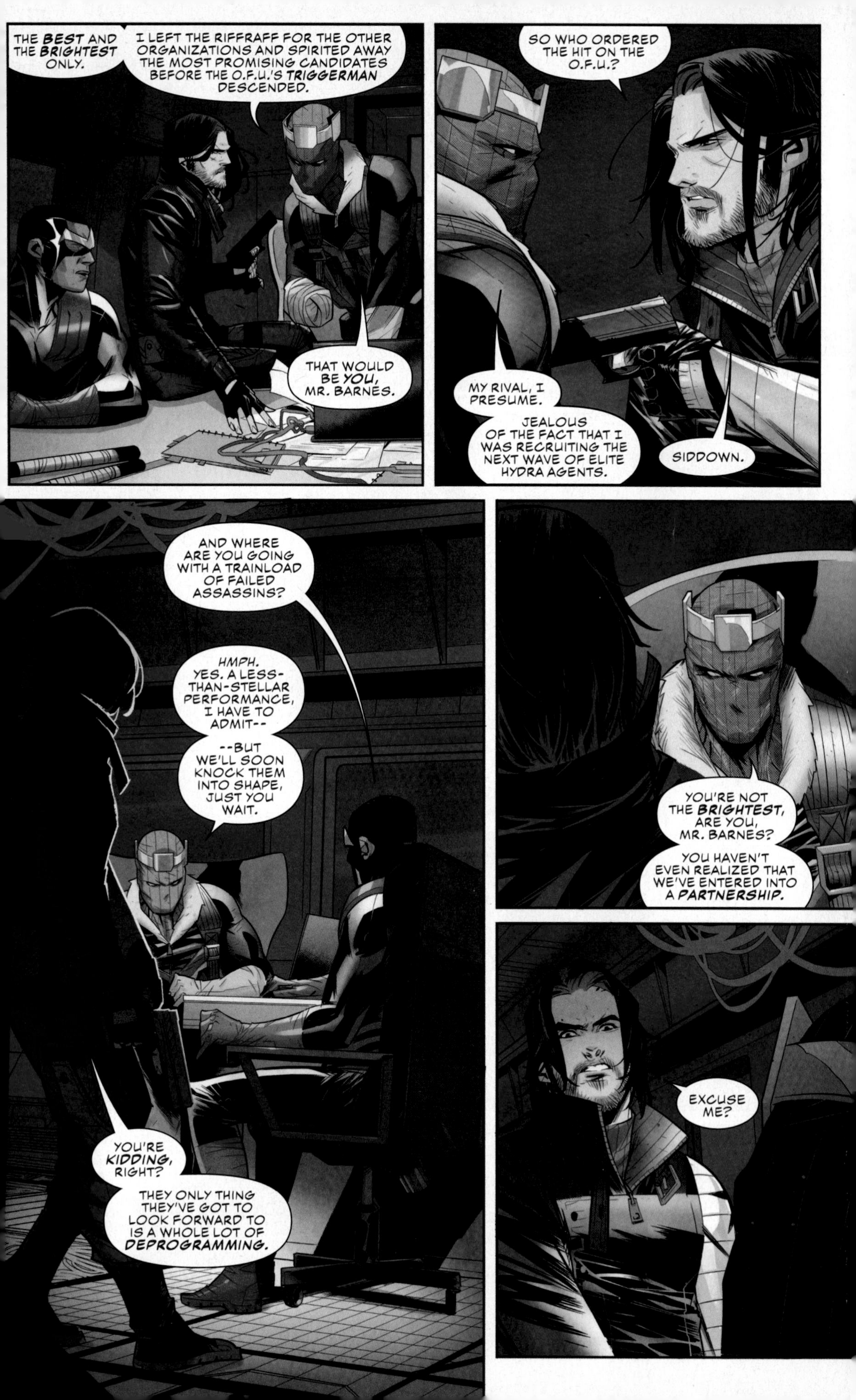
THE BEST AND THE BRIGHTEST ONLY.
I LEFT THE RIFFRAFF FOR THE OTHER ORGANIZATIONS AND SPIRITED AWAY THE MOST PROMISING CANDIDATES BEFORE THE O.F.U.'S TRIGGERMAN DESCENDED.
THAT WOULD BE YOU, MR. BARNES.
SO WHO ORDERED THE HIT ON THE O.F.U.?
MY RIVAL, I PRESUME.
JEALOUS OF THE FACT THAT I WAS RECRUITING THE NEXT WAVE OF ELITE HYDRA AGENTS.
SIDDOWN.
AND WHERE ARE YOU GOING WITH A TRAINLOAD OF FAILED ASSASSINS?
HMPH. YES. A LESS-THAN-STELLAR PERFORMANCE, I HAVE TO ADMIT--
--BUT WE'LL SOON KNOCK THEM INTO SHAPE, JUST YOU WAIT.
YOU'RE KIDDING, RIGHT?
THEY ONLY THING THEY'VE GOT TO LOOK FORWARD TO IS A WHOLE LOT OF DEPROGRAMMING.
YOU'RE NOT THE BRIGHTEST, ARE YOU, MR. BARNES?
YOU HAVEN'T EVEN REALIZED THAT WE'VE ENTERED INTO A PARTNERSHIP.
EXCUSE ME?

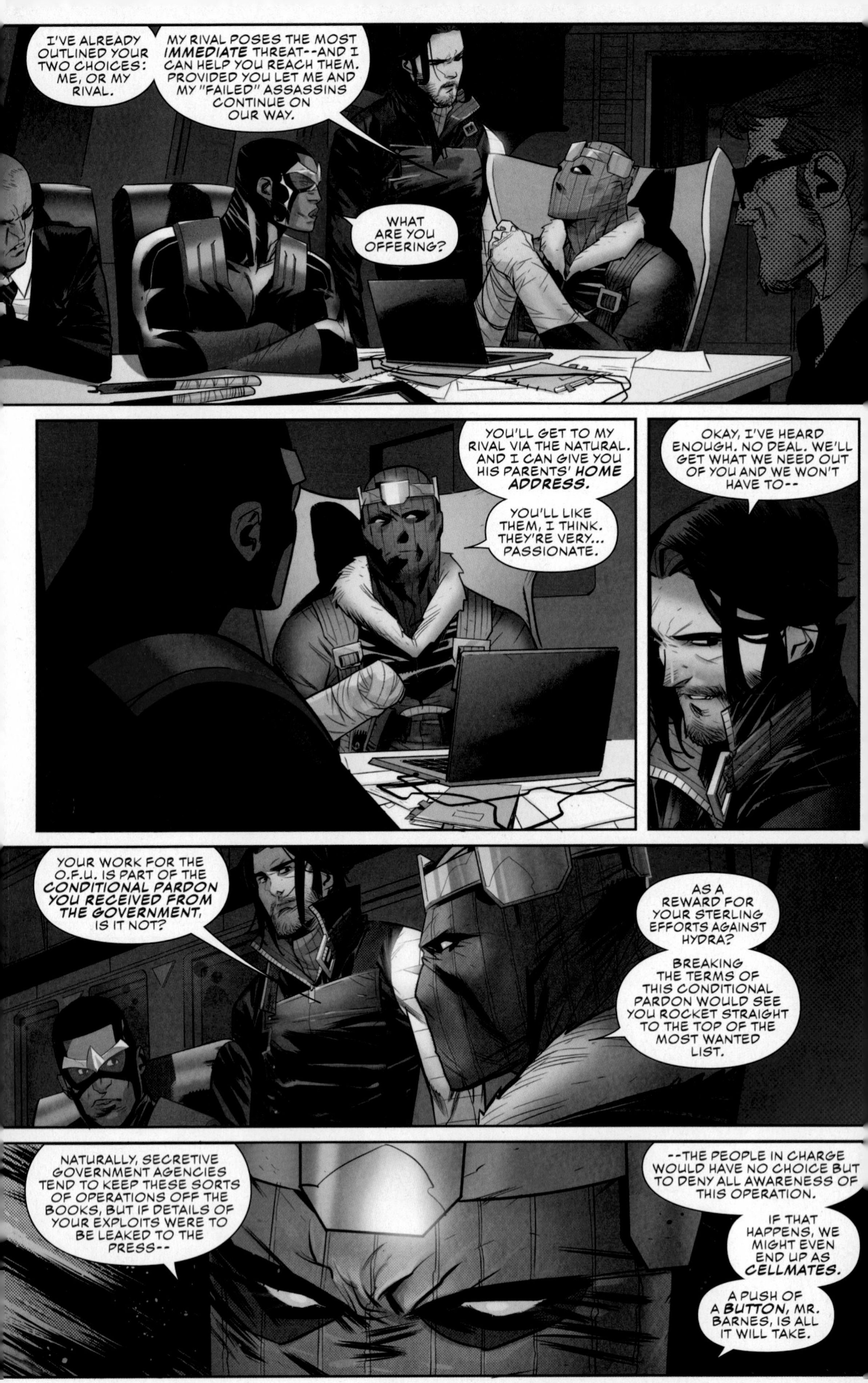
I'VE ALREADY OUTLINED YOUR TWO CHOICES: ME, OR MY RIVAL.
MY RIVAL POSES THE MOST IMMEDIATE THREAT--AND I CAN HELP YOU REACH THEM. PROVIDED YOU LET ME AND MY "FAILED" ASSASSINS CONTINUE ON OUR WAY.
WHAT ARE YOU OFFERING?
YOU'LL GET TO MY RIVAL VIA THE NATURAL. AND I CAN GIVE YOU HIS PARENTS' HOME ADDRESS.
YOU'LL LIKE THEM, I THINK. THEY'RE VERY... PASSIONATE.
OKAY, I'VE HEARD ENOUGH. NO DEAL. WE'LL GET WHAT WE NEED OUT OF YOU AND WE WON'T HAVE TO--
YOUR WORK FOR THE O.F.U. IS PART OF THE CONDITIONAL PARDON YOU RECEIVED FROM THE GOVERNMENT, IS IT NOT?
AS A REWARD FOR YOUR STERLING EFFORTS AGAINST HYDRA?
BREAKING THE TERMS OF THIS CONDITIONAL PARDON WOULD SEE YOU ROCKET STRAIGHT TO THE TOP OF THE MOST WANTED LIST.
NATURALLY, SECRETIVE GOVERNMENT AGENCIES TEND TO KEEP THESE SORTS OF OPERATIONS OFF THE BOOKS, BUT IF DETAILS OF YOUR EXPLOITS WERE TO BE LEAKED TO THE PRESS--
--THE PEOPLE IN CHARGE WOULD HAVE NO CHOICE BUT TO DENY ALL AWARENESS OF THIS OPERATION.
IF THAT HAPPENS, WE MIGHT EVEN END UP AS CELLMATES.
A PUSH OF A BUTTON, MR. BARNES, IS ALL IT WILL TAKE.

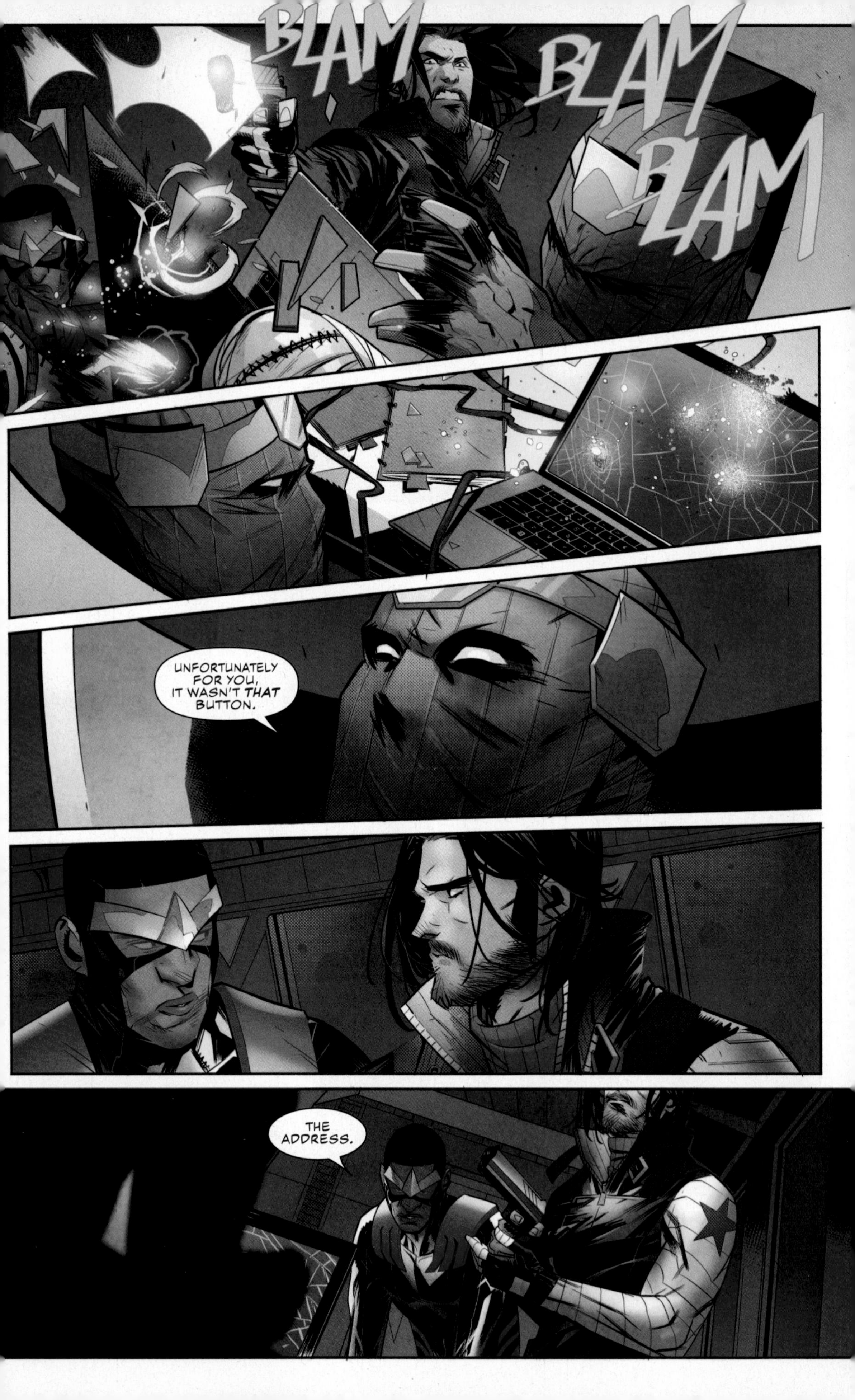
BLAM
BLAM
BLAM
BLAM
UNFORTUNATELY FOR YOU, IT WASN'T *THAT* BUTTON.
THE ADDRESS.

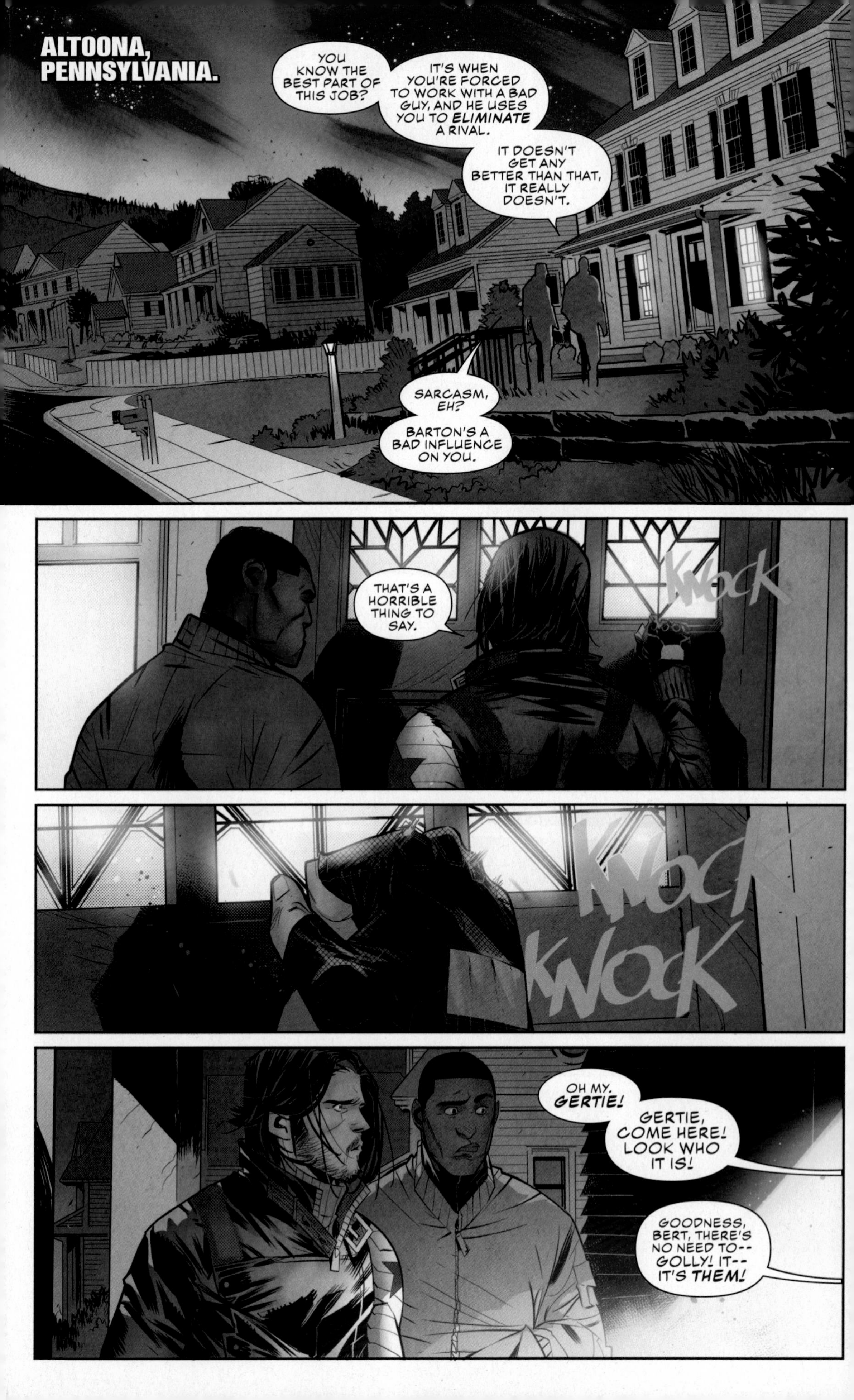
ALTOONA, PENNSYLVANIA.
YOU KNOW THE BEST PART OF THIS JOB?
IT'S WHEN YOU'RE FORCED TO WORK WITH A BAD GUY, AND HE USES YOU TO ELIMINATE A RIVAL.
IT DOESN'T GET ANY BETTER THAN THAT, IT REALLY DOESN'T.
SARCASM, EH?
BARTON'S A BAD INFLUENCE ON YOU.
THAT'S A HORRIBLE THING TO SAY.
KNOCK
KNOCK
KNOCK
OH MY. GERTIE!
GERTIE, COME HERE! LOOK WHO IT IS!
GOODNESS, BERT, THERE'S NO NEED TO-- GOLLY! IT-- IT'S THEM!

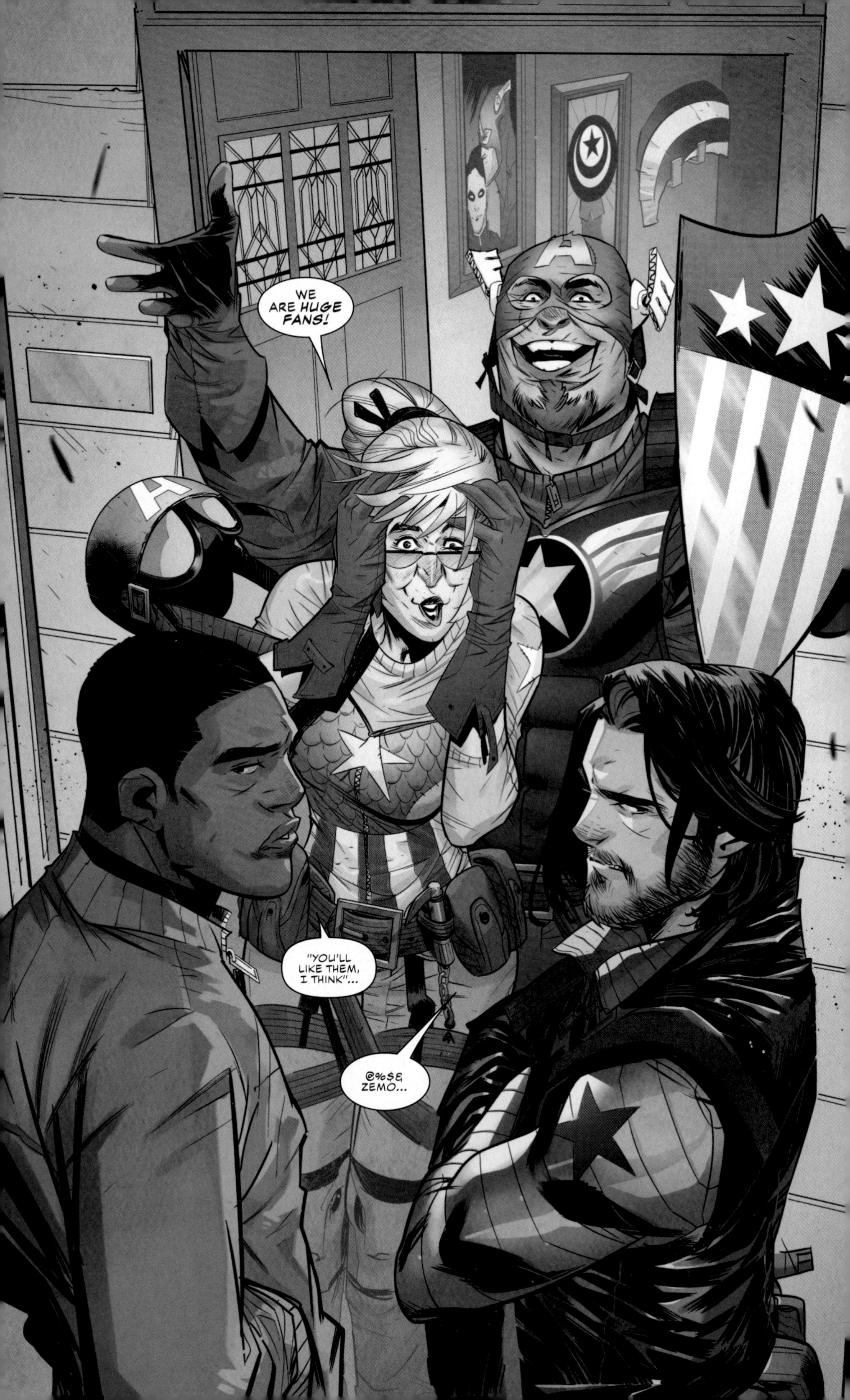
WE ARE HUGE FANS!
"YOU'LL LIKE THEM, I THINK"...
@%$&, ZEMO...

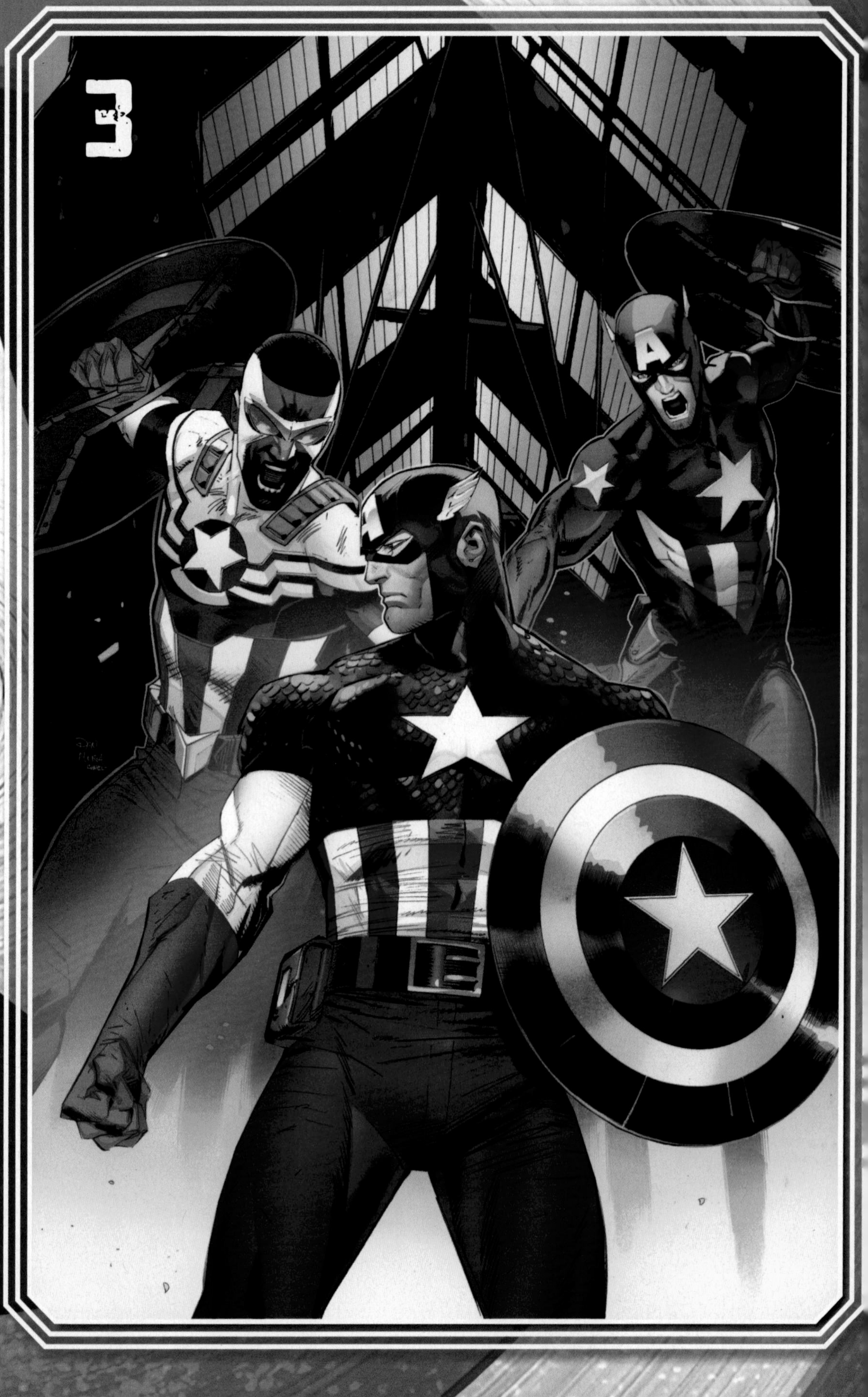
3

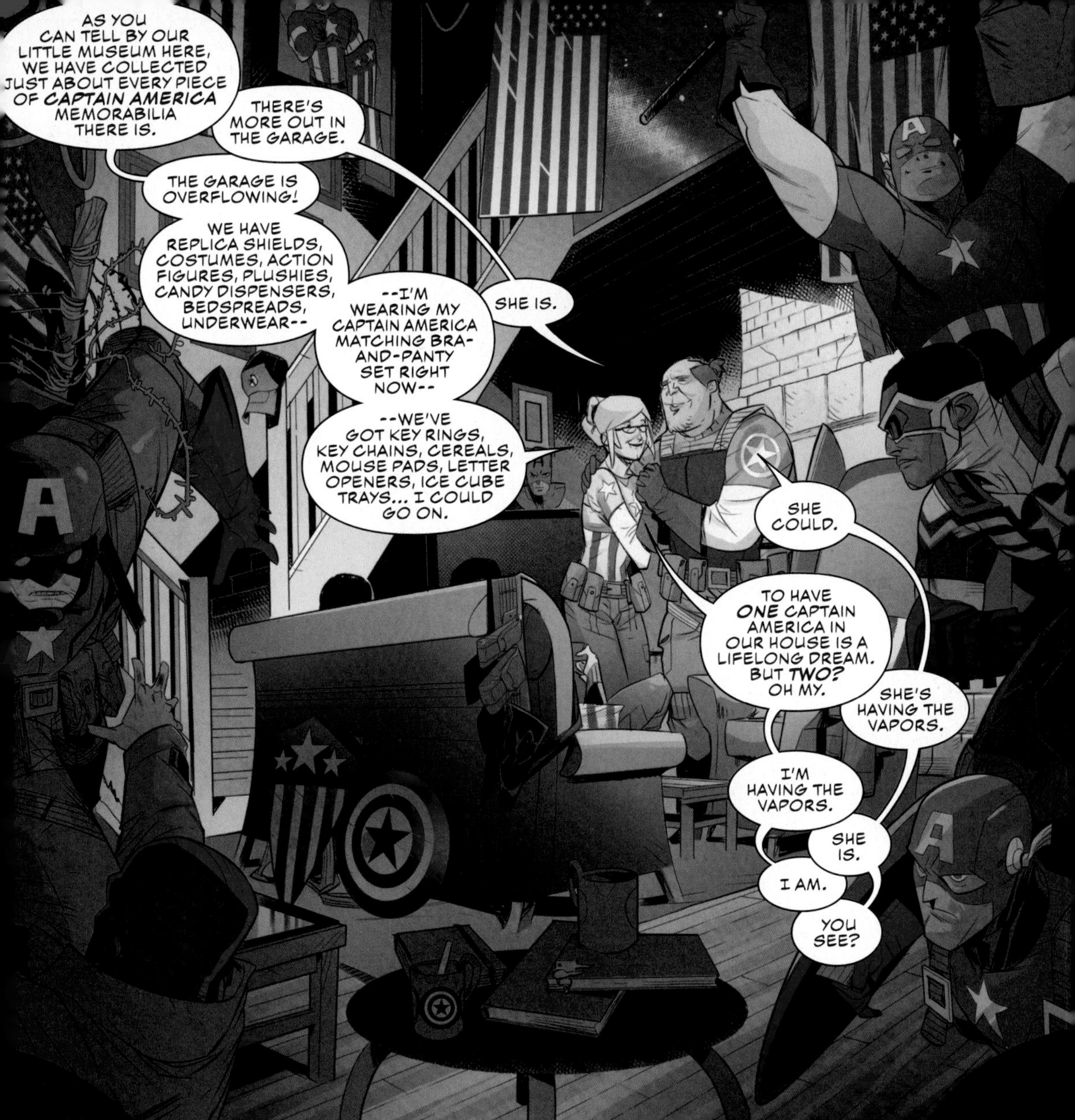
AS YOU CAN TELL BY OUR LITTLE MUSEUM HERE, WE HAVE COLLECTED JUST ABOUT EVERY PIECE OF CAPTAIN AMERICA MEMORABILIA THERE IS.
THERE'S MORE OUT IN THE GARAGE.
THE GARAGE IS OVERFLOWING!
WE HAVE REPLICA SHIELDS, COSTUMES, ACTION FIGURES, PLUSHIES, CANDY DISPENSERS, BEDSPREADS, UNDERWEAR--
--I'M WEARING MY CAPTAIN AMERICA MATCHING BRA-AND-PANTY SET RIGHT NOW--
SHE IS.
--WE'VE GOT KEY RINGS, KEY CHAINS, CEREALS, MOUSE PADS, LETTER OPENERS, ICE CUBE TRAYS... I COULD GO ON.
SHE COULD.
TO HAVE ONE CAPTAIN AMERICA IN OUR HOUSE IS A LIFELONG DREAM. BUT TWO? OH MY.
SHE'S HAVING THE VAPORS.
I'M HAVING THE VAPORS.
SHE IS.
I AM.
YOU SEE?

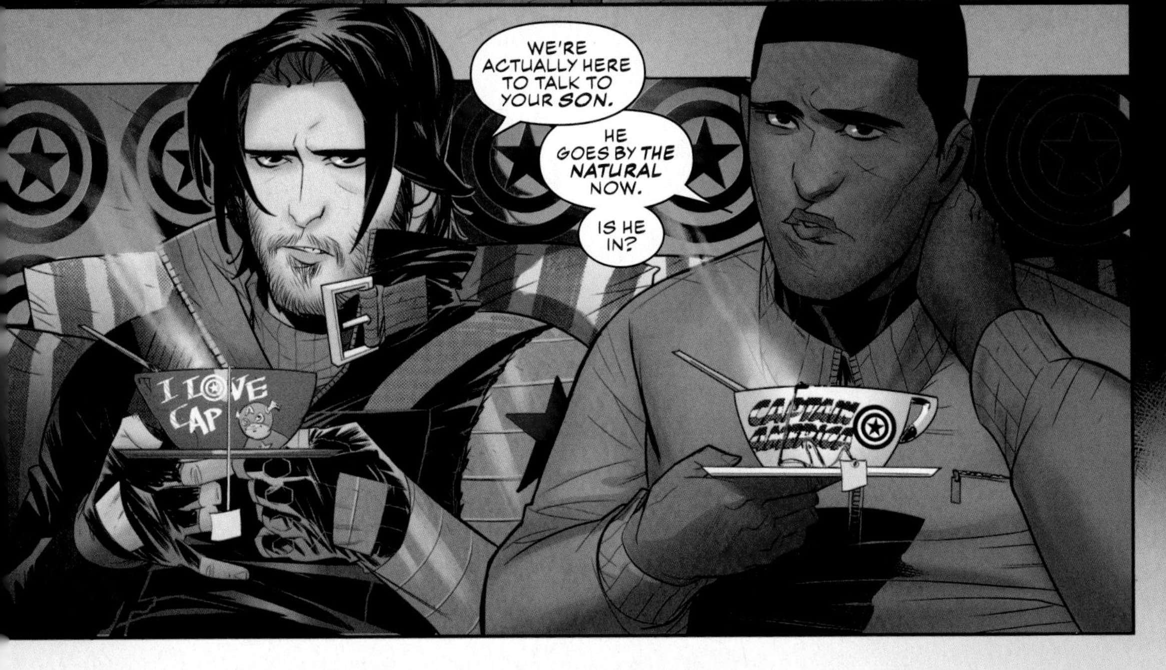
WE'RE ACTUALLY HERE TO TALK TO YOUR SON.
HE GOES BY THE NATURAL NOW.
IS HE IN?
I LOVE CAP
CAPTAIN AMERICA

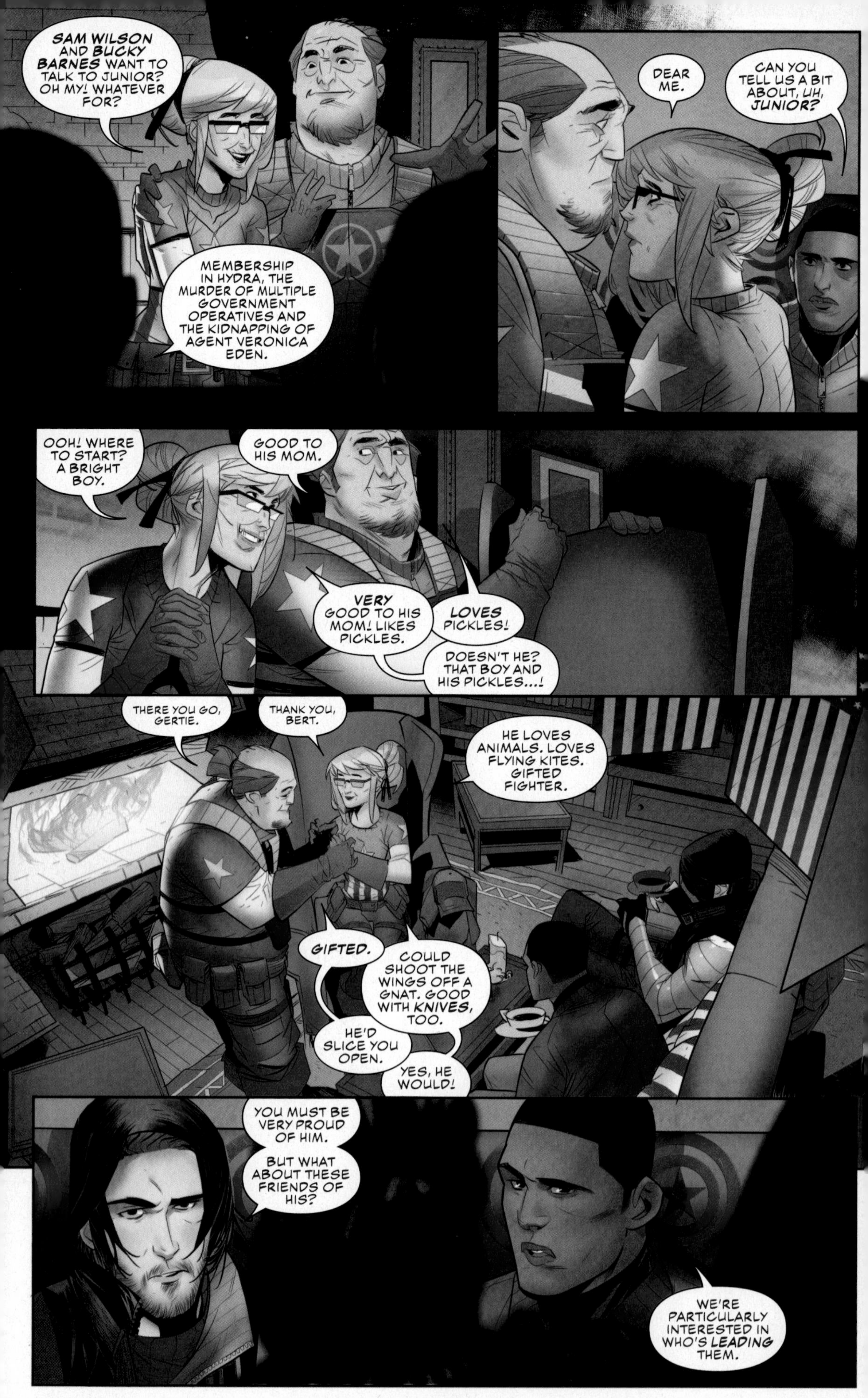
SAM WILSON AND BUCKY BARNES WANT TO TALK TO JUNIOR? OH MY! WHATEVER FOR?
MEMBERSHIP IN HYDRA, THE MURDER OF MULTIPLE GOVERNMENT OPERATIVES AND THE KIDNAPPING OF AGENT VERONICA EDEN.
DEAR ME.
CAN YOU TELL US A BIT ABOUT, UH, JUNIOR?
OOH! WHERE TO START? A BRIGHT BOY.
GOOD TO HIS MOM.
VERY GOOD TO HIS MOM! LIKES PICKLES.
LOVES PICKLES!
DOESN'T HE? THAT BOY AND HIS PICKLES...!
THERE YOU GO, GERTIE.
THANK YOU, BERT.
HE LOVES ANIMALS. LOVES FLYING KITES. GIFTED FIGHTER.
GIFTED.
COULD SHOOT THE WINGS OFF A GNAT. GOOD WITH KNIVES, TOO.
HE'D SLICE YOU OPEN.
YES, HE WOULD!
YOU MUST BE VERY PROUD OF HIM.
BUT WHAT ABOUT THESE FRIENDS OF HIS?
WE'RE PARTICULARLY INTERESTED IN WHO'S LEADING THEM.

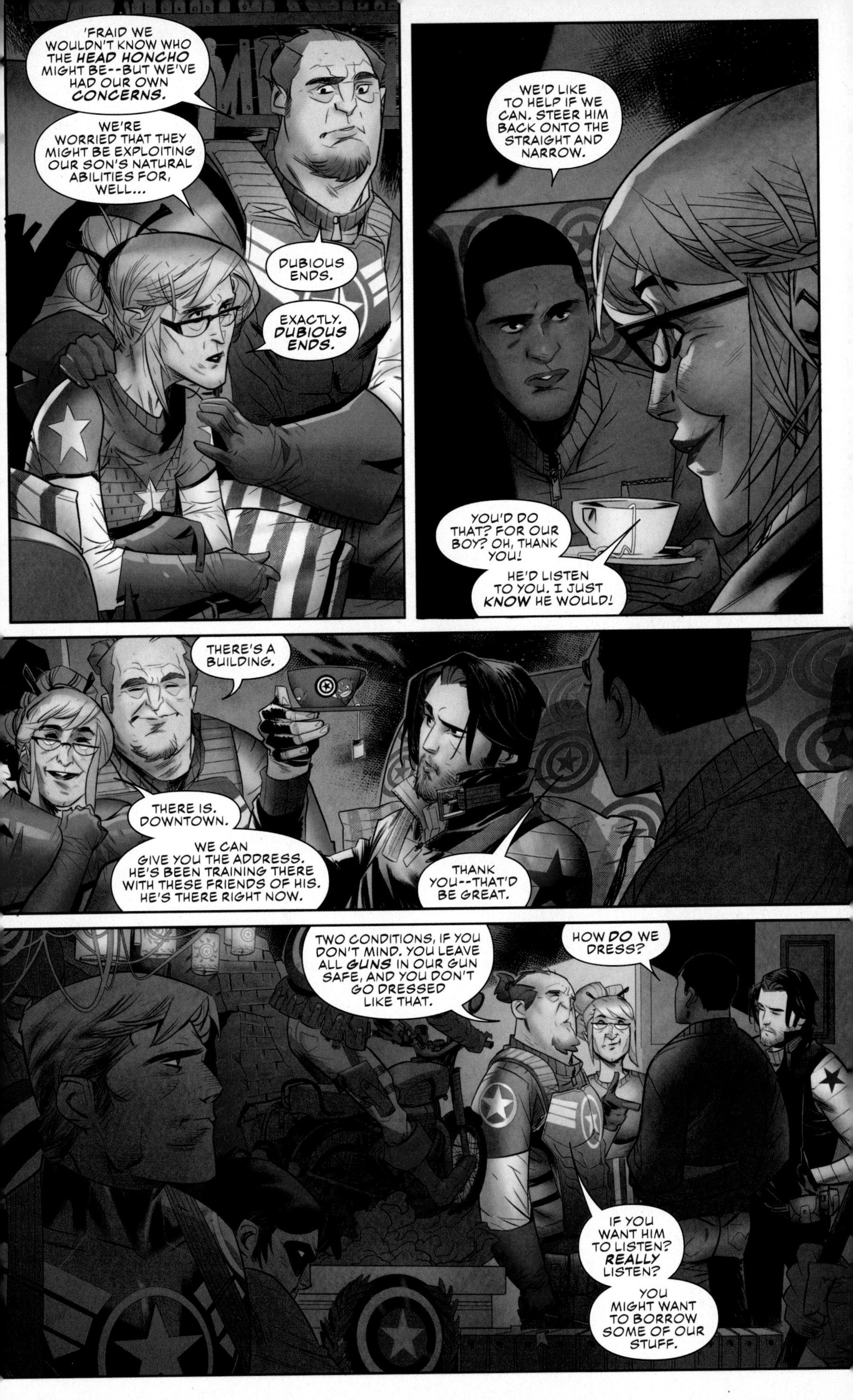

'FRAID WE WOULDN'T KNOW WHO THE HEAD HONCHO MIGHT BE--BUT WE'VE HAD OUR OWN CONCERNS.
WE'RE WORRIED THAT THEY MIGHT BE EXPLOITING OUR SON'S NATURAL ABILITIES FOR, WELL...
DUBIOUS ENDS.
EXACTLY. DUBIOUS ENDS.
WE'D LIKE TO HELP IF WE CAN. STEER HIM BACK ONTO THE STRAIGHT AND NARROW.
YOU'D DO THAT? FOR OUR BOY? OH, THANK YOU!
HE'D LISTEN TO YOU. I JUST KNOW HE WOULD!
THERE'S A BUILDING.
THERE IS. DOWNTOWN.
WE CAN GIVE YOU THE ADDRESS. HE'S BEEN TRAINING THERE WITH THESE FRIENDS OF HIS. HE'S THERE RIGHT NOW.
THANK YOU--THAT'D BE GREAT.
TWO CONDITIONS, IF YOU DON'T MIND. YOU LEAVE ALL GUNS IN OUR GUN SAFE, AND YOU DON'T GO DRESSED LIKE THAT.
HOW DO WE DRESS?
IF YOU WANT HIM TO LISTEN? REALLY LISTEN?
YOU MIGHT WANT TO BORROW SOME OF OUR STUFF.

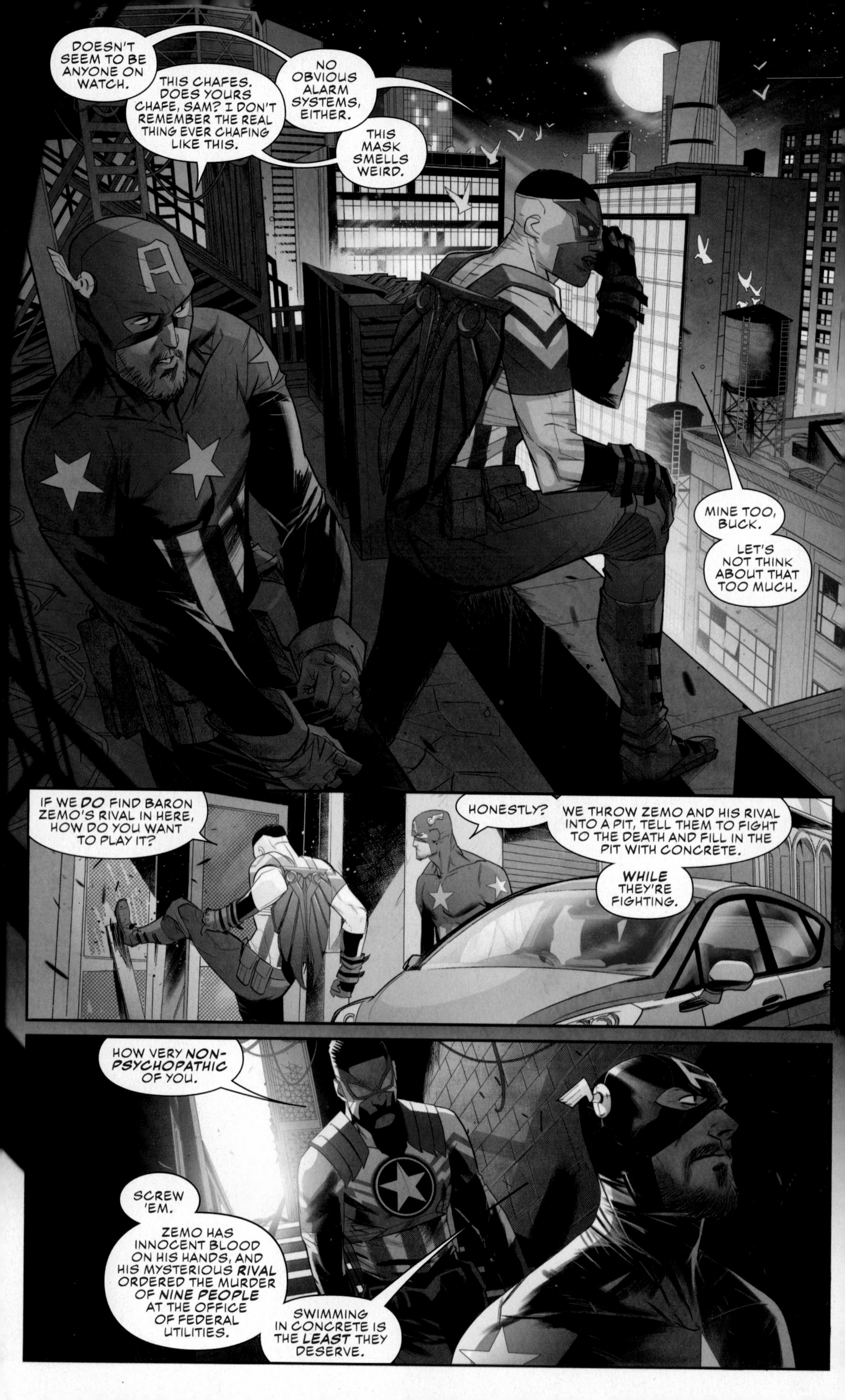
DOESN'T SEEM TO BE ANYONE ON WATCH.
THIS CHAFES. DOES YOURS CHAFE, SAM? I DON'T REMEMBER THE REAL THING EVER CHAFING LIKE THIS.
NO OBVIOUS ALARM SYSTEMS, EITHER.
THIS MASK SMELLS WEIRD.
MINE TOO, BUCK.
LET'S NOT THINK ABOUT THAT TOO MUCH.
IF WE DO FIND BARON ZEMO'S RIVAL IN HERE, HOW DO YOU WANT TO PLAY IT?
HONESTLY?
WE THROW ZEMO AND HIS RIVAL INTO A PIT, TELL THEM TO FIGHT TO THE DEATH AND FILL IN THE PIT WITH CONCRETE.
WHILE THEY'RE FIGHTING.
HOW VERY NON-PSYCHOPATHIC OF YOU.
SCREW 'EM.
ZEMO HAS INNOCENT BLOOD ON HIS HANDS, AND HIS MYSTERIOUS RIVAL ORDERED THE MURDER OF NINE PEOPLE AT THE OFFICE OF FEDERAL UTILITIES.
SWIMMING IN CONCRETE IS THE LEAST THEY DESERVE.

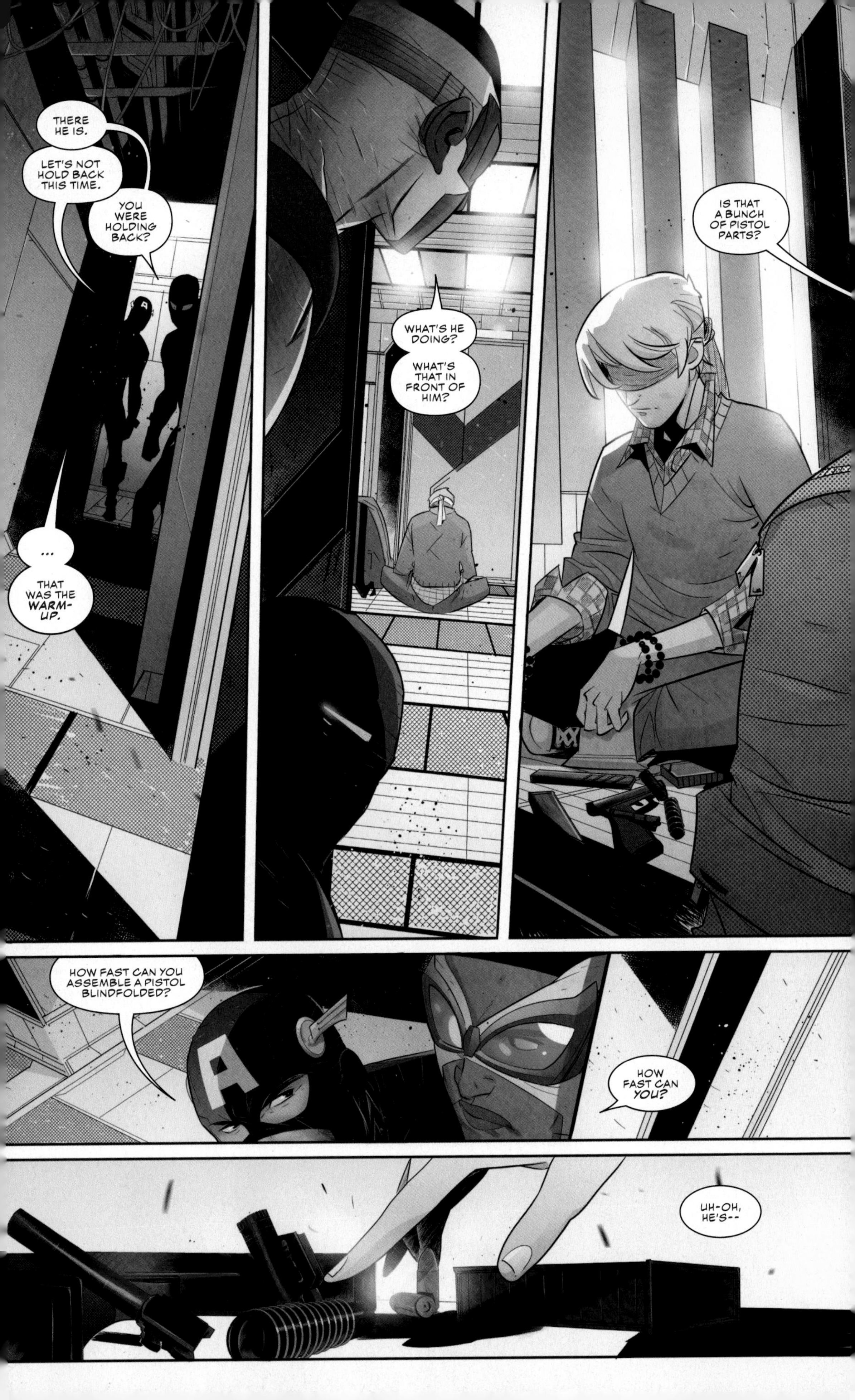

THERE HE IS.
LET'S NOT HOLD BACK THIS TIME.
YOU WERE HOLDING BACK?
...
THAT WAS THE WARM-UP.
WHAT'S HE DOING?
WHAT'S THAT IN FRONT OF HIM?
IS THAT A BUNCH OF PISTOL PARTS?
HOW FAST CAN YOU ASSEMBLE A PISTOL BLINDFOLDED?
HOW FAST CAN YOU?
UH-OH, HE'S--

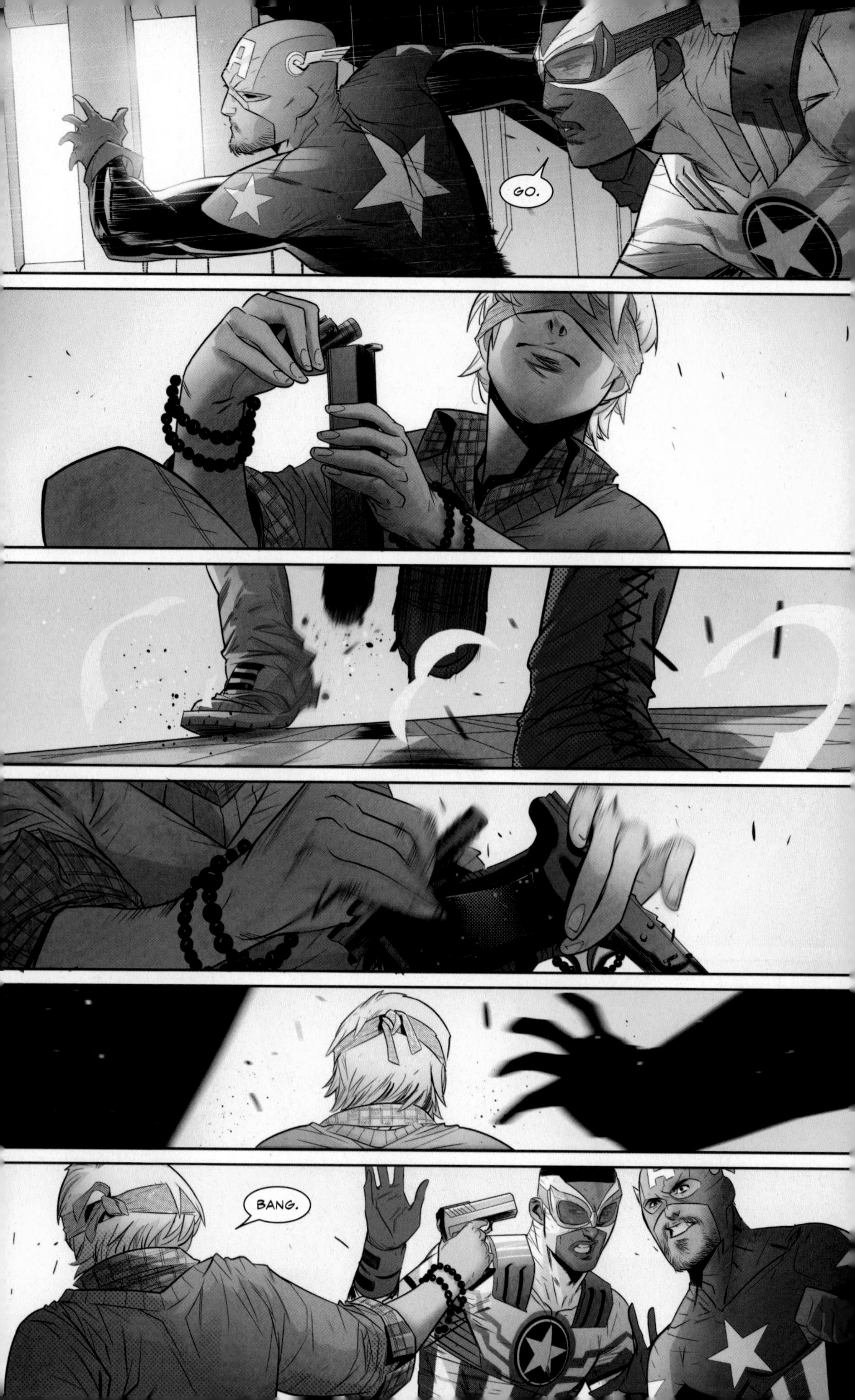
GO.
BANG.

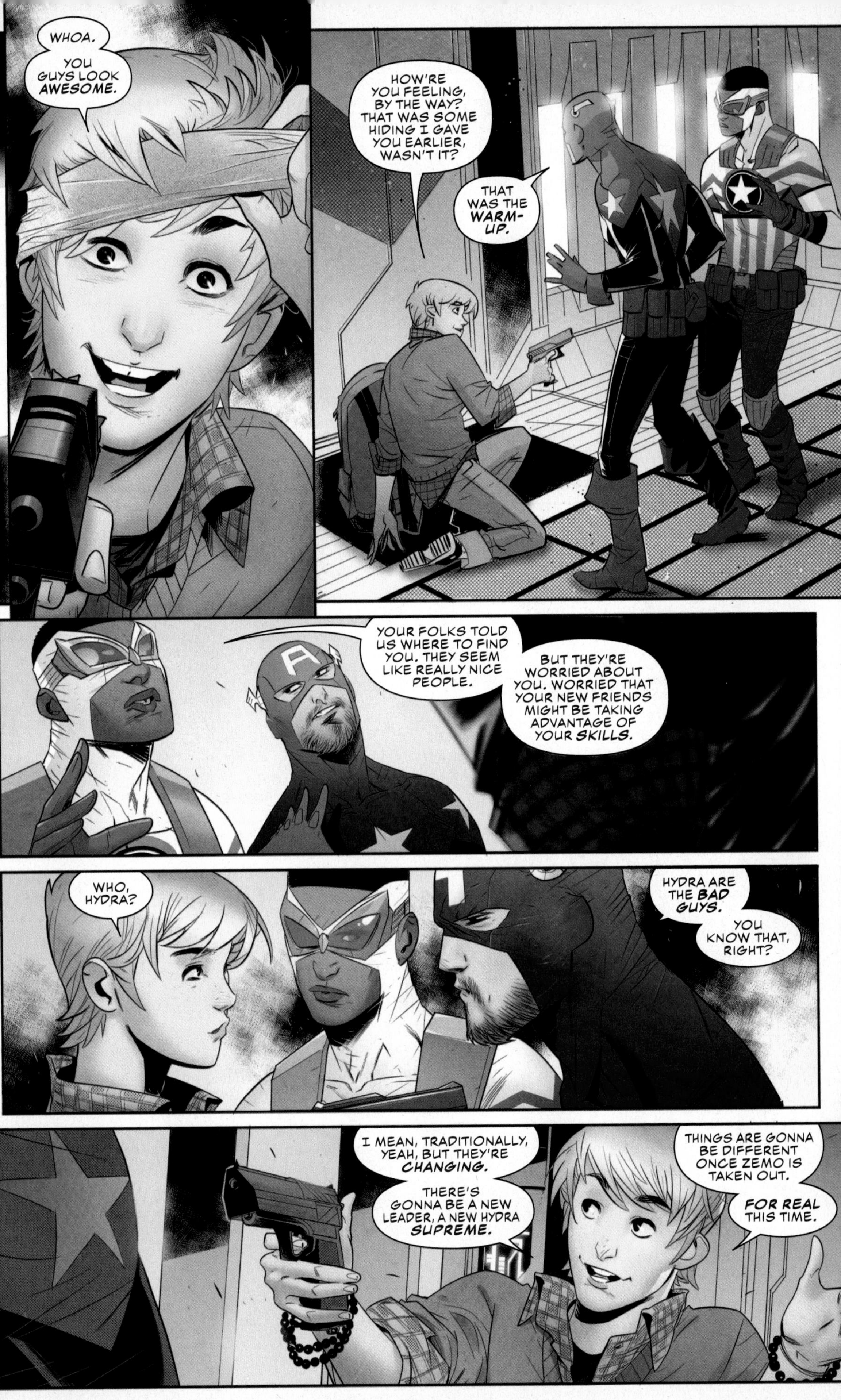
WHOA.
YOU GUYS LOOK AWESOME.
HOW'RE YOU FEELING, BY THE WAY? THAT WAS SOME HIDING I GAVE YOU EARLIER, WASN'T IT?
THAT WAS THE WARM-UP.
YOUR FOLKS TOLD US WHERE TO FIND YOU. THEY SEEM LIKE REALLY NICE PEOPLE.
BUT THEY'RE WORRIED ABOUT YOU. WORRIED THAT YOUR NEW FRIENDS MIGHT BE TAKING ADVANTAGE OF YOUR SKILLS.
WHO, HYDRA?
HYDRA ARE THE BAD GUYS.
YOU KNOW THAT, RIGHT?
I MEAN, TRADITIONALLY, YEAH, BUT THEY'RE CHANGING.
THERE'S GONNA BE A NEW LEADER, A NEW HYDRA SUPREME.
THINGS ARE GONNA BE DIFFERENT ONCE ZEMO IS TAKEN OUT.
FOR REAL THIS TIME.

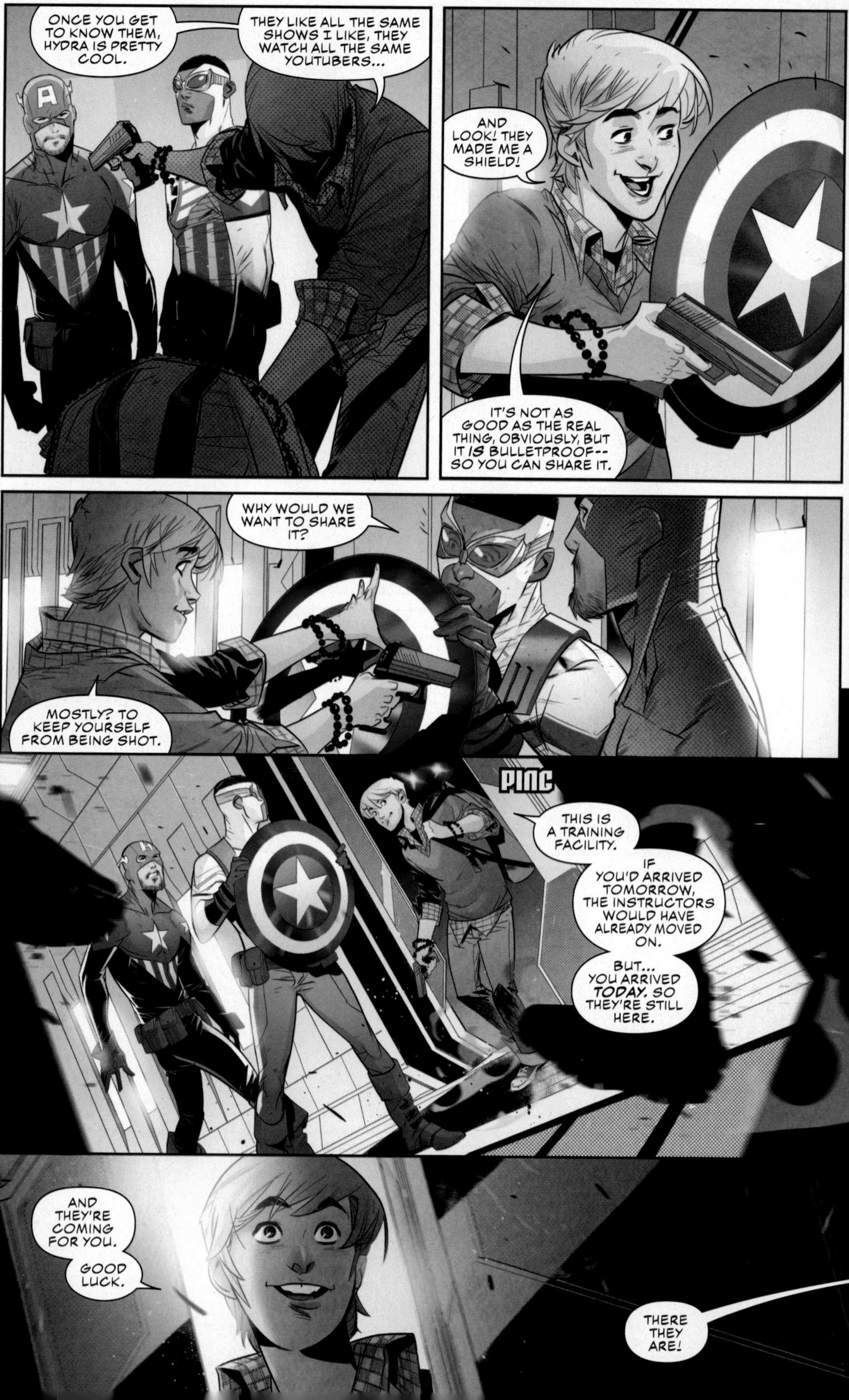
ONCE YOU GET TO KNOW THEM, HYDRA IS PRETTY COOL.
THEY LIKE ALL THE SAME SHOWS I LIKE, THEY WATCH ALL THE SAME YOUTUBERS...
AND LOOK! THEY MADE ME A SHIELD!
IT'S NOT AS GOOD AS THE REAL THING, OBVIOUSLY, BUT IT *IS* BULLETPROOF-- SO YOU CAN SHARE IT.
WHY WOULD WE WANT TO SHARE IT?
MOSTLY? TO KEEP YOURSELF FROM BEING SHOT.
PING
THIS IS A TRAINING FACILITY.
IF YOU'D ARRIVED TOMORROW, THE INSTRUCTORS WOULD HAVE ALREADY MOVED ON.
BUT... YOU ARRIVED **TODAY**. SO THEY'RE STILL HERE.
AND THEY'RE COMING FOR YOU.
GOOD LUCK.
THERE THEY ARE!

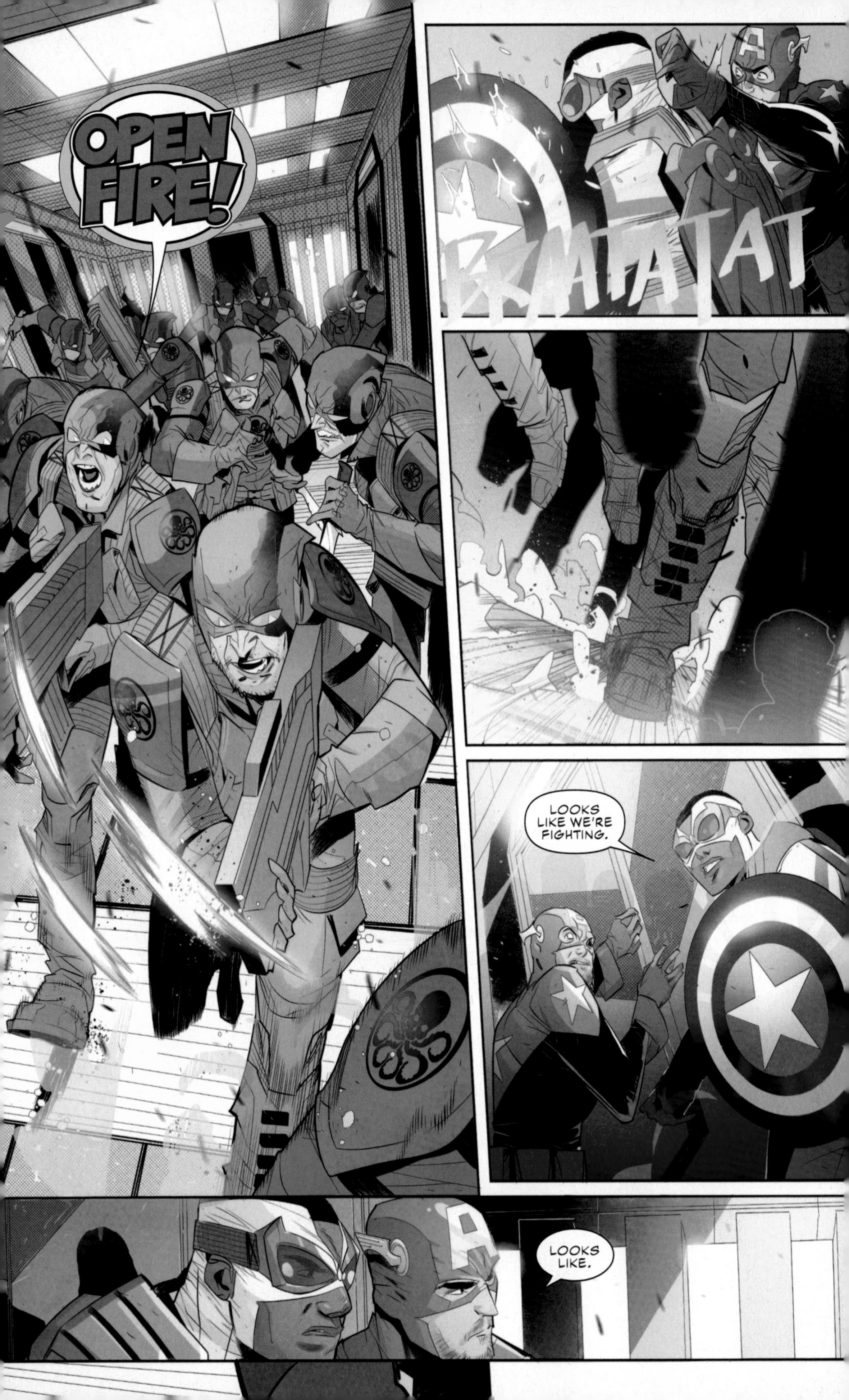
OPEN FIRE!
BRRATATAT
LOOKS LIKE WE'RE FIGHTING.
LOOKS LIKE.

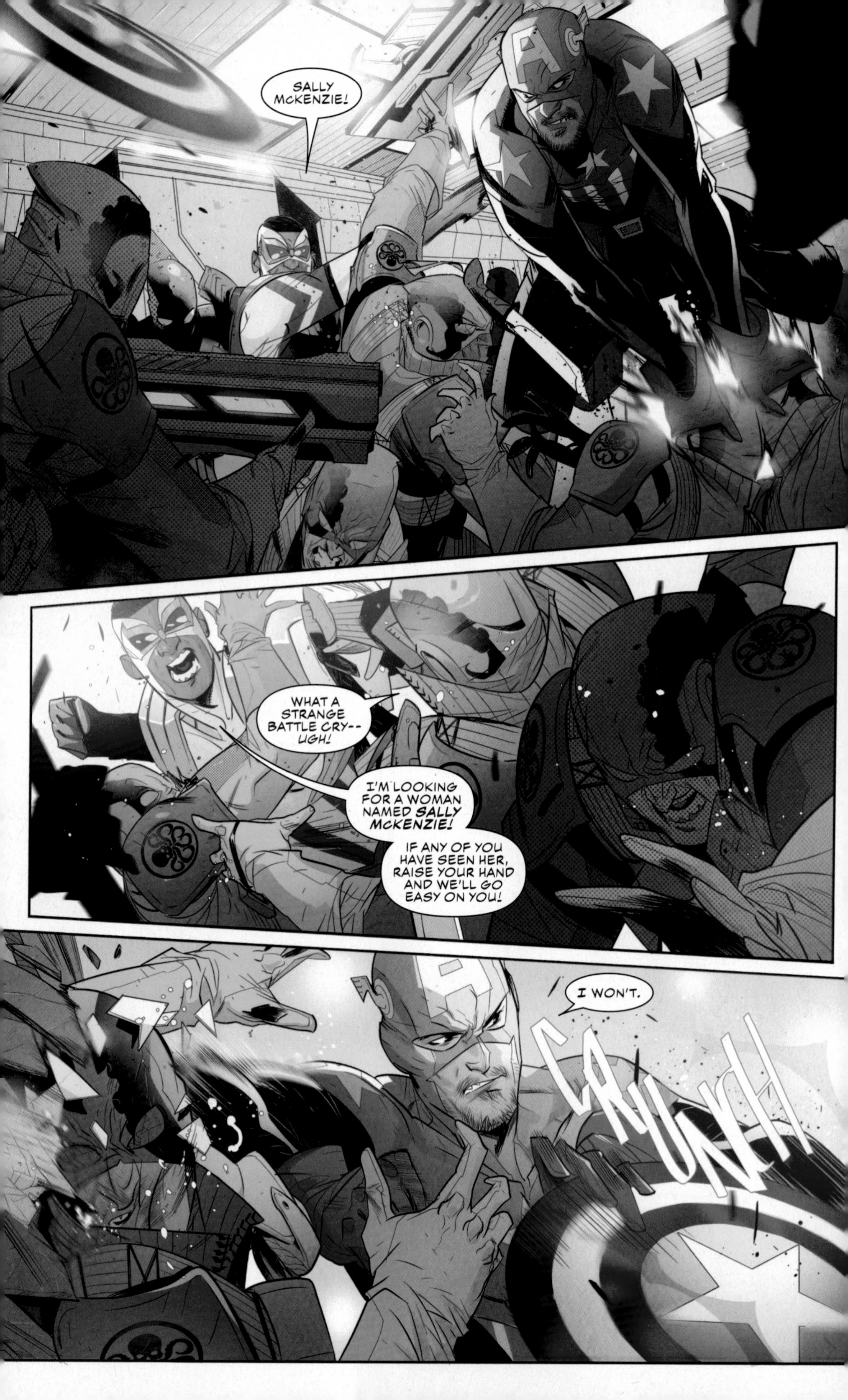

SALLY MCKENZIE!
WHAT A STRANGE BATTLE CRY-- UGH!
I'M LOOKING FOR A WOMAN NAMED SALLY MCKENZIE!
IF ANY OF YOU HAVE SEEN HER, RAISE YOUR HAND AND WE'LL GO EASY ON YOU!
I WON'T.
CRUNCH

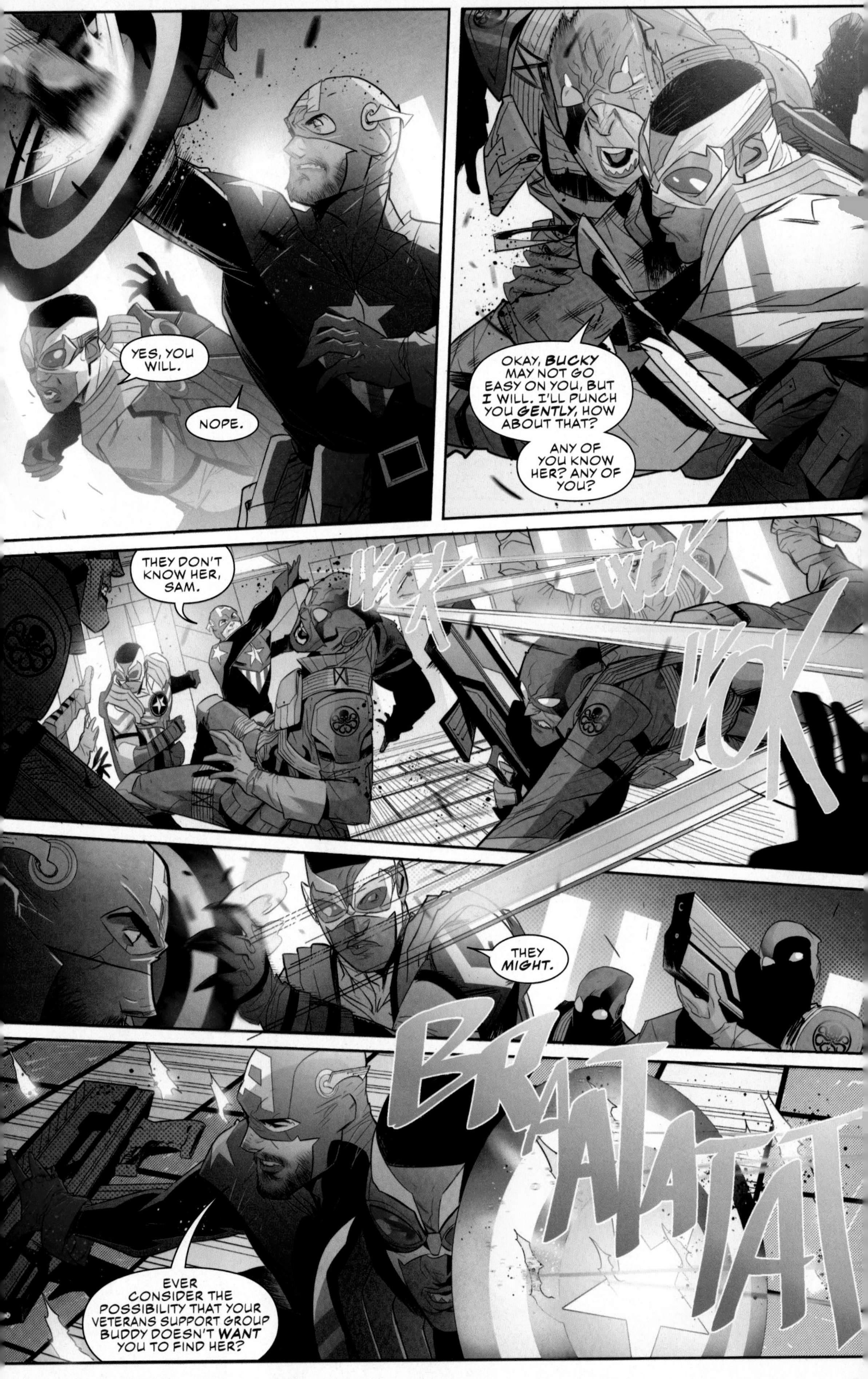
YES, YOU WILL.
NOPE.
OKAY, BUCKY MAY NOT GO EASY ON YOU, BUT I WILL. I'LL PUNCH YOU GENTLY, HOW ABOUT THAT?
ANY OF YOU KNOW HER? ANY OF YOU?
THEY DON'T KNOW HER, SAM.
WOK
WOK
WOK
THEY MIGHT.
BRATATATAT
EVER CONSIDER THE POSSIBILITY THAT YOUR VETERANS SUPPORT GROUP BUDDY DOESN'T WANT YOU TO FIND HER?

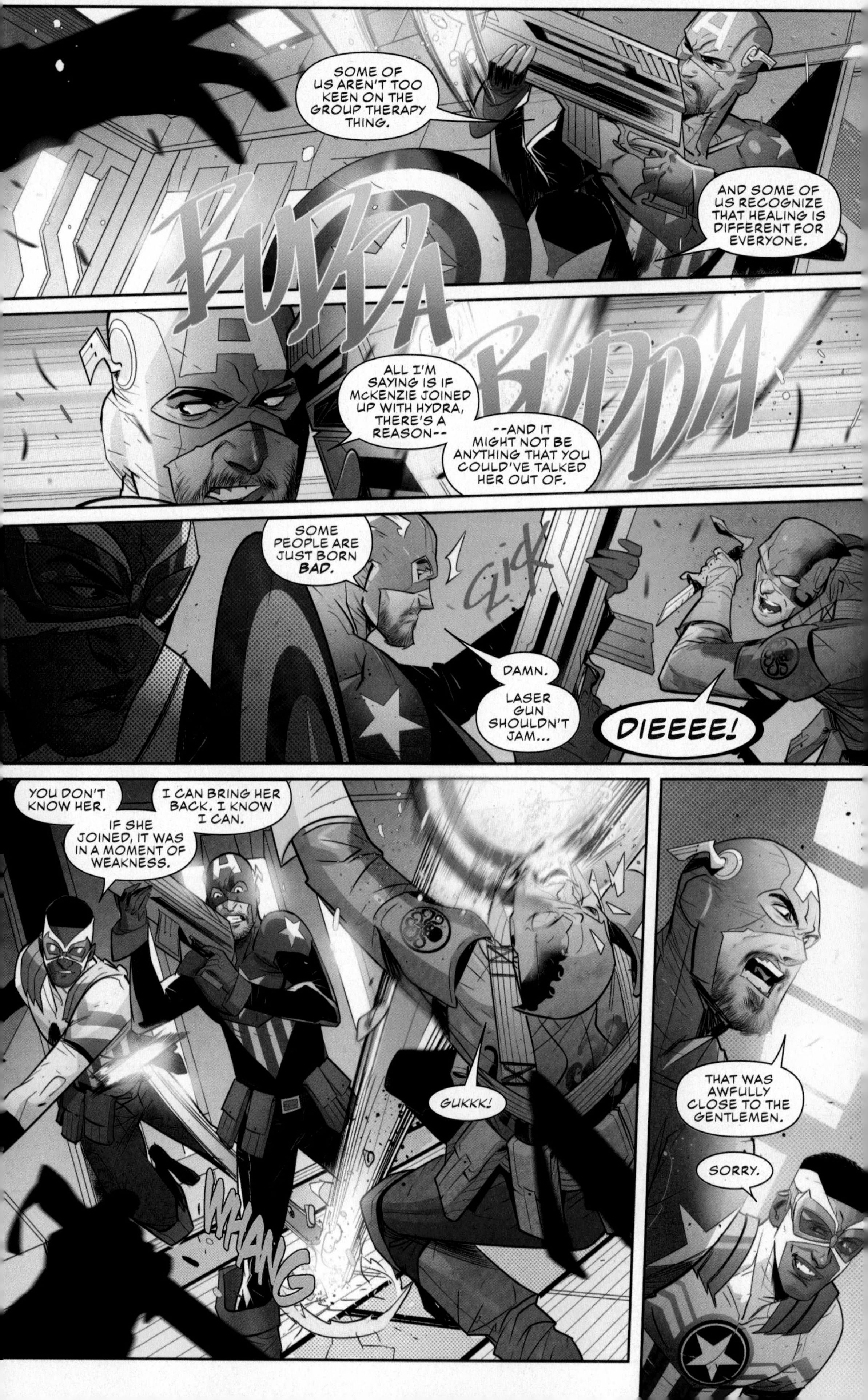

SOME OF US AREN'T TOO KEEN ON THE GROUP THERAPY THING.
AND SOME OF US RECOGNIZE THAT HEALING IS DIFFERENT FOR EVERYONE.
BUDDA
BUDDA
ALL I'M SAYING IS IF McKENZIE JOINED UP WITH HYDRA, THERE'S A REASON--
--AND IT MIGHT NOT BE ANYTHING THAT YOU COULD'VE TALKED HER OUT OF.
SOME PEOPLE ARE JUST BORN BAD.
CLICK
DAMN.
LASER GUN SHOULDN'T JAM...
DIEEEE!
YOU DON'T KNOW HER.
IF SHE JOINED, IT WAS IN A MOMENT OF WEAKNESS.
I CAN BRING HER BACK. I KNOW I CAN.
GUKKK!
WHANG
THAT WAS AWFULLY CLOSE TO THE GENTLEMEN.
SORRY.

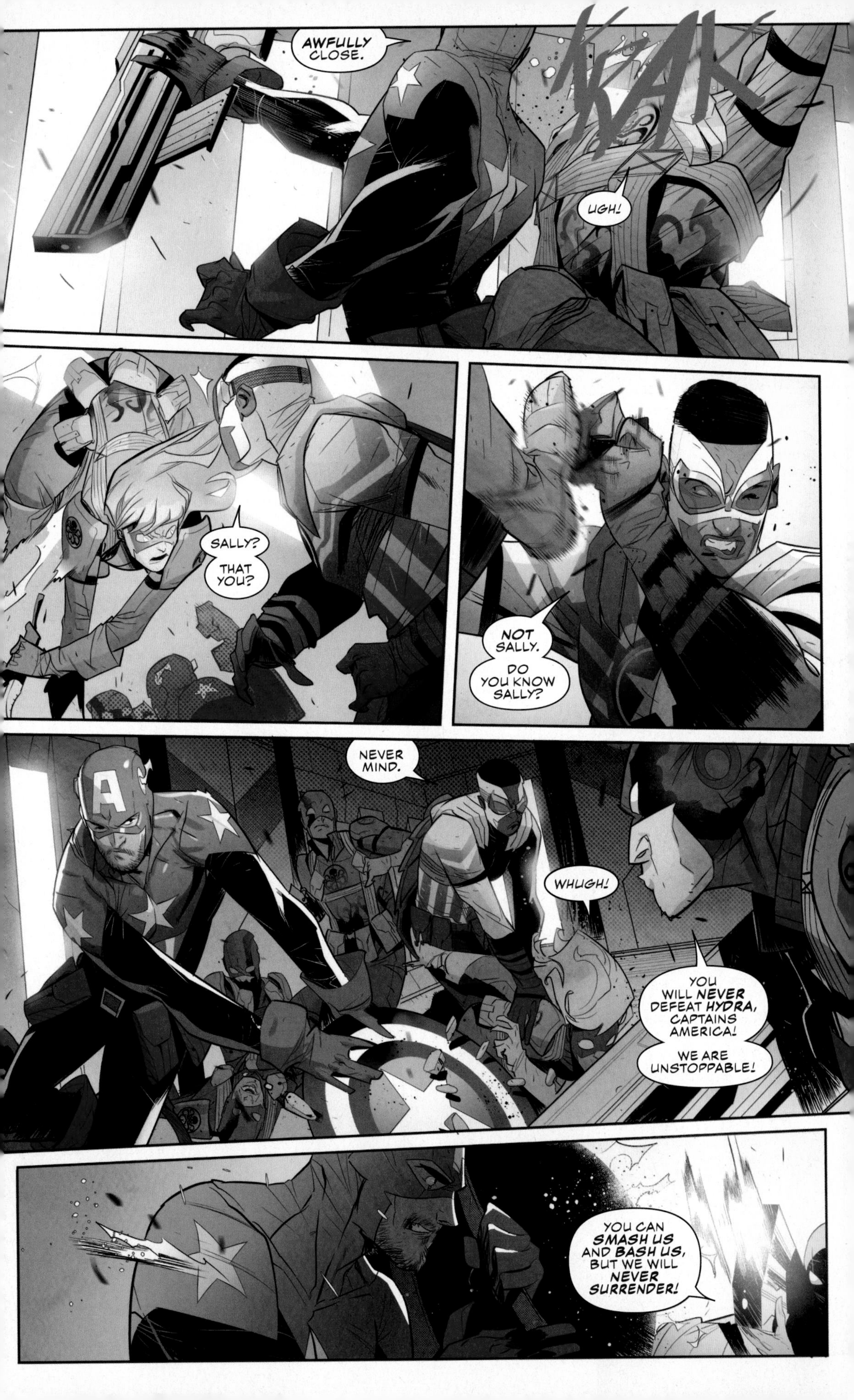

AWFULLY CLOSE.
KRAK
UGH!
SALLY? THAT YOU?
NOT SALLY.
DO YOU KNOW SALLY?
NEVER MIND.
WHUGH!
YOU WILL NEVER DEFEAT HYDRA, CAPTAINS AMERICA!
WE ARE UNSTOPPABLE!
YOU CAN SMASH US AND BASH US, BUT WE WILL NEVER SURRENDER!

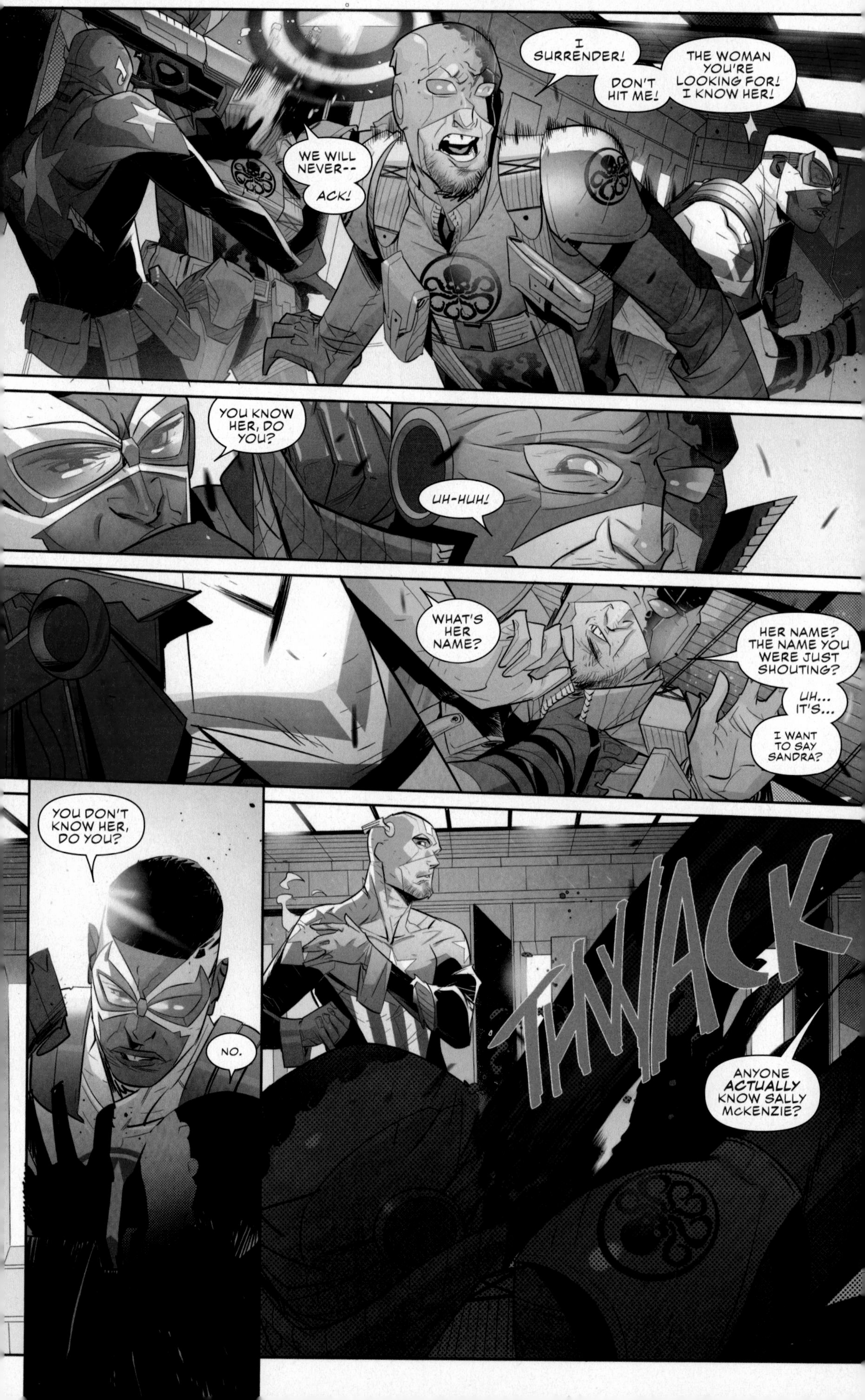
I SURRENDER!
DON'T HIT ME!
THE WOMAN YOU'RE LOOKING FOR! I KNOW HER!
WE WILL NEVER--
ACK!
YOU KNOW HER, DO YOU?
UH-HUH!
WHAT'S HER NAME?
HER NAME? THE NAME YOU WERE JUST SHOUTING?
UH... IT'S...
I WANT TO SAY SANDRA?
YOU DON'T KNOW HER, DO YOU?
NO.
THWACK
ANYONE ACTUALLY KNOW SALLY McKENZIE?

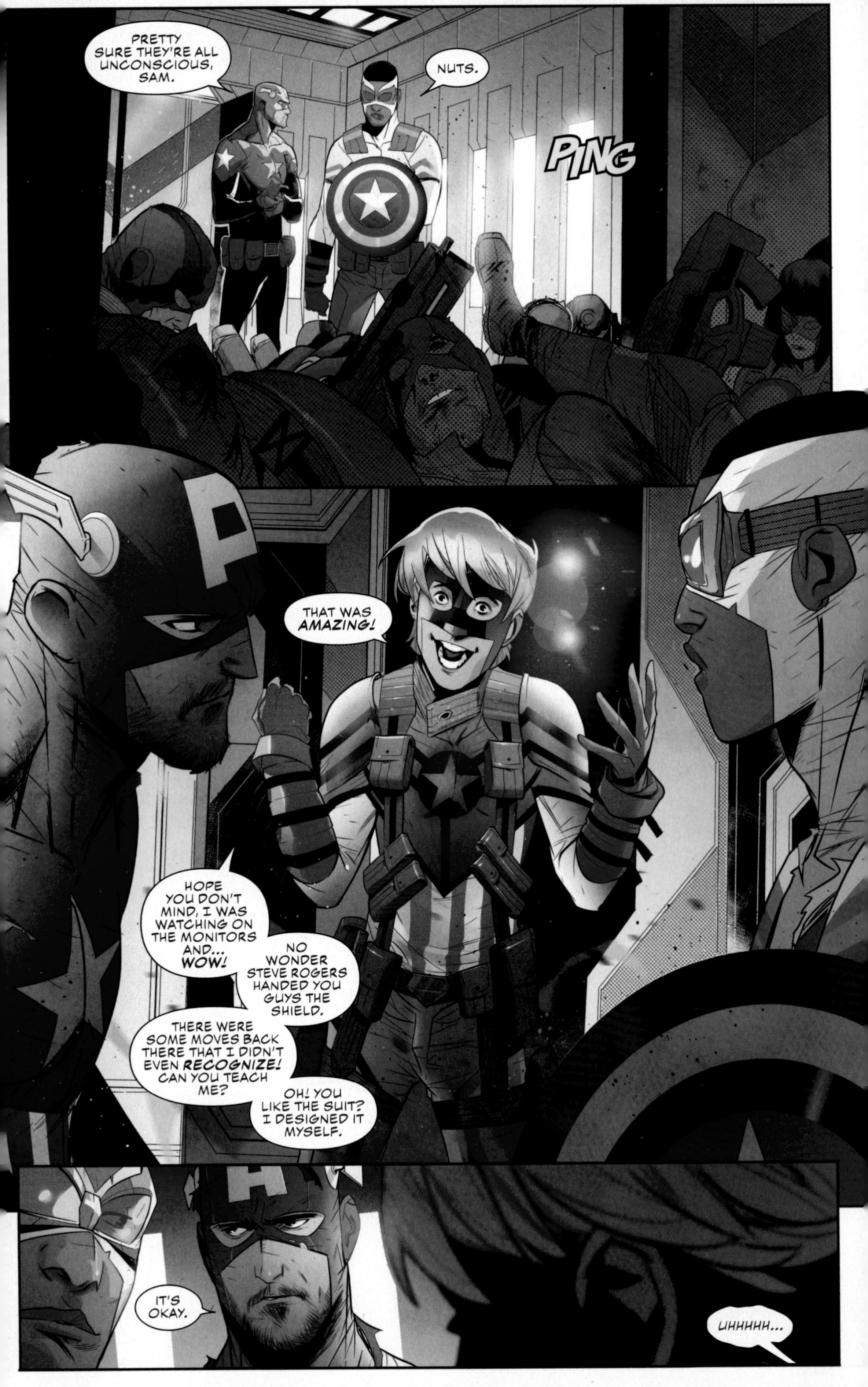
PRETTY SURE THEY'RE ALL UNCONSCIOUS, SAM.
NUTS.
PING
THAT WAS AMAZING!
HOPE YOU DON'T MIND, I WAS WATCHING ON THE MONITORS AND... WOW!
NO WONDER STEVE ROGERS HANDED YOU GUYS THE SHIELD.
THERE WERE SOME MOVES BACK THERE THAT I DIDN'T EVEN RECOGNIZE! CAN YOU TEACH ME?
OH! YOU LIKE THE SUIT? I DESIGNED IT MYSELF.
IT'S OKAY.
UHHHHH...

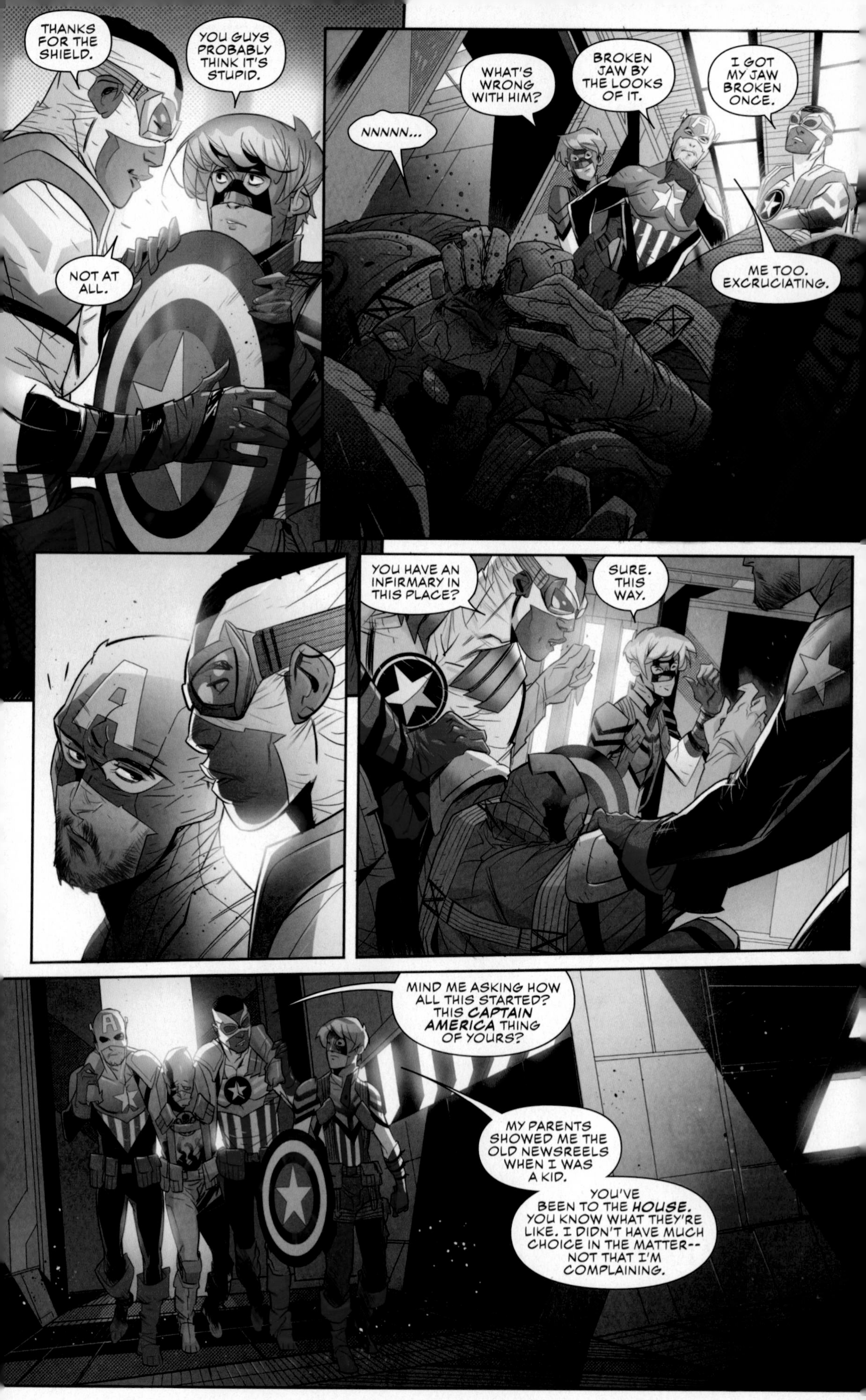
THANKS FOR THE SHIELD.
YOU GUYS PROBABLY THINK IT'S STUPID.
NOT AT ALL.
NNNNN...
WHAT'S WRONG WITH HIM?
BROKEN JAW BY THE LOOKS OF IT.
I GOT MY JAW BROKEN ONCE.
ME TOO. EXCRUCIATING.
YOU HAVE AN INFIRMARY IN THIS PLACE?
SURE. THIS WAY.
MIND ME ASKING HOW ALL THIS STARTED? THIS *CAPTAIN AMERICA* THING OF YOURS?
MY PARENTS SHOWED ME THE OLD NEWSREELS WHEN I WAS A KID.
YOU'VE BEEN TO THE *HOUSE*. YOU KNOW WHAT THEY'RE LIKE. I DIDN'T HAVE MUCH CHOICE IN THE MATTER-- NOT THAT I'M COMPLAINING.

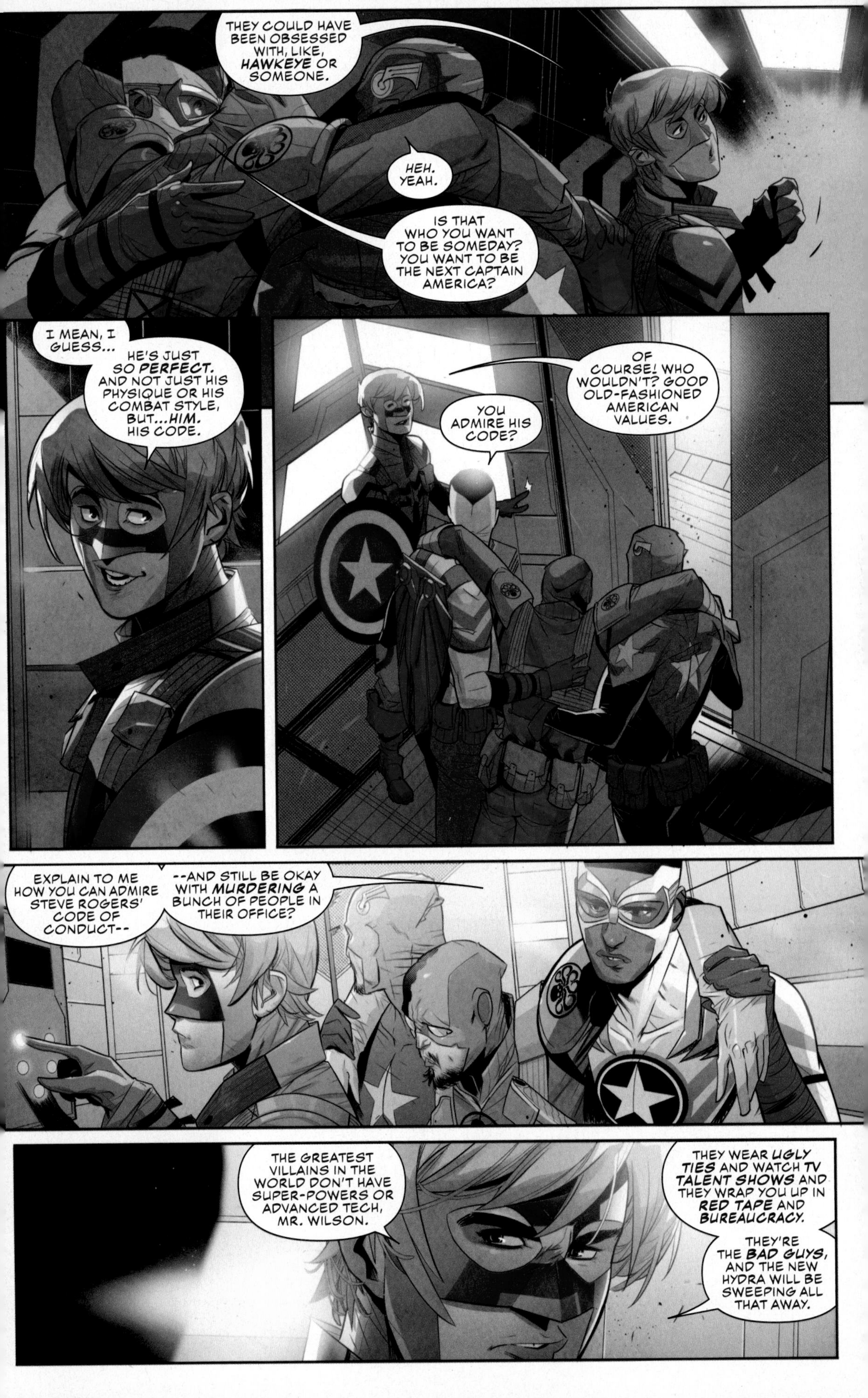
THEY COULD HAVE BEEN OBSESSED WITH, LIKE, HAWKEYE OR SOMEONE.
HEH. YEAH.
IS THAT WHO YOU WANT TO BE SOMEDAY? YOU WANT TO BE THE NEXT CAPTAIN AMERICA?
I MEAN, I GUESS...
HE'S JUST SO PERFECT. AND NOT JUST HIS PHYSIQUE OR HIS COMBAT STYLE, BUT...HIM. HIS CODE.
YOU ADMIRE HIS CODE?
OF COURSE! WHO WOULDN'T? GOOD OLD-FASHIONED AMERICAN VALUES.
EXPLAIN TO ME HOW YOU CAN ADMIRE STEVE ROGERS' CODE OF CONDUCT--
--AND STILL BE OKAY WITH MURDERING A BUNCH OF PEOPLE IN THEIR OFFICE?
THE GREATEST VILLAINS IN THE WORLD DON'T HAVE SUPER-POWERS OR ADVANCED TECH, MR. WILSON.
THEY WEAR UGLY TIES AND WATCH TV TALENT SHOWS AND THEY WRAP YOU UP IN RED TAPE AND BUREAUCRACY.
THEY'RE THE BAD GUYS, AND THE NEW HYDRA WILL BE SWEEPING ALL THAT AWAY.

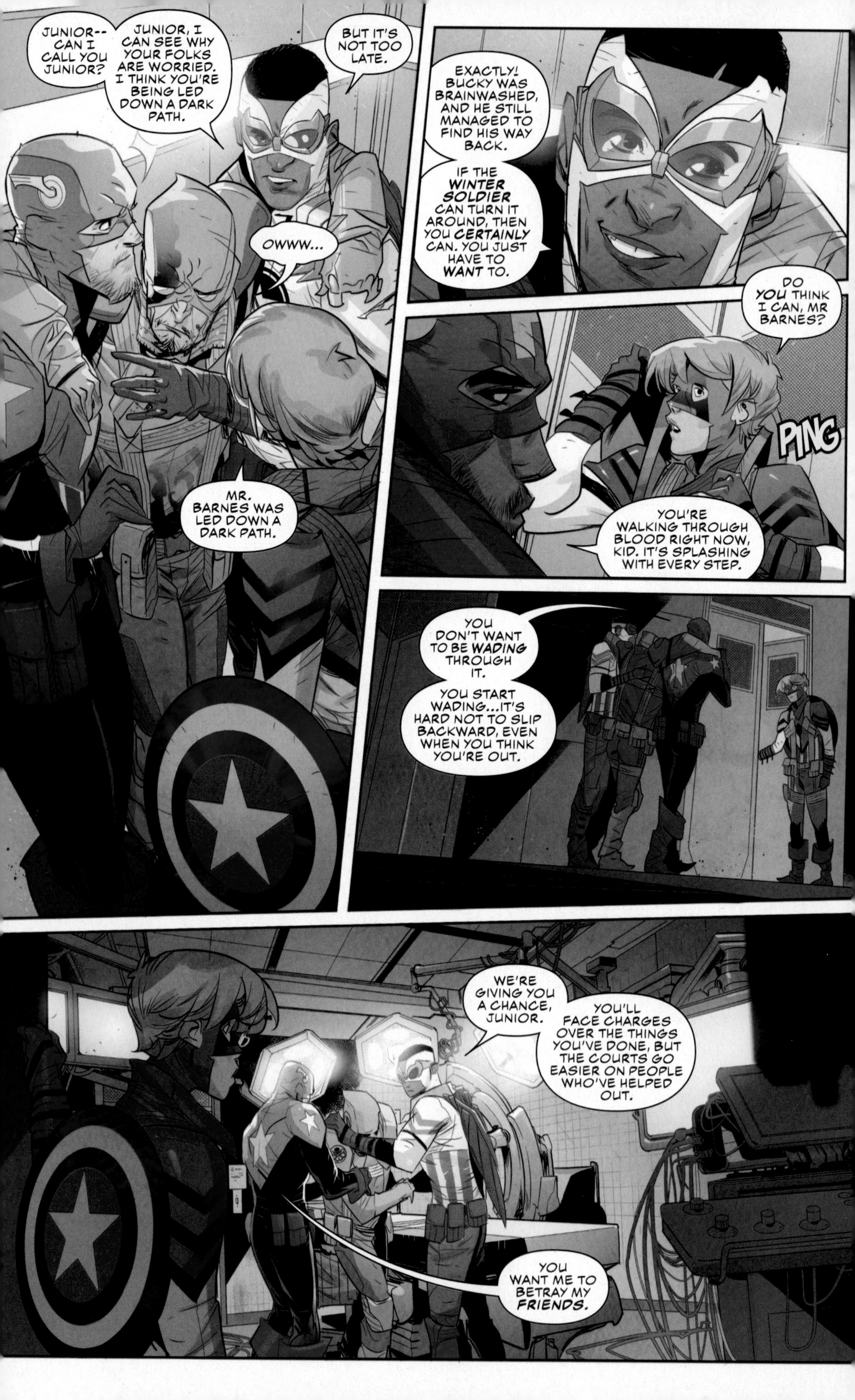
JUNIOR-- CAN I CALL YOU JUNIOR?
JUNIOR, I CAN SEE WHY YOUR FOLKS ARE WORRIED. I THINK YOU'RE BEING LED DOWN A DARK PATH.
BUT IT'S NOT TOO LATE.
OWWW...
MR. BARNES WAS LED DOWN A DARK PATH.
EXACTLY! BUCKY WAS BRAINWASHED, AND HE STILL MANAGED TO FIND HIS WAY BACK.
IF THE WINTER SOLDIER CAN TURN IT AROUND, THEN YOU CERTAINLY CAN. YOU JUST HAVE TO WANT TO.
DO YOU THINK I CAN, MR BARNES?
PING
YOU'RE WALKING THROUGH BLOOD RIGHT NOW, KID. IT'S SPLASHING WITH EVERY STEP.
YOU DON'T WANT TO BE WADING THROUGH IT.
YOU START WADING...IT'S HARD NOT TO SLIP BACKWARD, EVEN WHEN YOU THINK YOU'RE OUT.
WE'RE GIVING YOU A CHANCE, JUNIOR.
YOU'LL FACE CHARGES OVER THE THINGS YOU'VE DONE, BUT THE COURTS GO EASIER ON PEOPLE WHO'VE HELPED OUT.
YOU WANT ME TO BETRAY MY FRIENDS.

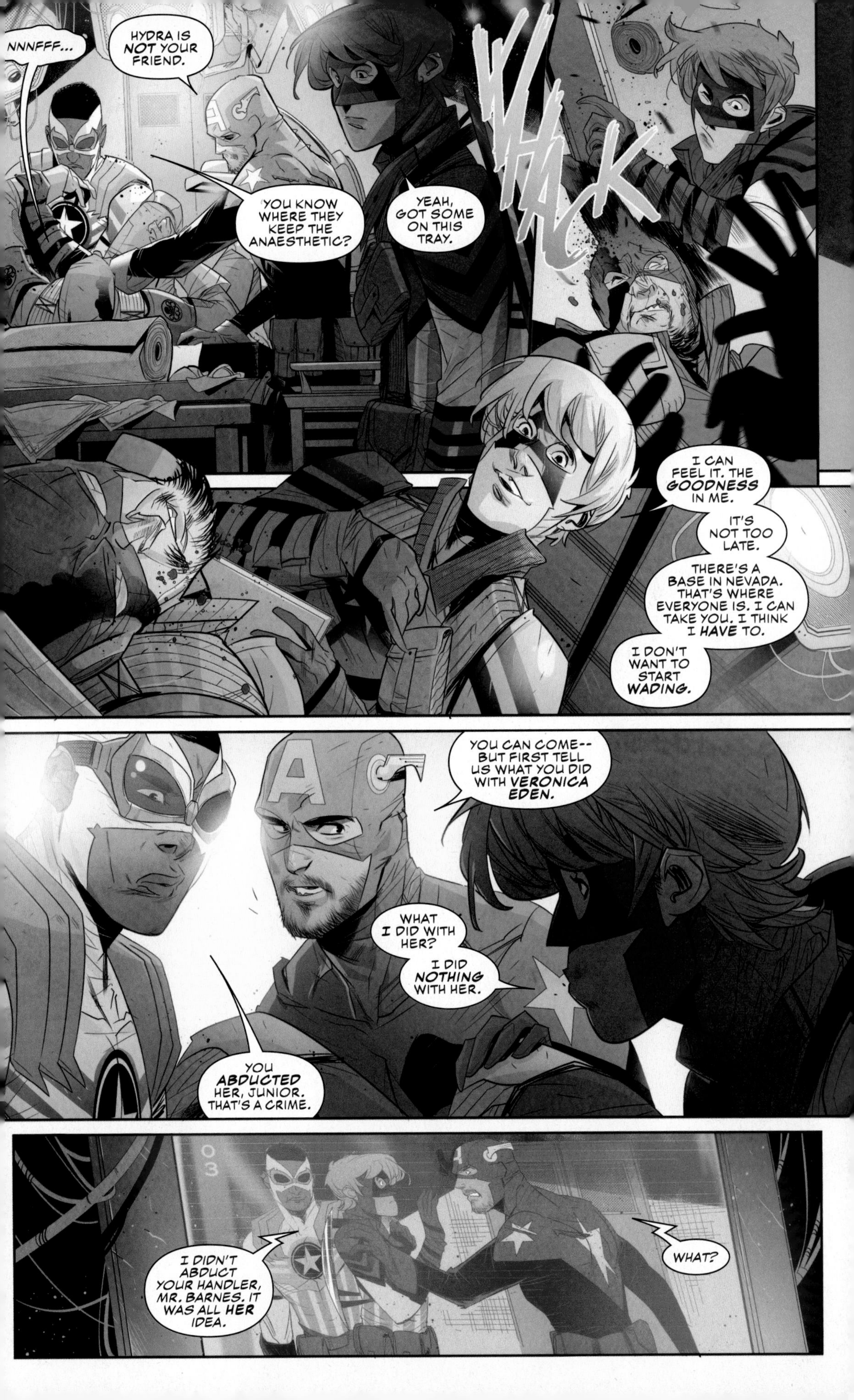
NNNFFF...
HYDRA IS NOT YOUR FRIEND.
YOU KNOW WHERE THEY KEEP THE ANAESTHETIC?
YEAH, GOT SOME ON THIS TRAY.
WHACK
I CAN FEEL IT. THE GOODNESS IN ME.
IT'S NOT TOO LATE.
THERE'S A BASE IN NEVADA. THAT'S WHERE EVERYONE IS. I CAN TAKE YOU. I THINK I HAVE TO.
I DON'T WANT TO START WADING.
YOU CAN COME-- BUT FIRST TELL US WHAT YOU DID WITH VERONICA EDEN.
WHAT I DID WITH HER?
I DID NOTHING WITH HER.
YOU ABDUCTED HER, JUNIOR. THAT'S A CRIME.
I DIDN'T ABDUCT YOUR HANDLER, MR. BARNES. IT WAS ALL HER IDEA.
WHAT?

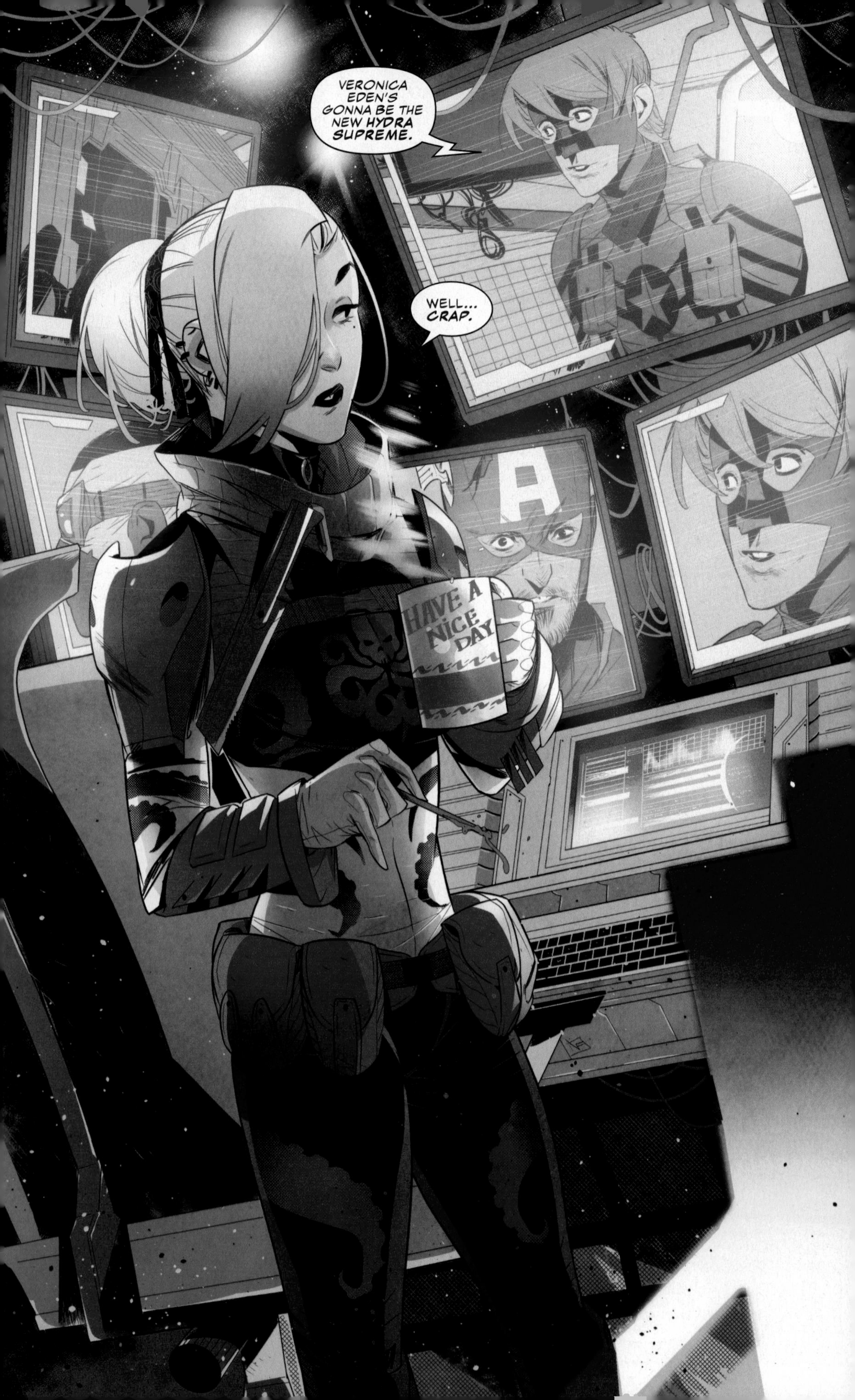
VERONICA EDEN'S GONNA BE THE NEW HYDRA SUPREME.
WELL... CRAP.
HAVE A NICE DAY

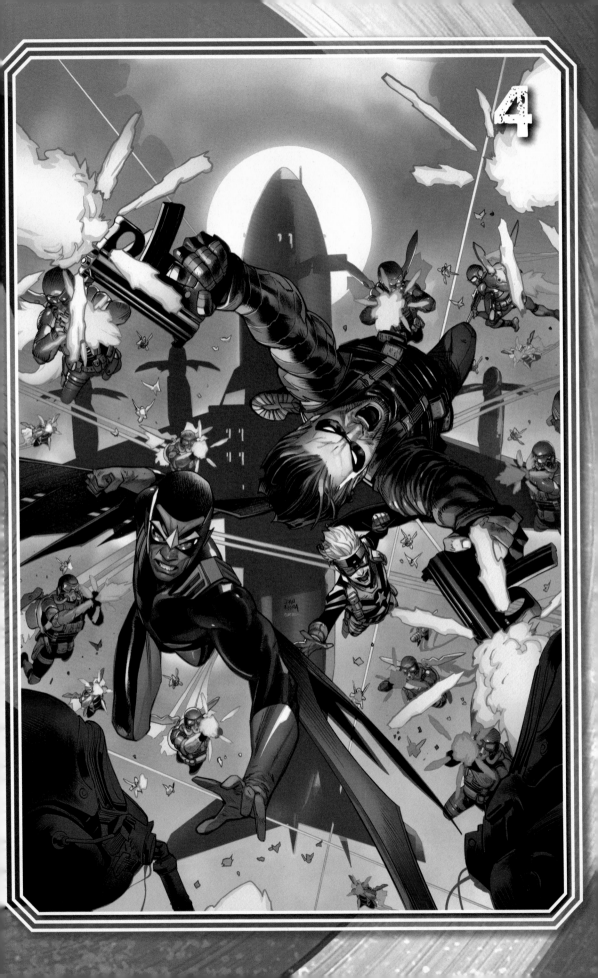

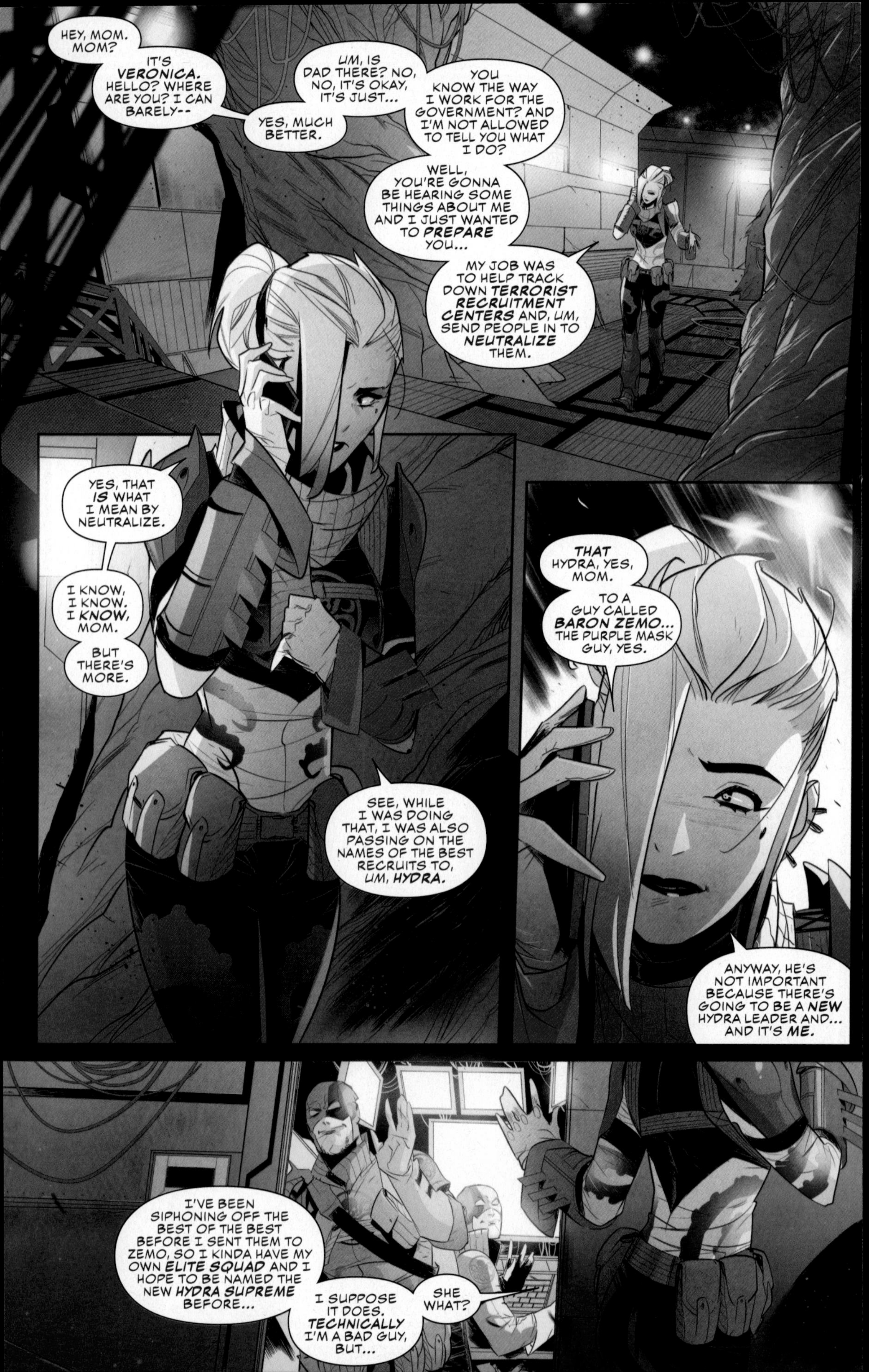
HEY, MOM. MOM?
IT'S VERONICA. HELLO? WHERE ARE YOU? I CAN BARELY--
YES, MUCH BETTER.
UM, IS DAD THERE? NO, NO, IT'S OKAY, IT'S JUST...
YOU KNOW THE WAY I WORK FOR THE GOVERNMENT? AND I'M NOT ALLOWED TO TELL YOU WHAT I DO?
WELL, YOU'RE GONNA BE HEARING SOME THINGS ABOUT ME AND I JUST WANTED TO PREPARE YOU...
MY JOB WAS TO HELP TRACK DOWN TERRORIST RECRUITMENT CENTERS AND, UM, SEND PEOPLE IN TO NEUTRALIZE THEM.
YES, THAT IS WHAT I MEAN BY NEUTRALIZE.
I KNOW, I KNOW. I KNOW, MOM.
BUT THERE'S MORE.
SEE, WHILE I WAS DOING THAT, I WAS ALSO PASSING ON THE NAMES OF THE BEST RECRUITS TO, UM, HYDRA.
THAT HYDRA, YES, MOM.
TO A GUY CALLED BARON ZEMO... THE PURPLE MASK GUY, YES.
ANYWAY, HE'S NOT IMPORTANT BECAUSE THERE'S GOING TO BE A NEW HYDRA LEADER AND... AND IT'S ME.
I'VE BEEN SIPHONING OFF THE BEST OF THE BEST BEFORE I SENT THEM TO ZEMO, SO I KINDA HAVE MY OWN ELITE SQUAD AND I HOPE TO BE NAMED THE NEW HYDRA SUPREME BEFORE...
I SUPPOSE IT DOES. TECHNICALLY I'M A BAD GUY, BUT...
SHE WHAT?

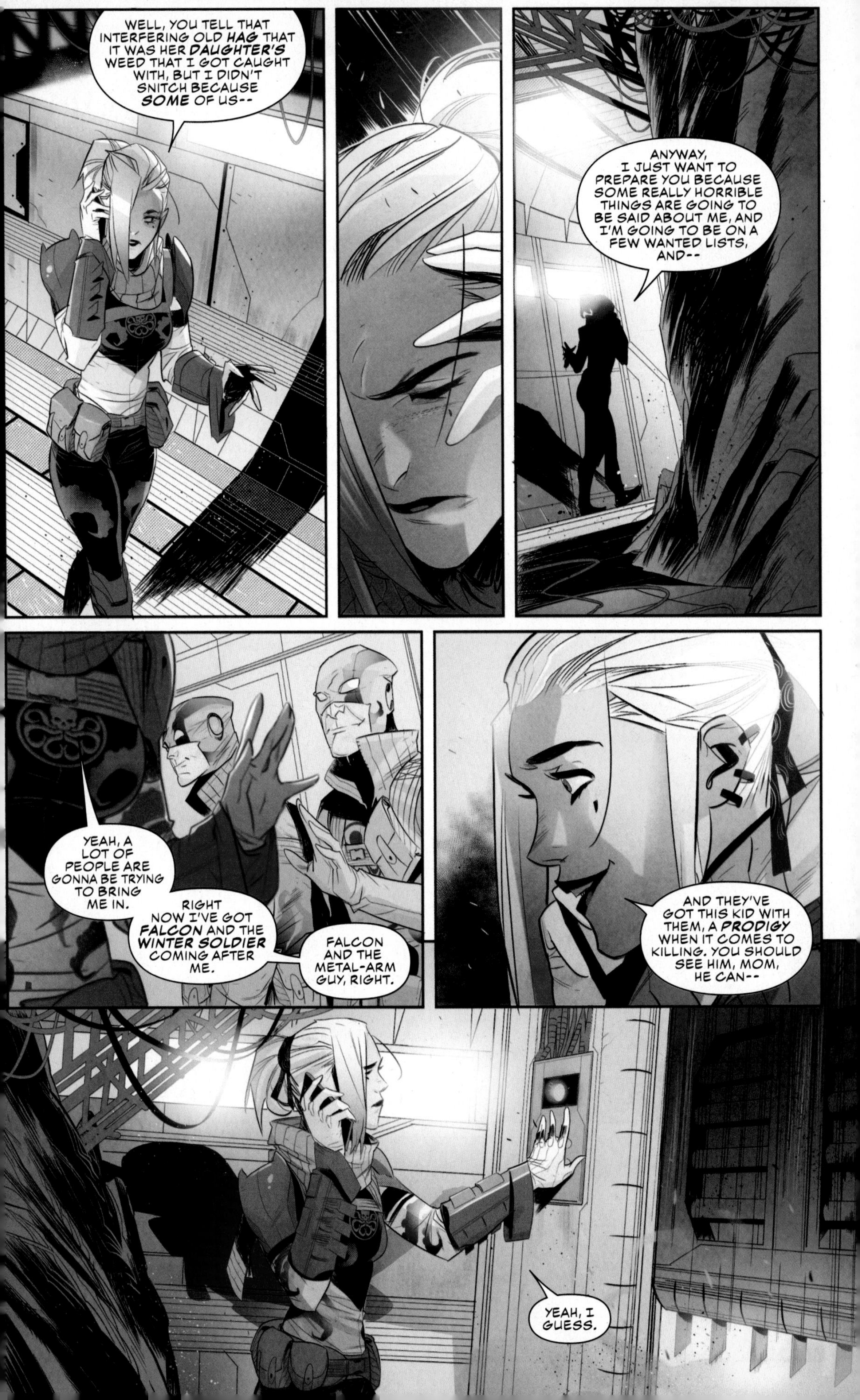
WELL, YOU TELL THAT INTERFERING OLD HAG THAT IT WAS HER DAUGHTER'S WEED THAT I GOT CAUGHT WITH, BUT I DIDN'T SNITCH BECAUSE SOME OF US--
ANYWAY, I JUST WANT TO PREPARE YOU BECAUSE SOME REALLY HORRIBLE THINGS ARE GOING TO BE SAID ABOUT ME, AND I'M GOING TO BE ON A FEW WANTED LISTS, AND--
YEAH, A LOT OF PEOPLE ARE GONNA BE TRYING TO BRING ME IN.
RIGHT NOW I'VE GOT FALCON AND THE WINTER SOLDIER COMING AFTER ME.
FALCON AND THE METAL-ARM GUY, RIGHT.
AND THEY'VE GOT THIS KID WITH THEM, A PRODIGY WHEN IT COMES TO KILLING. YOU SHOULD SEE HIM, MOM, HE CAN--
YEAH, I GUESS.

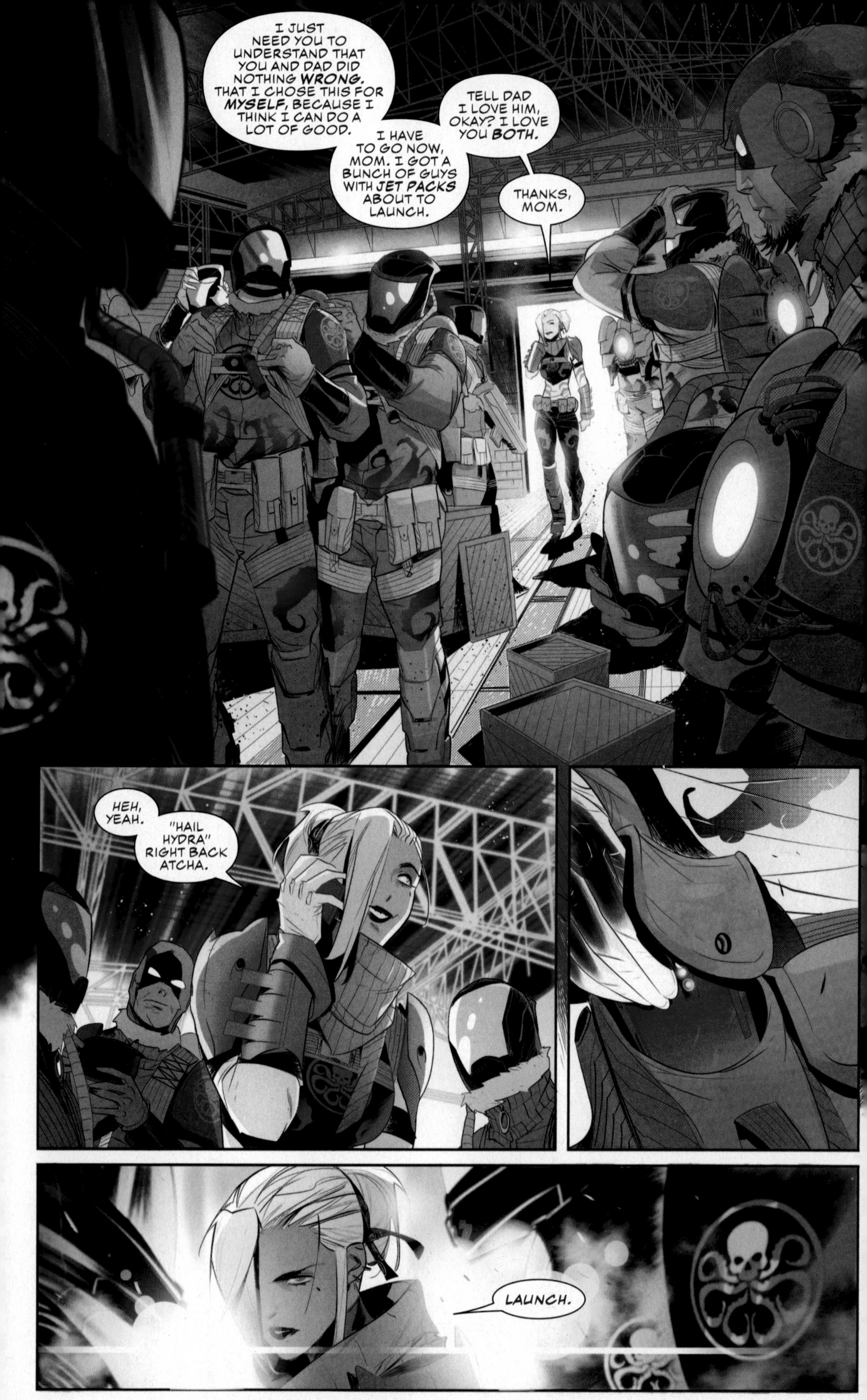
I JUST NEED YOU TO UNDERSTAND THAT YOU AND DAD DID NOTHING **WRONG.** THAT I CHOSE THIS FOR **MYSELF**, BECAUSE I THINK I CAN DO A LOT OF GOOD.
I HAVE TO GO NOW, MOM. I GOT A BUNCH OF GUYS WITH **JET PACKS** ABOUT TO LAUNCH.
TELL DAD I LOVE HIM, OKAY? I LOVE YOU **BOTH.**
THANKS, MOM.
HEH, YEAH.
"HAIL HYDRA" RIGHT BACK ATCHA.
LAUNCH.

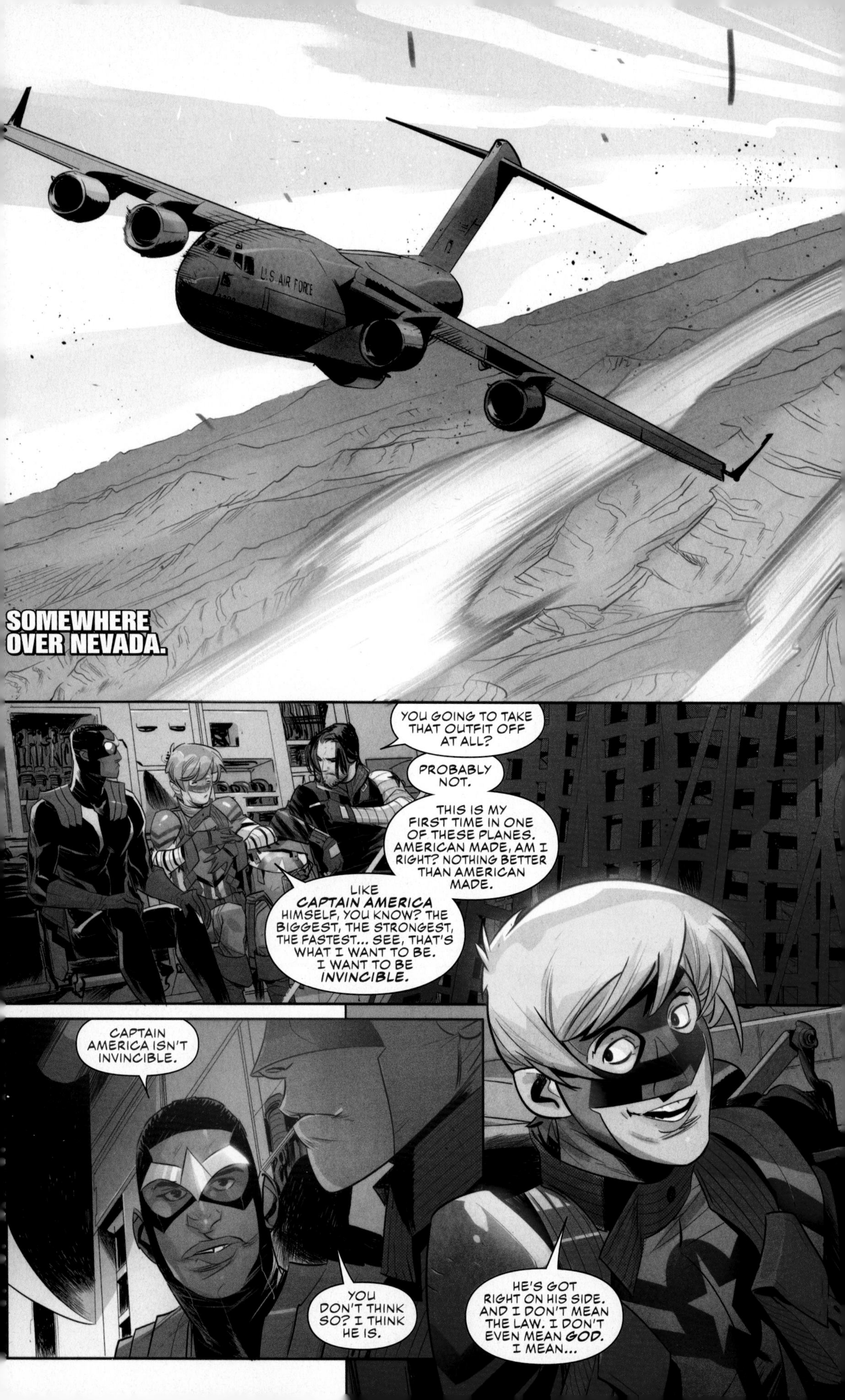

SOMEWHERE OVER NEVADA.
U.S. AIR FORCE
YOU GOING TO TAKE THAT OUTFIT OFF AT ALL?
PROBABLY NOT.
THIS IS MY FIRST TIME IN ONE OF THESE PLANES. AMERICAN MADE, AM I RIGHT? NOTHING BETTER THAN AMERICAN MADE.
LIKE *CAPTAIN AMERICA* HIMSELF, YOU KNOW? THE BIGGEST, THE STRONGEST, THE FASTEST... SEE, THAT'S WHAT I WANT TO BE. I WANT TO BE *INVINCIBLE.*
CAPTAIN AMERICA ISN'T INVINCIBLE.
YOU DON'T THINK SO? I THINK HE IS.
HE'S GOT RIGHT ON HIS SIDE. AND I DON'T MEAN THE LAW. I DON'T EVEN MEAN *GOD.* I MEAN...

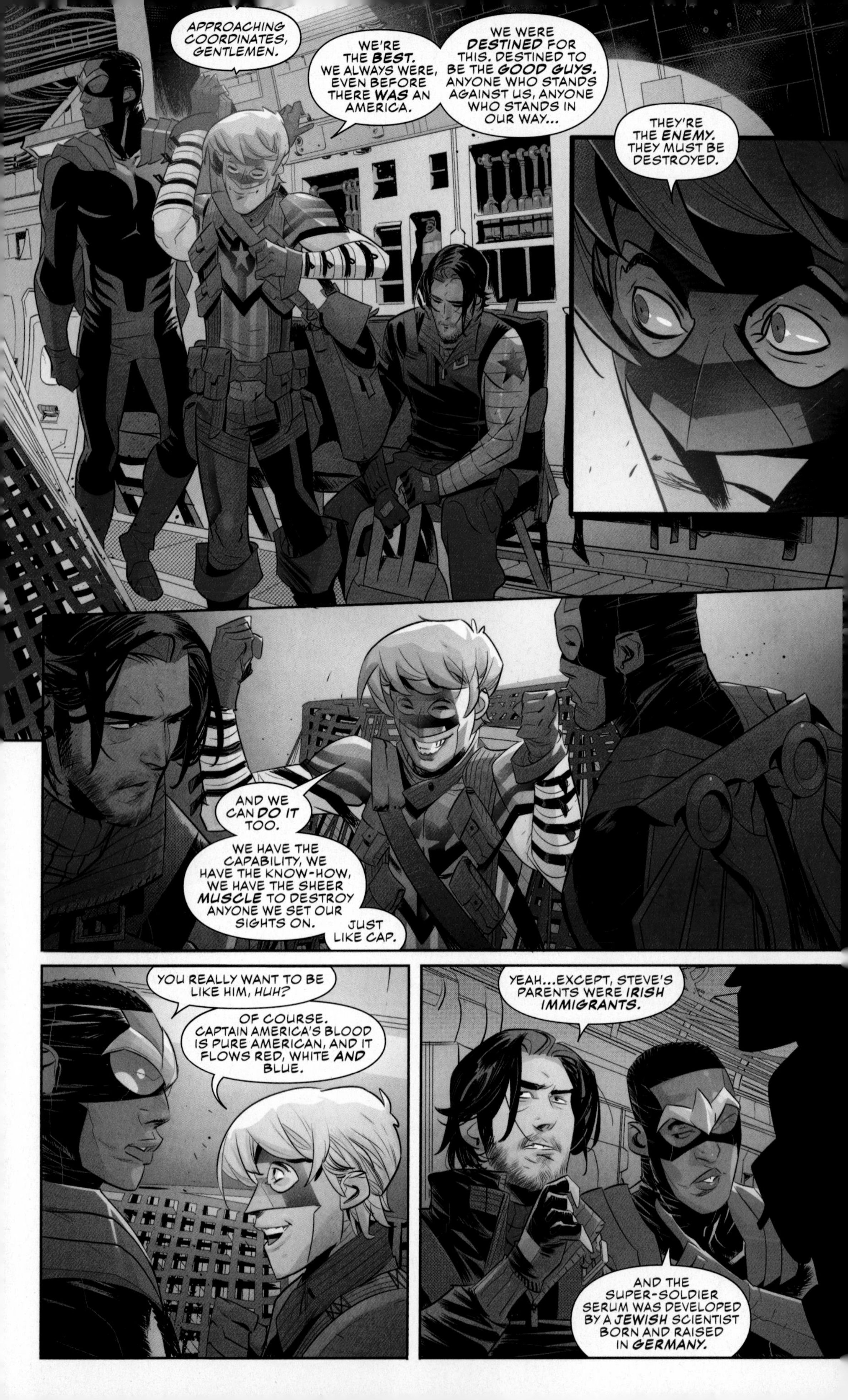

APPROACHING COORDINATES, GENTLEMEN.
WE'RE THE **BEST.** WE ALWAYS WERE, EVEN BEFORE THERE **WAS** AN AMERICA.
WE WERE **DESTINED** FOR THIS. DESTINED TO BE THE **GOOD GUYS.** ANYONE WHO STANDS AGAINST US, ANYONE WHO STANDS IN OUR WAY...
THEY'RE THE **ENEMY.** THEY MUST BE DESTROYED.
AND WE CAN **DO IT** TOO.
WE HAVE THE CAPABILITY, WE HAVE THE KNOW-HOW, WE HAVE THE SHEER **MUSCLE** TO DESTROY ANYONE WE SET OUR SIGHTS ON.
JUST LIKE CAP.
YOU REALLY WANT TO BE LIKE HIM, *HUH?*
OF COURSE. CAPTAIN AMERICA'S BLOOD IS PURE AMERICAN, AND IT FLOWS RED, WHITE **AND** BLUE.
YEAH...EXCEPT, STEVE'S PARENTS WERE ***IRISH IMMIGRANTS.***
AND THE SUPER-SOLDIER SERUM WAS DEVELOPED BY A ***JEWISH*** SCIENTIST BORN AND RAISED IN ***GERMANY.***

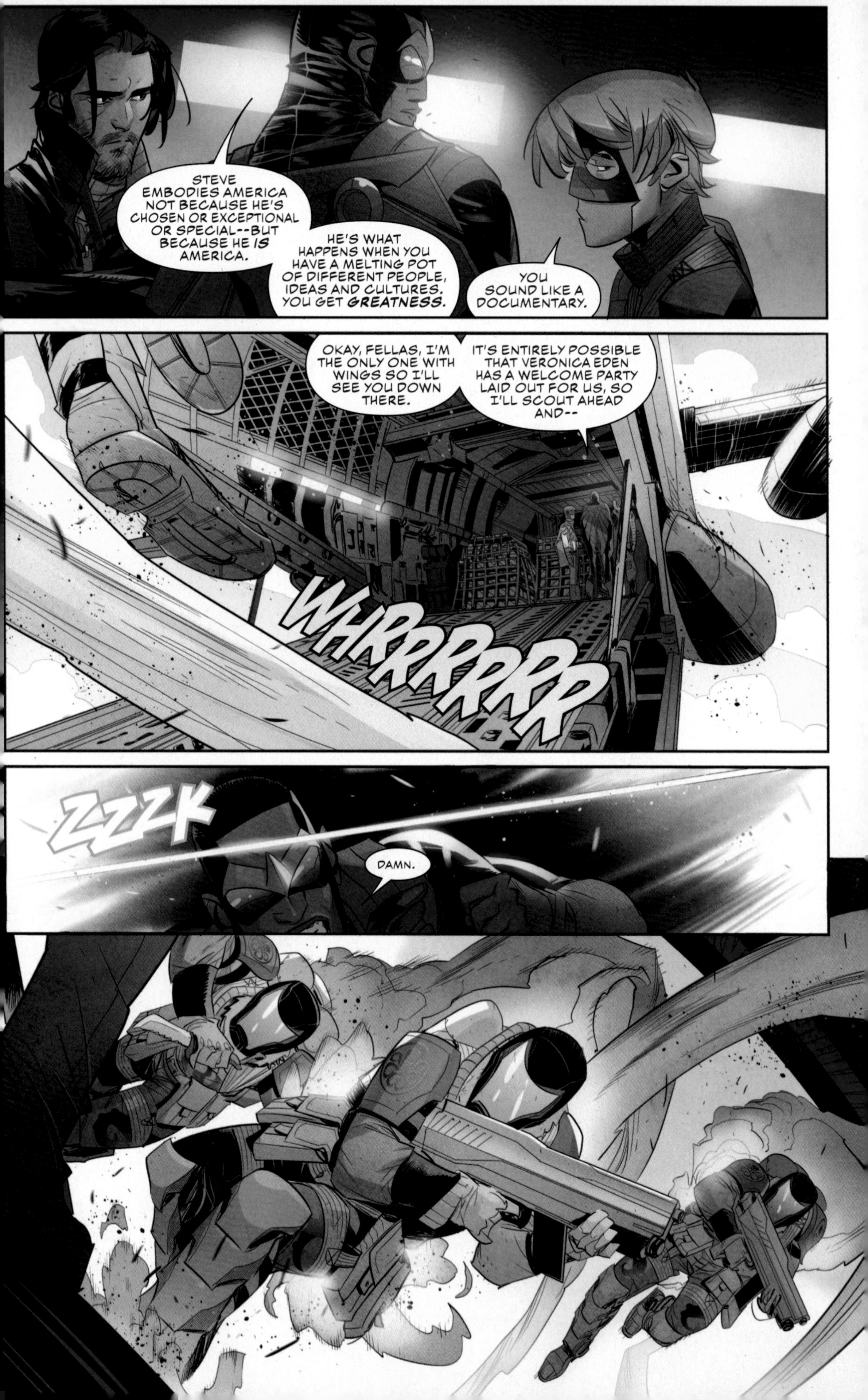
STEVE EMBODIES AMERICA NOT BECAUSE HE'S CHOSEN OR EXCEPTIONAL OR SPECIAL--BUT BECAUSE HE *IS* AMERICA.
HE'S WHAT HAPPENS WHEN YOU HAVE A MELTING POT OF DIFFERENT PEOPLE, IDEAS AND CULTURES. YOU GET **GREATNESS**.
YOU SOUND LIKE A DOCUMENTARY.
OKAY, FELLAS, I'M THE ONLY ONE WITH WINGS SO I'LL SEE YOU DOWN THERE.
IT'S ENTIRELY POSSIBLE THAT VERONICA EDEN HAS A WELCOME PARTY LAID OUT FOR US, SO I'LL SCOUT AHEAD AND--
WHRRRRRR
ZZZK
DAMN.

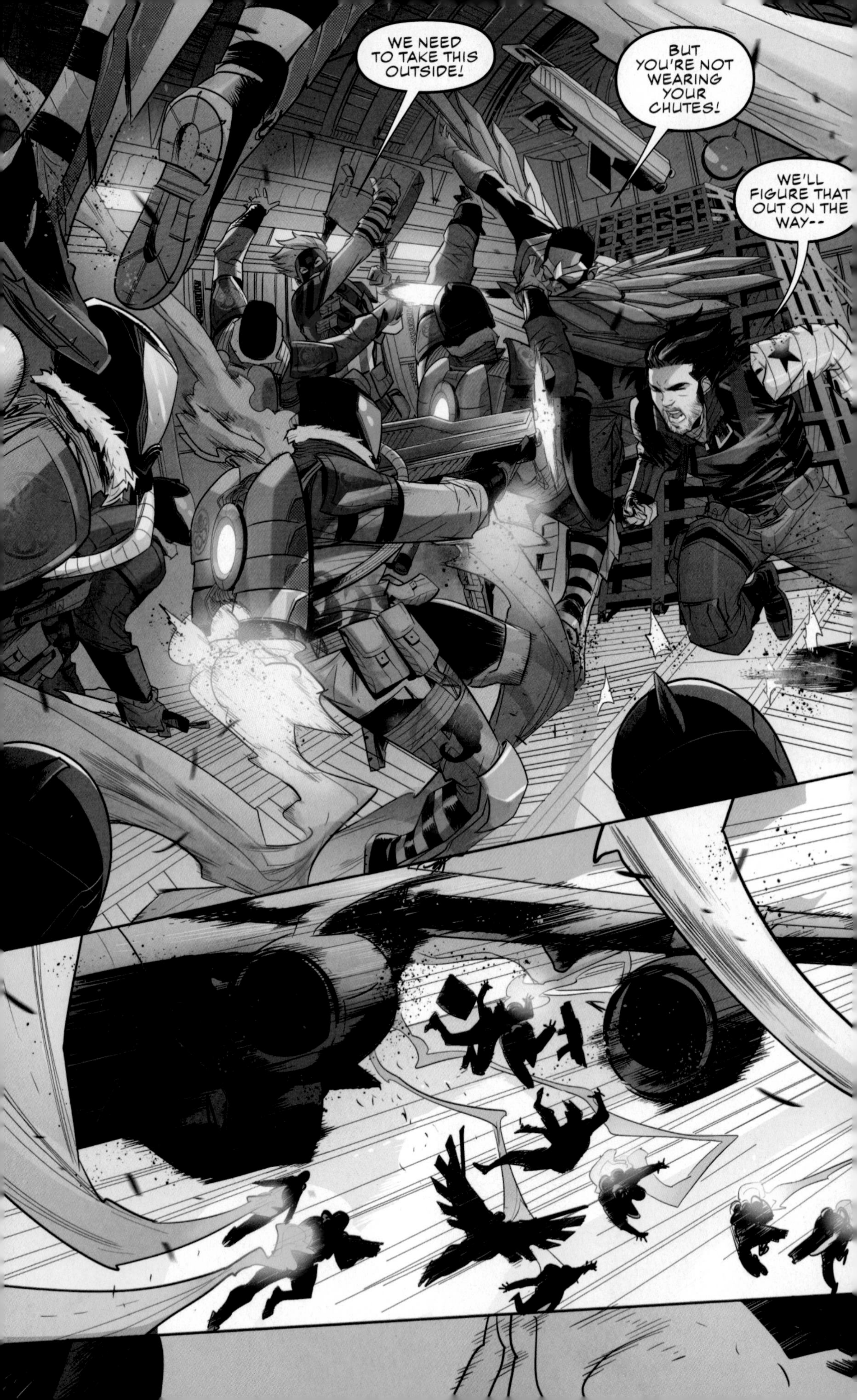
WE NEED TO TAKE THIS OUTSIDE!
BUT YOU'RE NOT WEARING YOUR CHUTES!
WE'LL FIGURE THAT OUT ON THE WAY--

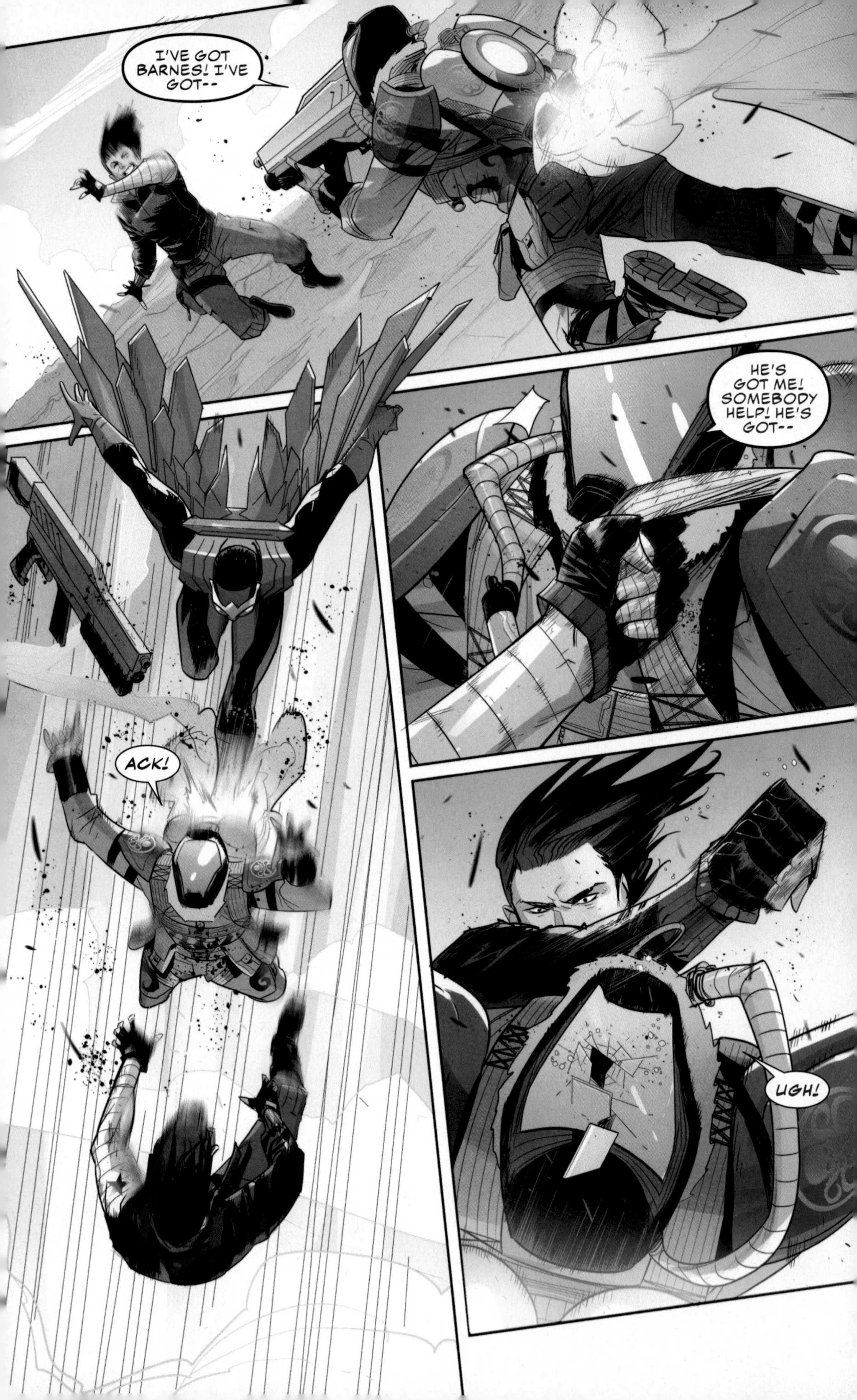
I'VE GOT BARNES! I'VE GOT--
HE'S GOT ME! SOMEBODY HELP! HE'S GOT--
ACK!
UGH!

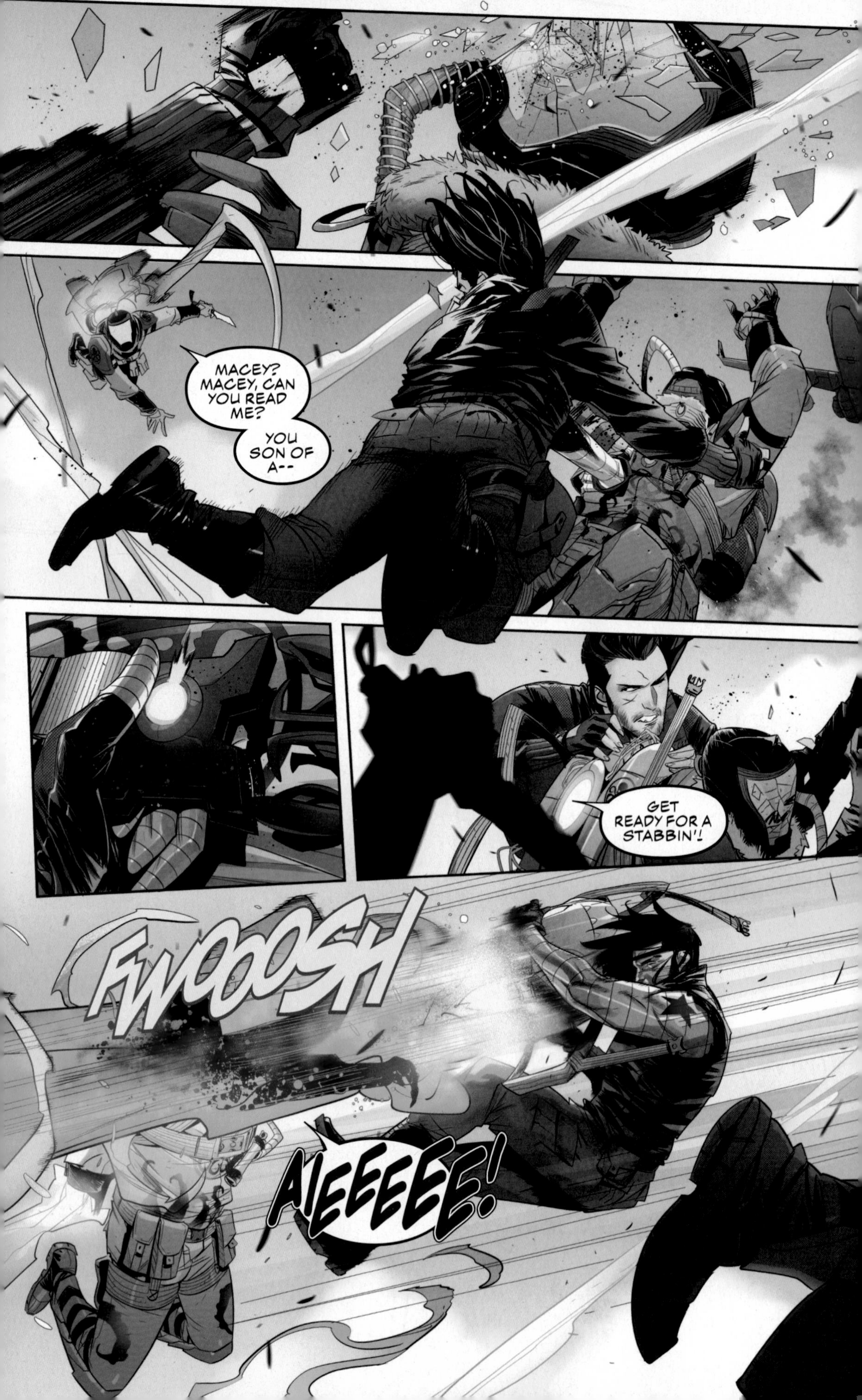
MACEY? MACEY, CAN YOU READ ME?
YOU SON OF A--
GET READY FOR A STABBIN'!
FWOOOSH
AIEEEEE!

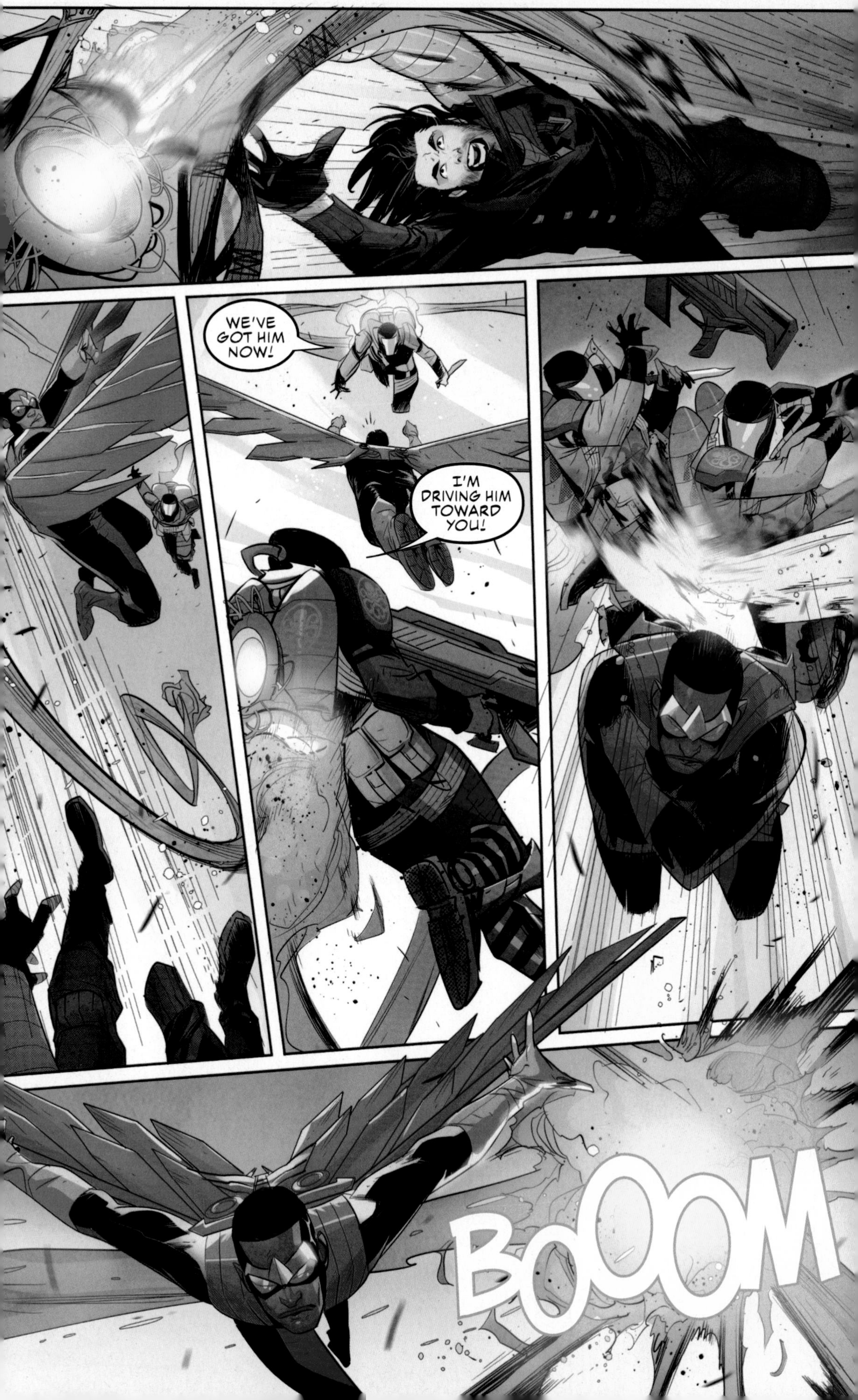
WE'VE GOT HIM NOW!
I'M DRIVING HIM TOWARD YOU!
BOOOOM

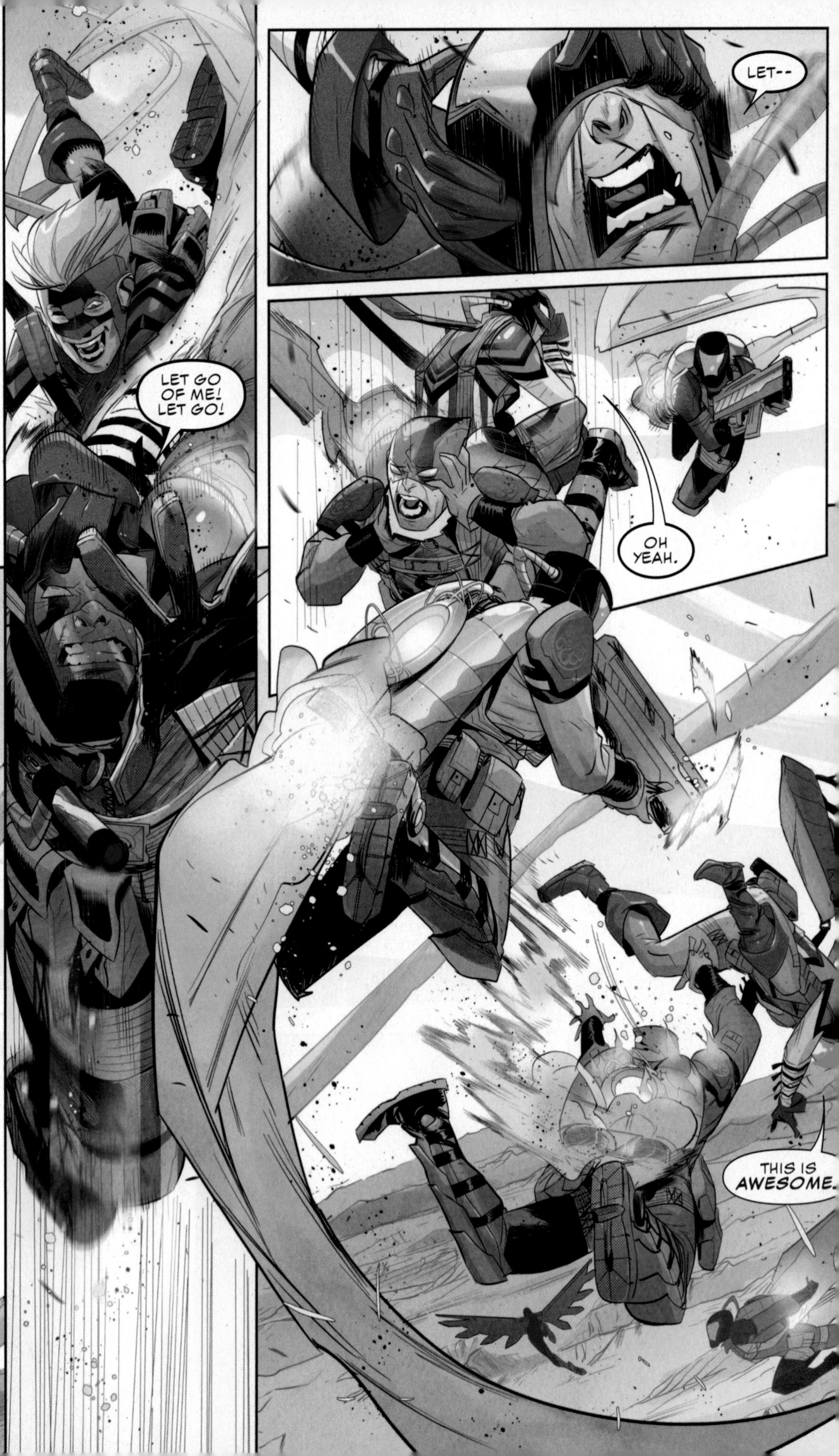
LET--
LET GO OF ME! LET GO!
OH YEAH.
THIS IS AWESOME.

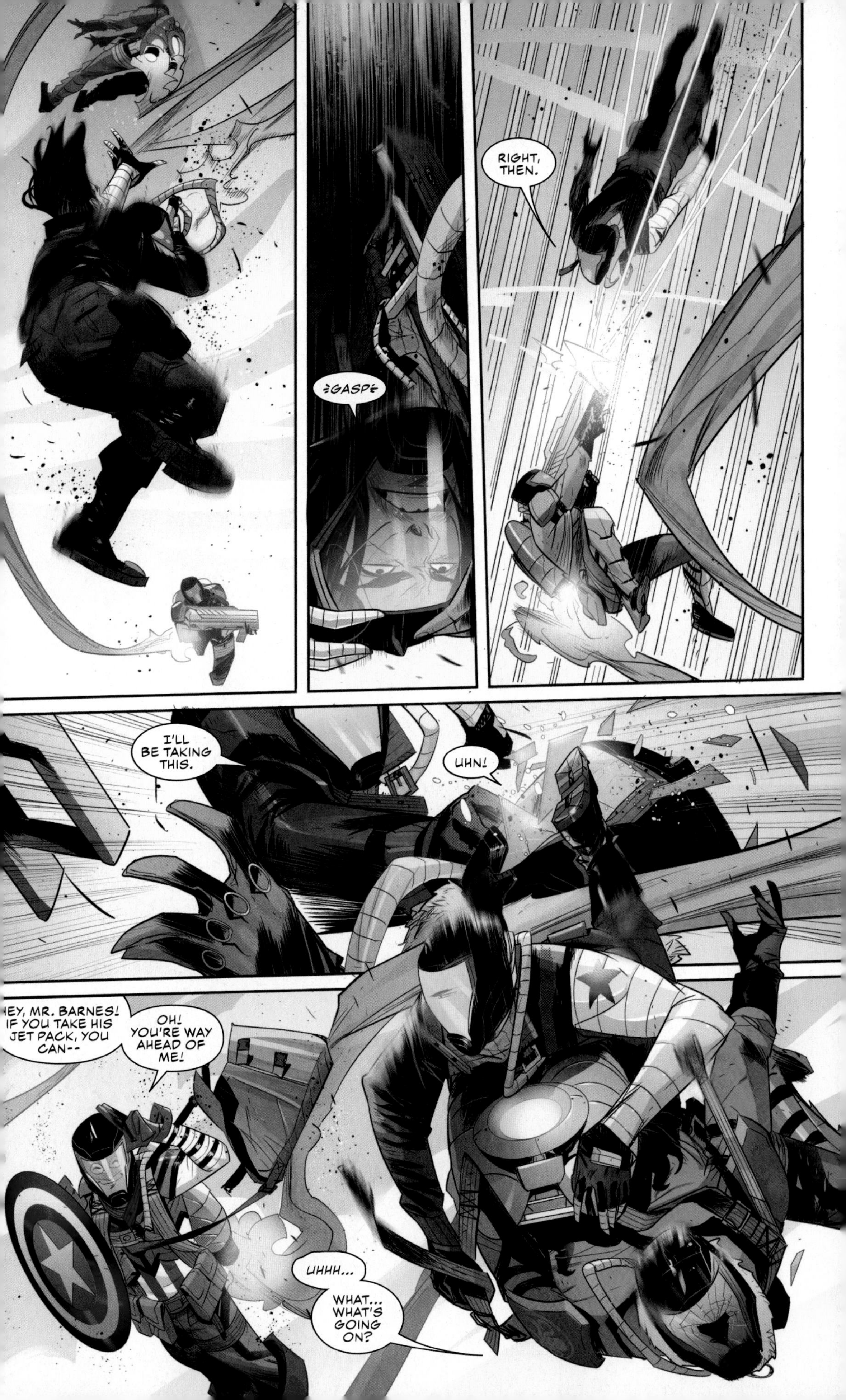
RIGHT, THEN.
≈GASP≈
I'LL BE TAKING THIS.
UHN!
EY, MR. BARNES! IF YOU TAKE HIS JET PACK, YOU CAN--
OH! YOU'RE WAY AHEAD OF ME!
UHHH...
WHAT... WHAT'S GOING ON?

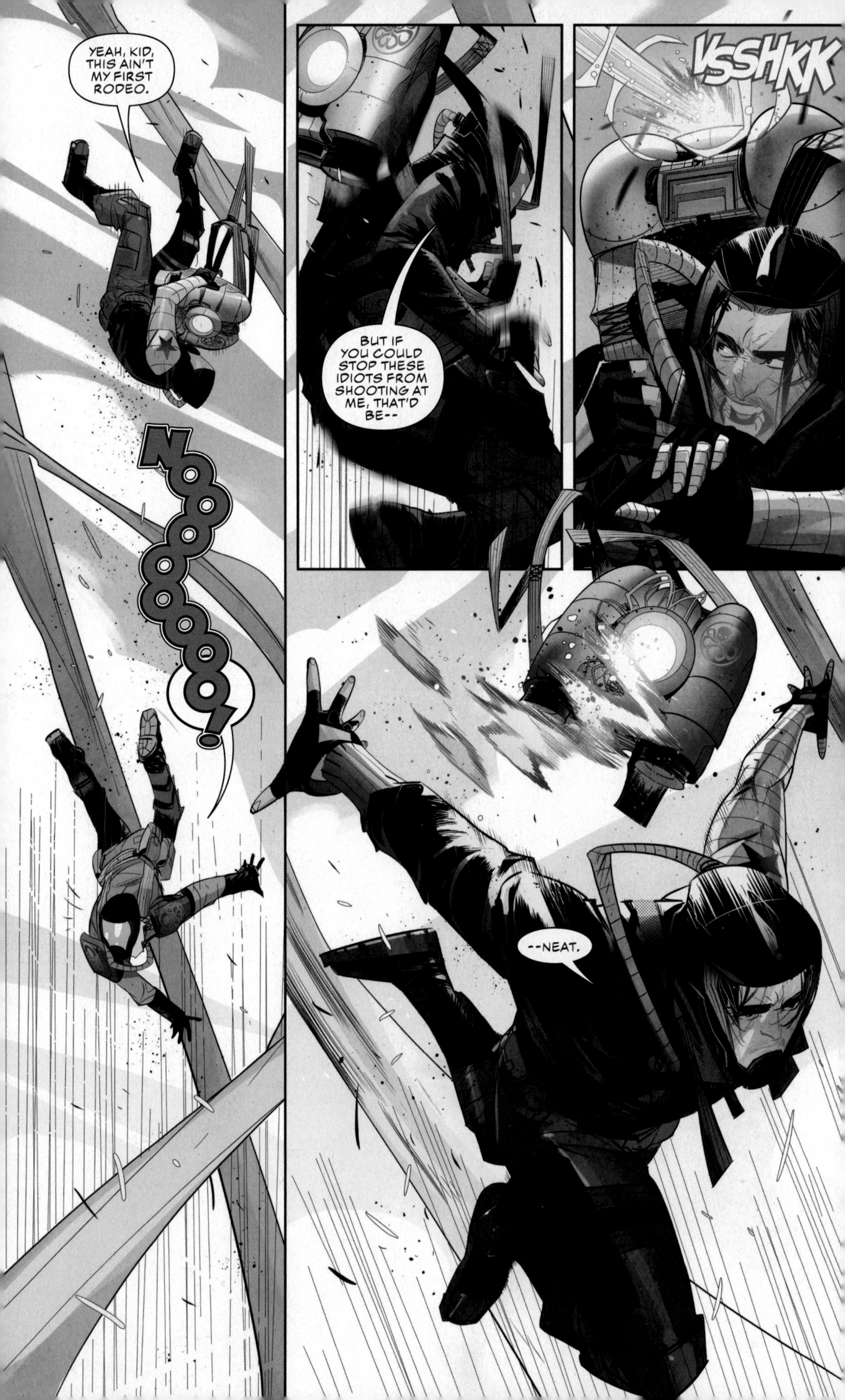
YEAH, KID, THIS AIN'T MY FIRST RODEO.
NOOOOOOOOO!
BUT IF YOU COULD STOP THESE IDIOTS FROM SHOOTING AT ME, THAT'D BE--
VSSHKK
--NEAT.

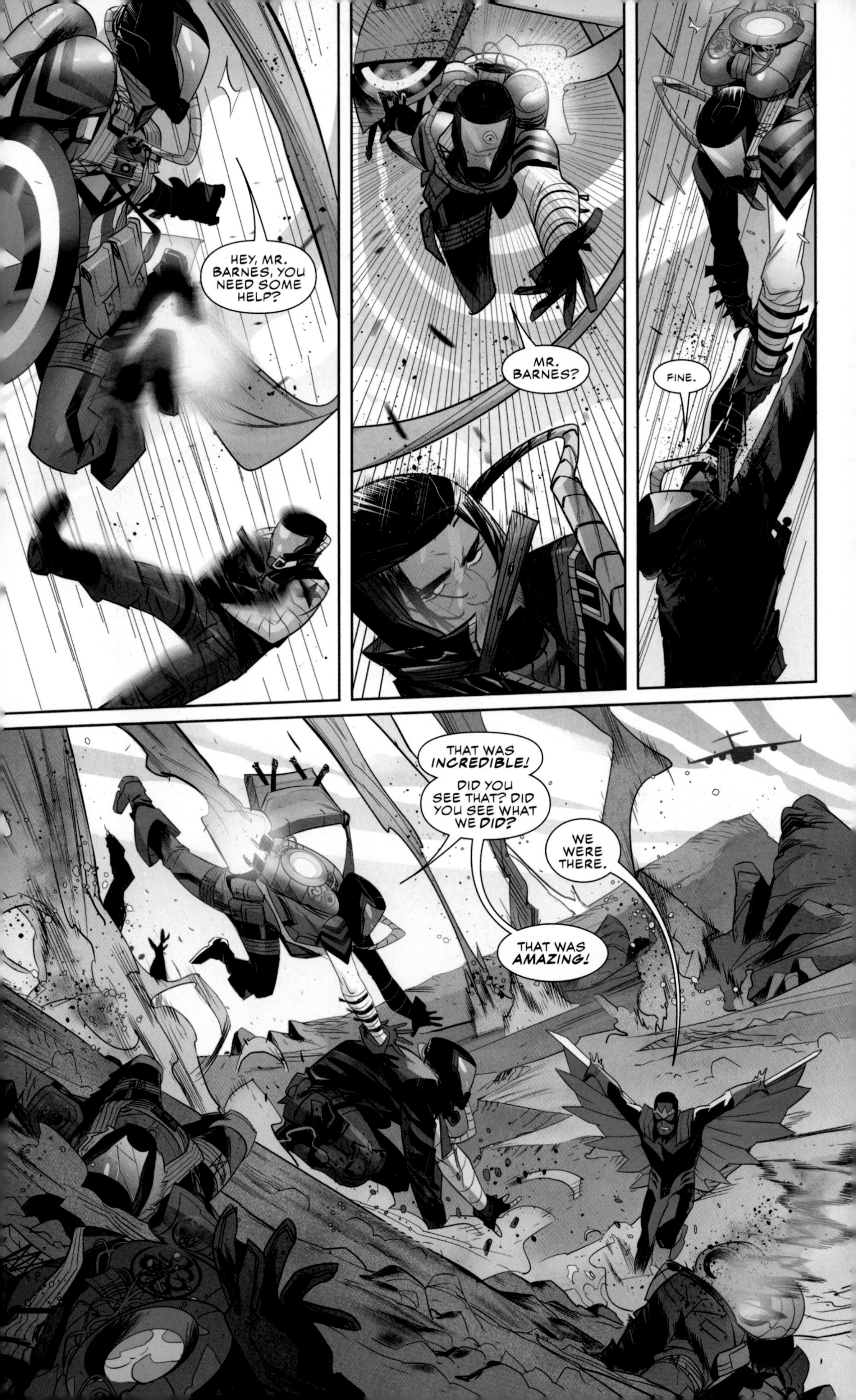
HEY, MR. BARNES, YOU NEED SOME HELP?
MR. BARNES?
FINE.
THAT WAS *INCREDIBLE!*
DID YOU SEE THAT? DID YOU SEE WHAT WE *DID?*
WE WERE THERE.
THAT WAS *AMAZING!*

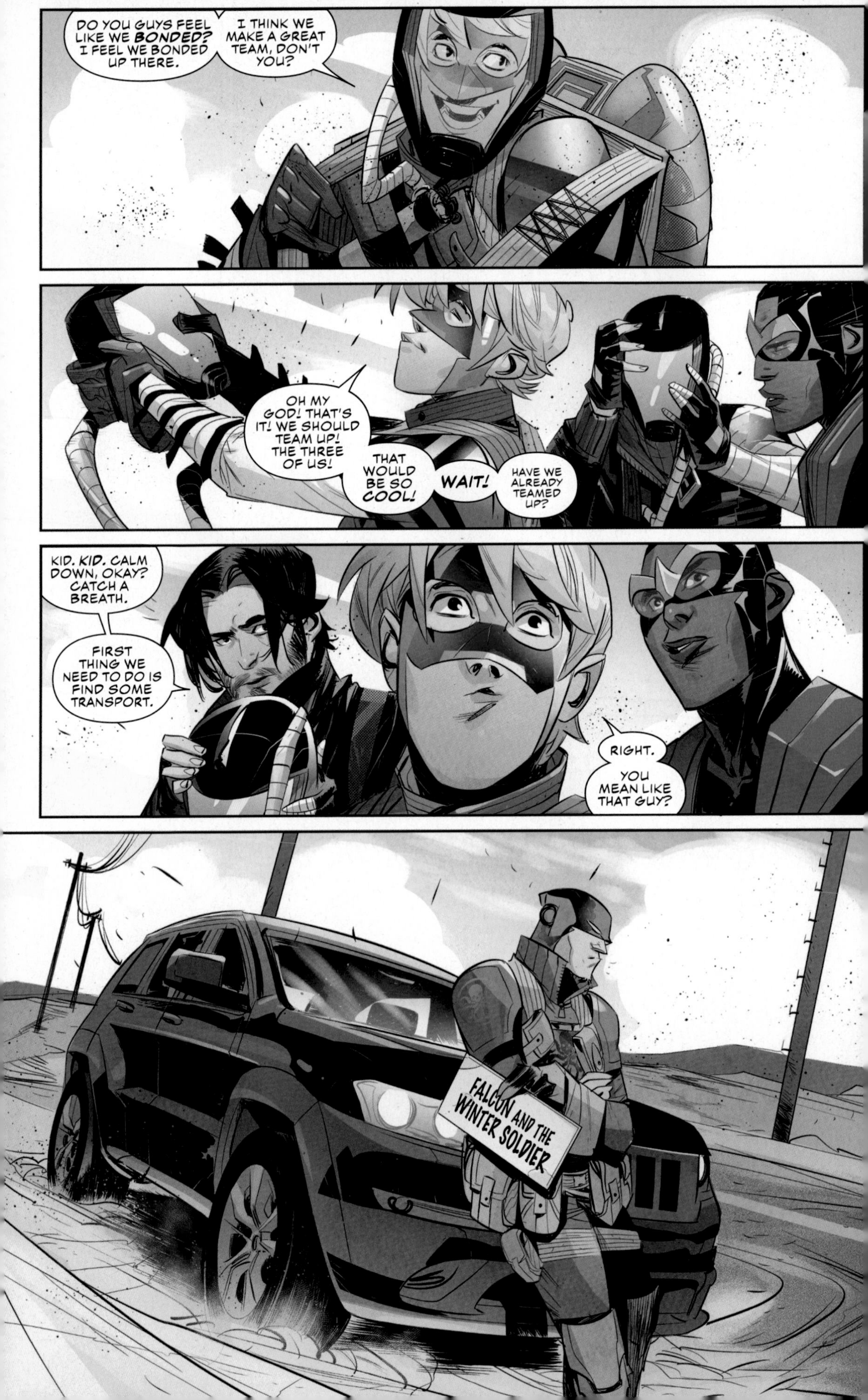
DO YOU GUYS FEEL LIKE WE BONDED? I FEEL WE BONDED UP THERE.
I THINK WE MAKE A GREAT TEAM, DON'T YOU?
OH MY GOD! THAT'S IT! WE SHOULD TEAM UP! THE THREE OF US!
THAT WOULD BE SO COOL!
WAIT!
HAVE WE ALREADY TEAMED UP?
KID. KID. CALM DOWN, OKAY? CATCH A BREATH.
FIRST THING WE NEED TO DO IS FIND SOME TRANSPORT.
RIGHT.
YOU MEAN LIKE THAT GUY?
FALCON AND THE WINTER SOLDIER

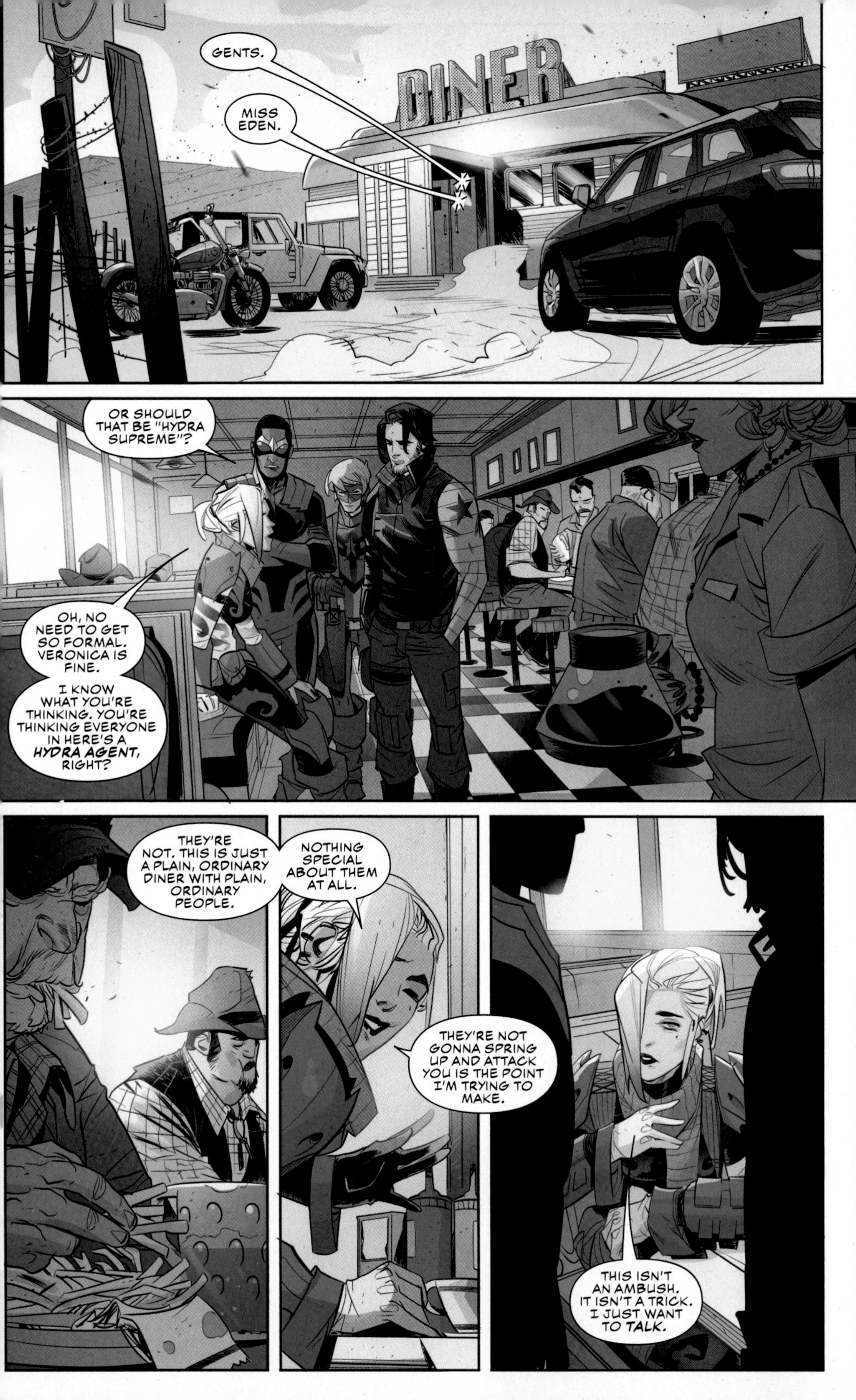
GENTS.
MISS EDEN.
DINER
OR SHOULD THAT BE "HYDRA SUPREME"?
OH, NO NEED TO GET SO FORMAL. VERONICA IS FINE.
I KNOW WHAT YOU'RE THINKING. YOU'RE THINKING EVERYONE IN HERE'S A *HYDRA AGENT*, RIGHT?
THEY'RE NOT. THIS IS JUST A PLAIN, ORDINARY DINER WITH PLAIN, ORDINARY PEOPLE.
NOTHING SPECIAL ABOUT THEM AT ALL.
THEY'RE NOT GONNA SPRING UP AND ATTACK YOU IS THE POINT I'M TRYING TO MAKE.
THIS ISN'T AN AMBUSH. IT ISN'T A TRICK. I JUST WANT TO *TALK*.

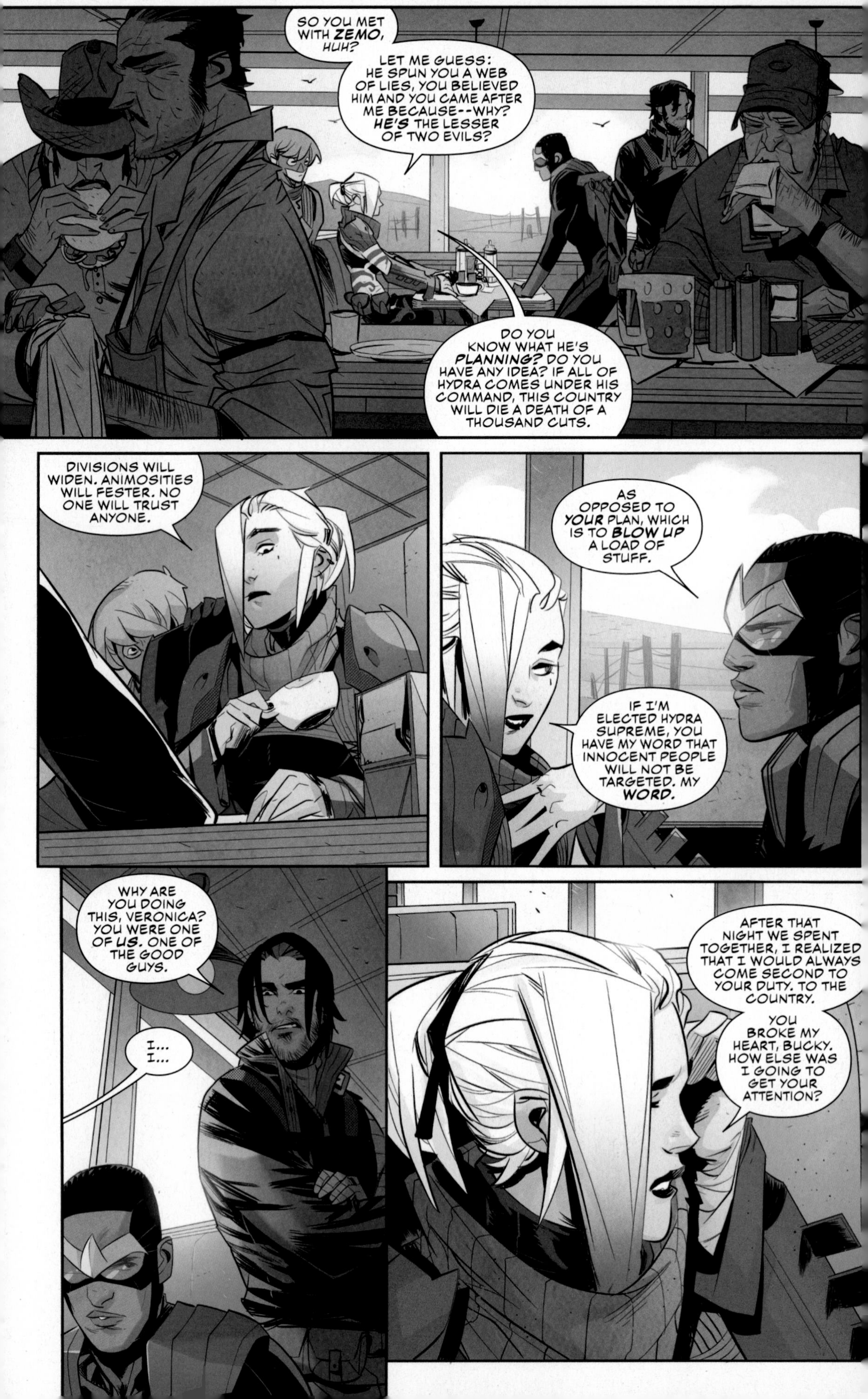
SO YOU MET WITH ZEMO, HUH?
LET ME GUESS: HE SPUN YOU A WEB OF LIES, YOU BELIEVED HIM AND YOU CAME AFTER ME BECAUSE--WHY? HE'S THE LESSER OF TWO EVILS?
DO YOU KNOW WHAT HE'S PLANNING? DO YOU HAVE ANY IDEA? IF ALL OF HYDRA COMES UNDER HIS COMMAND, THIS COUNTRY WILL DIE A DEATH OF A THOUSAND CUTS.
DIVISIONS WILL WIDEN. ANIMOSITIES WILL FESTER. NO ONE WILL TRUST ANYONE.
AS OPPOSED TO YOUR PLAN, WHICH IS TO BLOW UP A LOAD OF STUFF.
IF I'M ELECTED HYDRA SUPREME, YOU HAVE MY WORD THAT INNOCENT PEOPLE WILL NOT BE TARGETED. MY WORD.
WHY ARE YOU DOING THIS, VERONICA? YOU WERE ONE OF US. ONE OF THE GOOD GUYS.
I... I...
AFTER THAT NIGHT WE SPENT TOGETHER, I REALIZED THAT I WOULD ALWAYS COME SECOND TO YOUR DUTY. TO THE COUNTRY.
YOU BROKE MY HEART, BUCKY. HOW ELSE WAS I GOING TO GET YOUR ATTENTION?

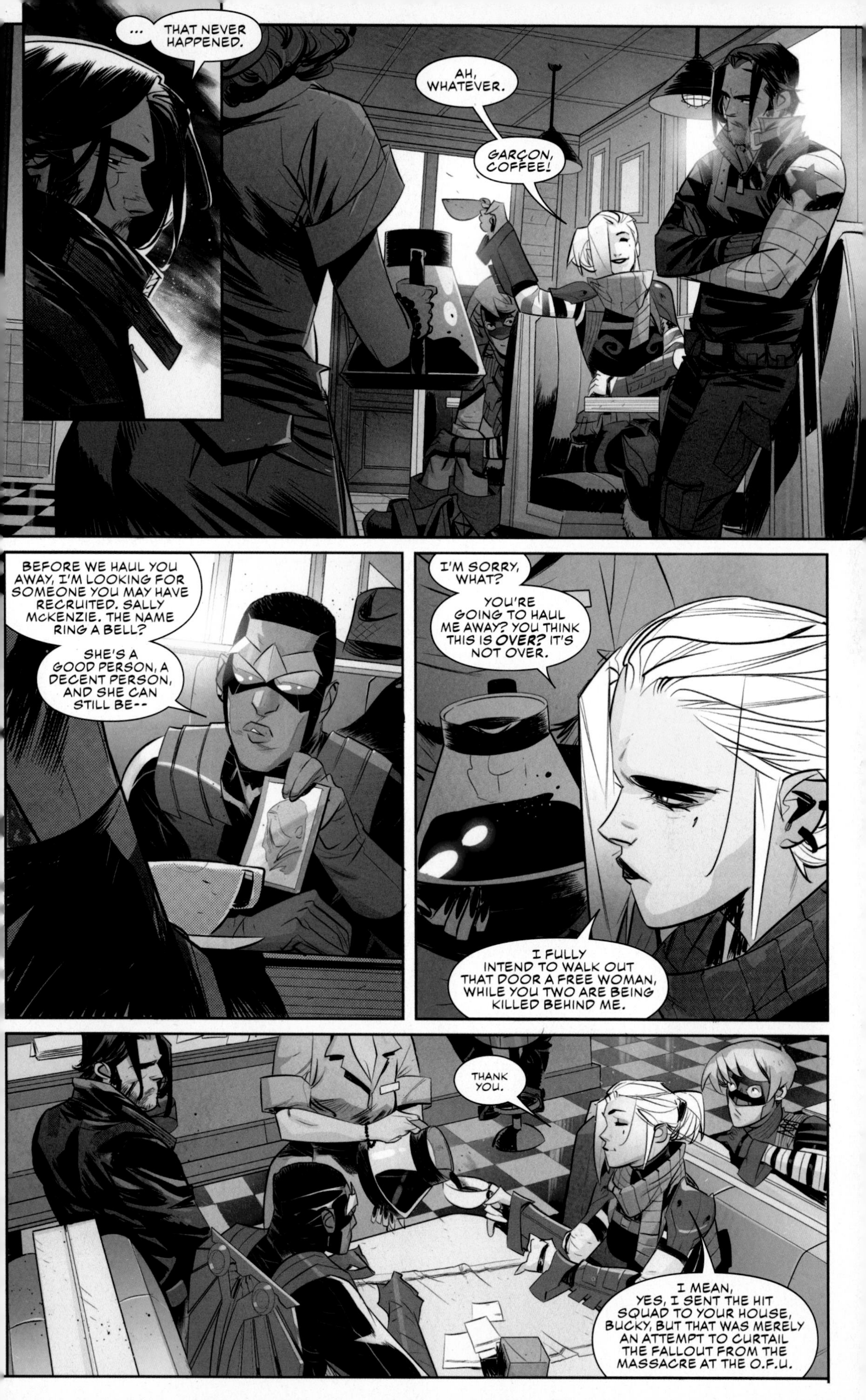
...
THAT NEVER HAPPENED.
AH, WHATEVER.
GARÇON, COFFEE!
BEFORE WE HAUL YOU AWAY, I'M LOOKING FOR SOMEONE YOU MAY HAVE RECRUITED. SALLY McKENZIE. THE NAME RING A BELL?
SHE'S A GOOD PERSON, A DECENT PERSON, AND SHE CAN STILL BE--
I'M SORRY, WHAT?
YOU'RE GOING TO HAUL ME AWAY? YOU THINK THIS IS OVER? IT'S NOT OVER.
I FULLY INTEND TO WALK OUT THAT DOOR A FREE WOMAN, WHILE YOU TWO ARE BEING KILLED BEHIND ME.
THANK YOU.
I MEAN, YES, I SENT THE HIT SQUAD TO YOUR HOUSE, BUCKY, BUT THAT WAS MERELY AN ATTEMPT TO CURTAIL THE FALLOUT FROM THE MASSACRE AT THE O.F.U.

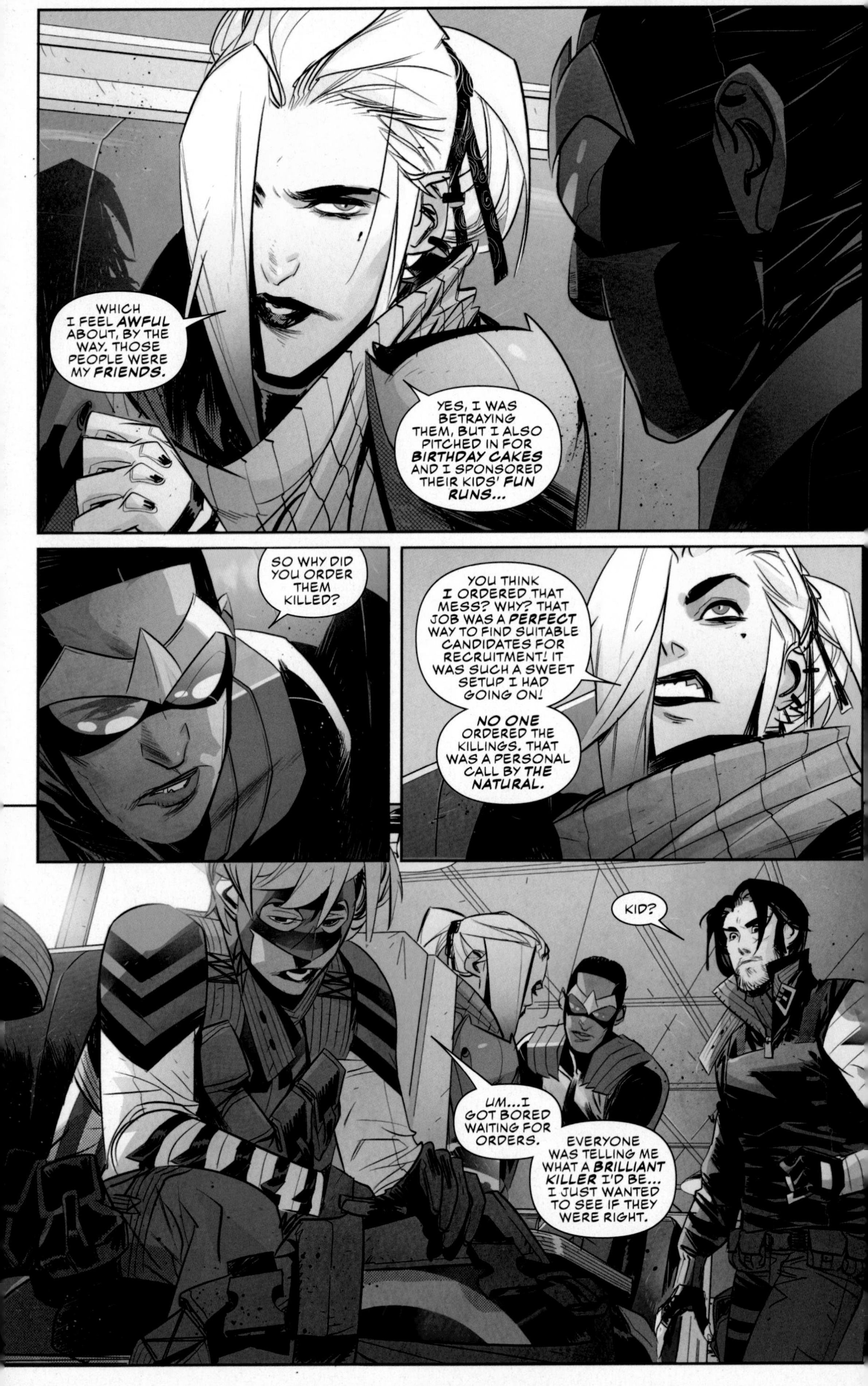
WHICH I FEEL **AWFUL** ABOUT, BY THE WAY. THOSE PEOPLE WERE MY **FRIENDS.**
YES, I WAS BETRAYING THEM, BUT I ALSO PITCHED IN FOR **BIRTHDAY CAKES** AND I SPONSORED THEIR KIDS' **FUN RUNS...**
SO WHY DID YOU ORDER THEM KILLED?
YOU THINK **I** ORDERED THAT MESS? WHY? THAT JOB WAS A **PERFECT** WAY TO FIND SUITABLE CANDIDATES FOR RECRUITMENT! IT WAS SUCH A SWEET SETUP I HAD GOING ON!
NO ONE ORDERED THE KILLINGS. THAT WAS A PERSONAL CALL BY **THE NATURAL.**
KID?
UM...I GOT BORED WAITING FOR ORDERS.
EVERYONE WAS TELLING ME WHAT A **BRILLIANT KILLER** I'D BE... I JUST WANTED TO SEE IF THEY WERE RIGHT.

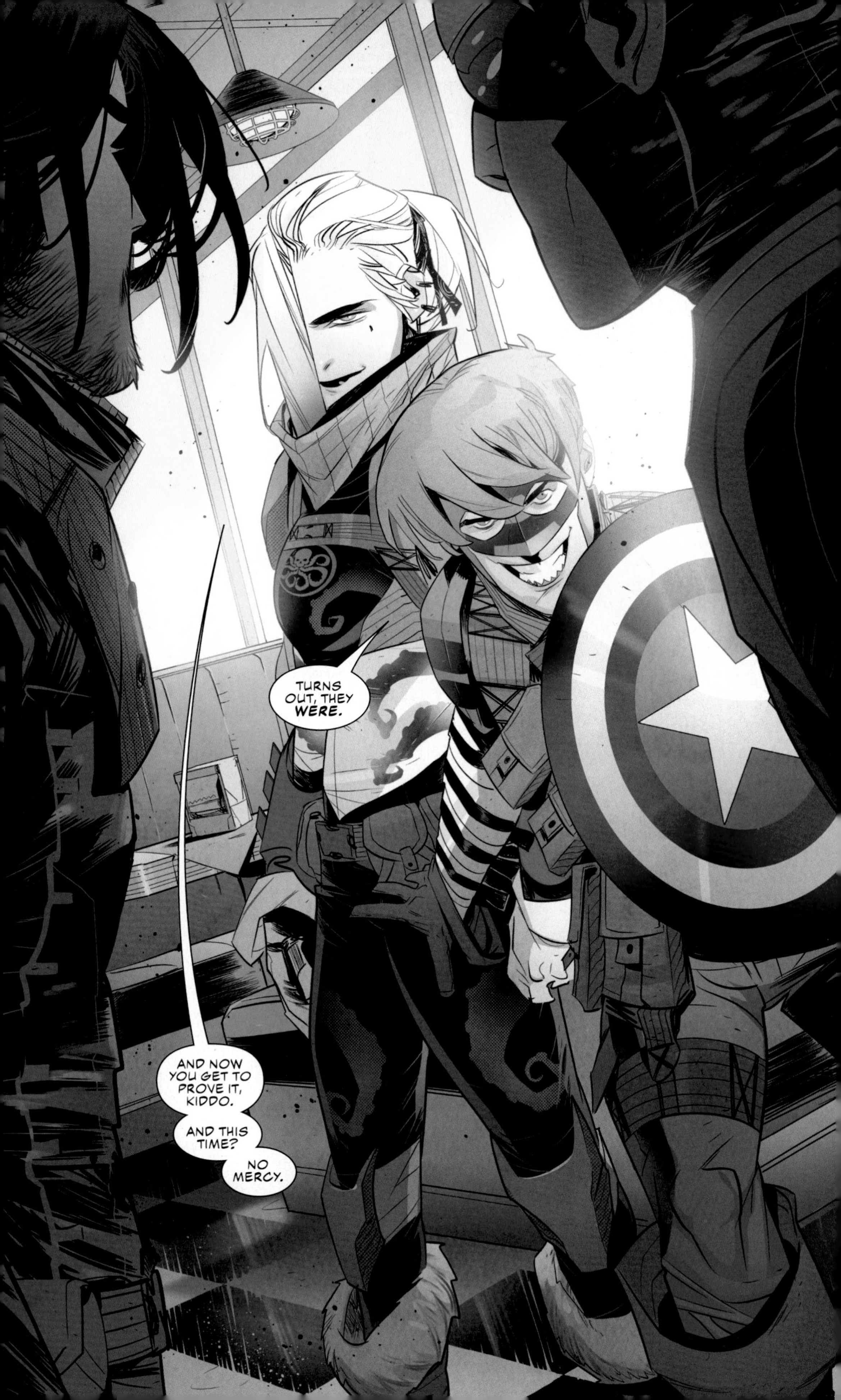
TURNS OUT, THEY WERE.
AND NOW YOU GET TO PROVE IT, KIDDO.
AND THIS TIME?
NO MERCY.

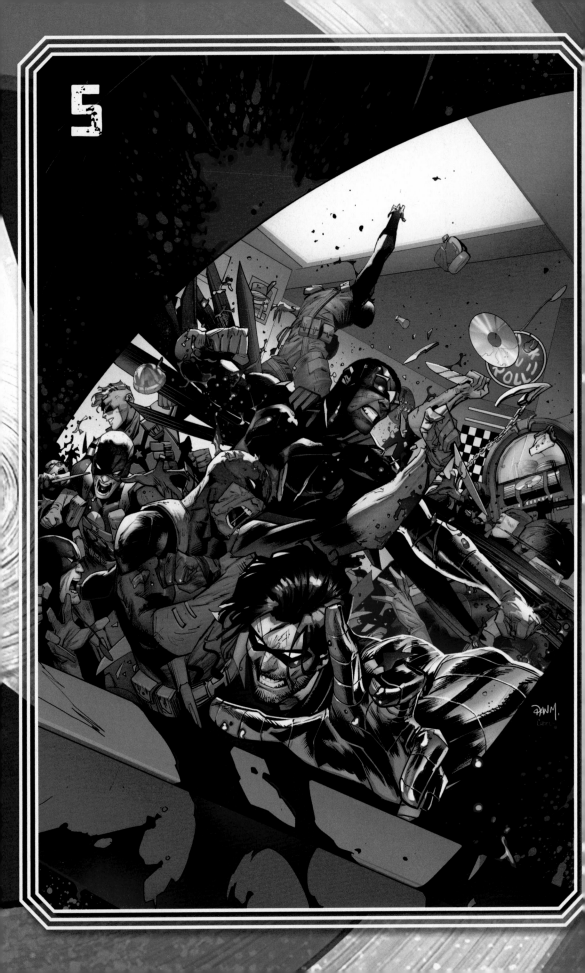

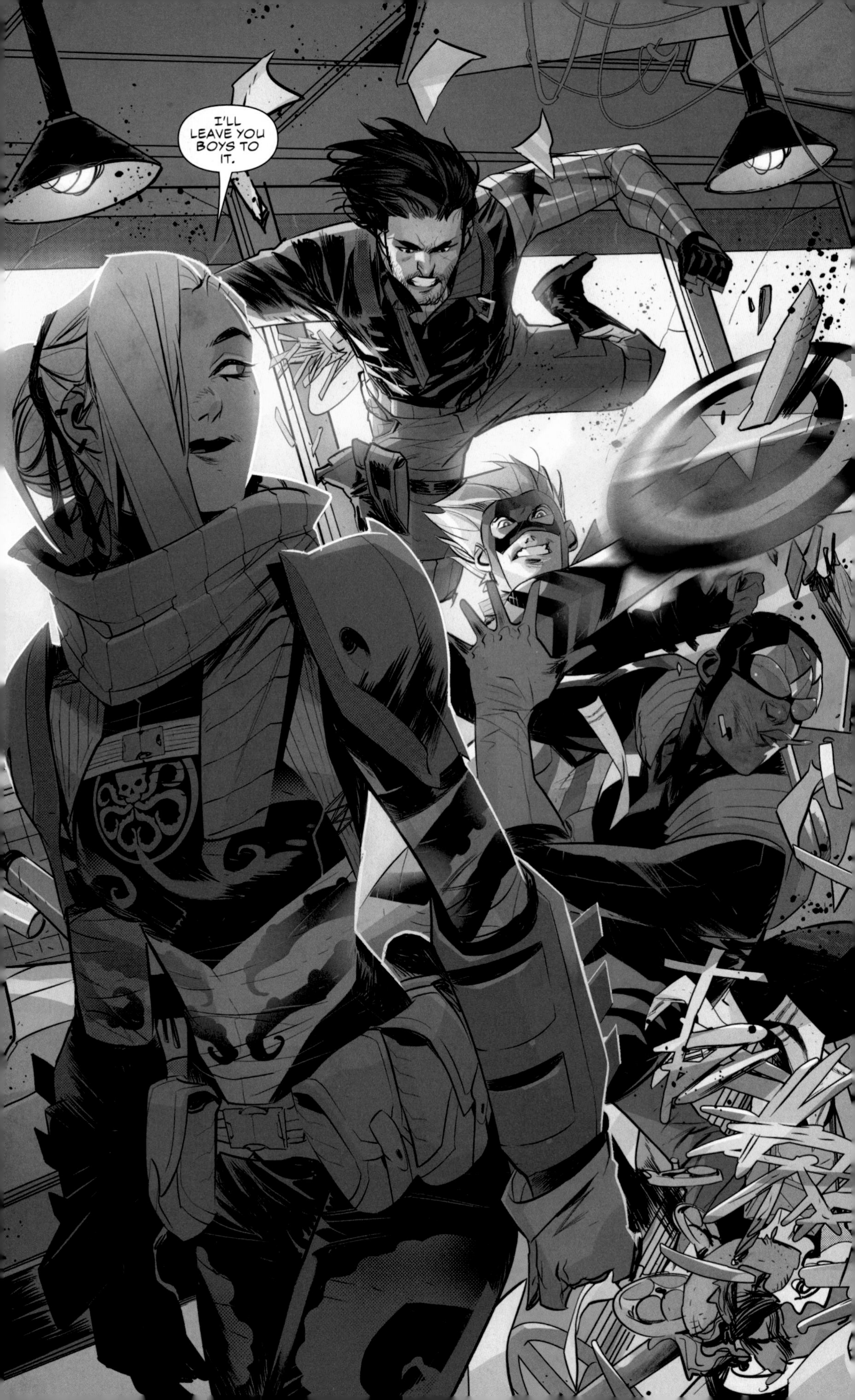
I'LL LEAVE YOU BOYS TO IT.

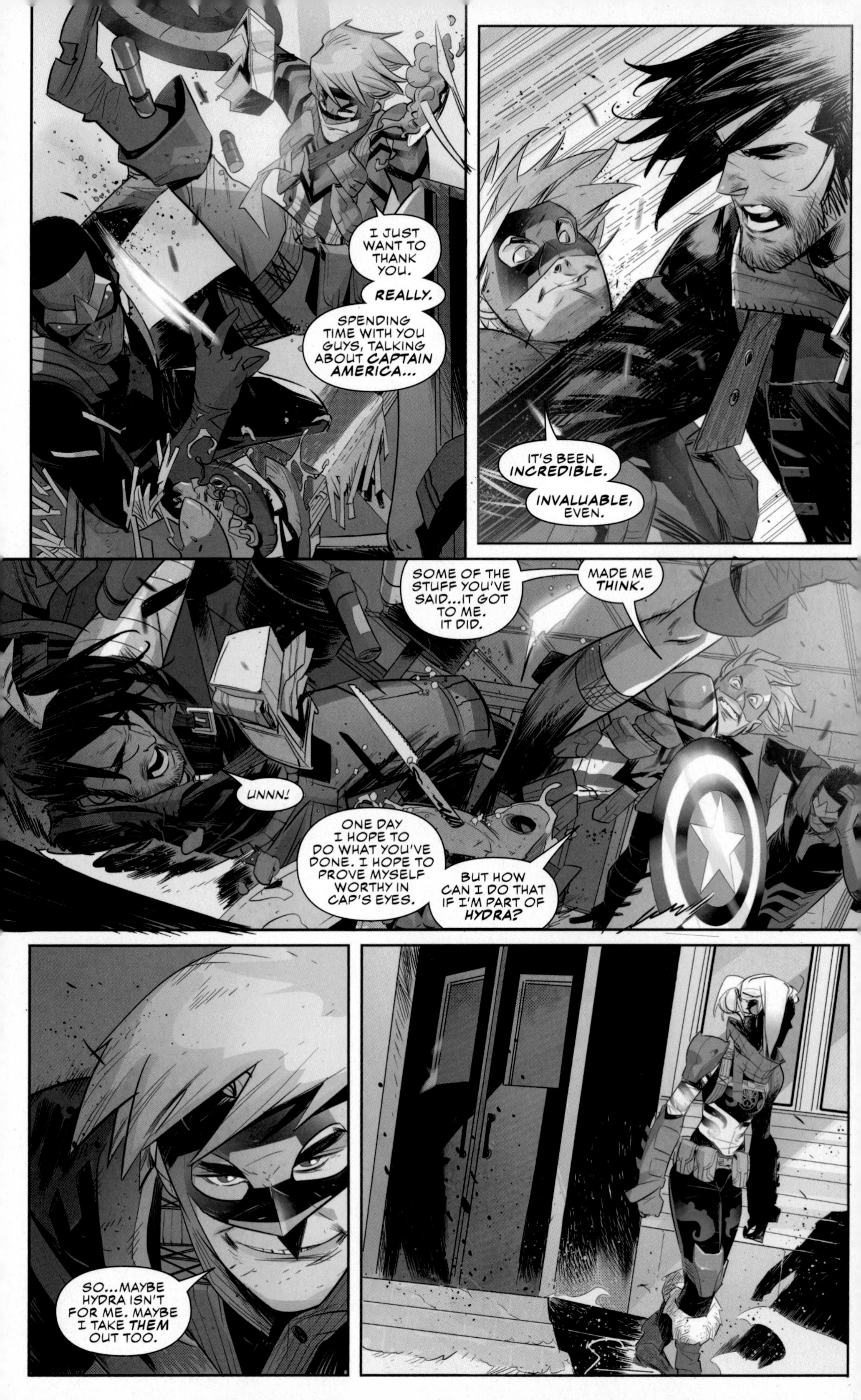
I JUST WANT TO THANK YOU.
REALLY.
SPENDING TIME WITH YOU GUYS, TALKING ABOUT CAPTAIN AMERICA...
IT'S BEEN INCREDIBLE.
INVALUABLE, EVEN.
SOME OF THE STUFF YOU'VE SAID...IT GOT TO ME. IT DID.
MADE ME THINK.
UNNN!
ONE DAY I HOPE TO DO WHAT YOU'VE DONE. I HOPE TO PROVE MYSELF WORTHY IN CAP'S EYES.
BUT HOW CAN I DO THAT IF I'M PART OF HYDRA?
SO...MAYBE HYDRA ISN'T FOR ME. MAYBE I TAKE THEM OUT TOO.

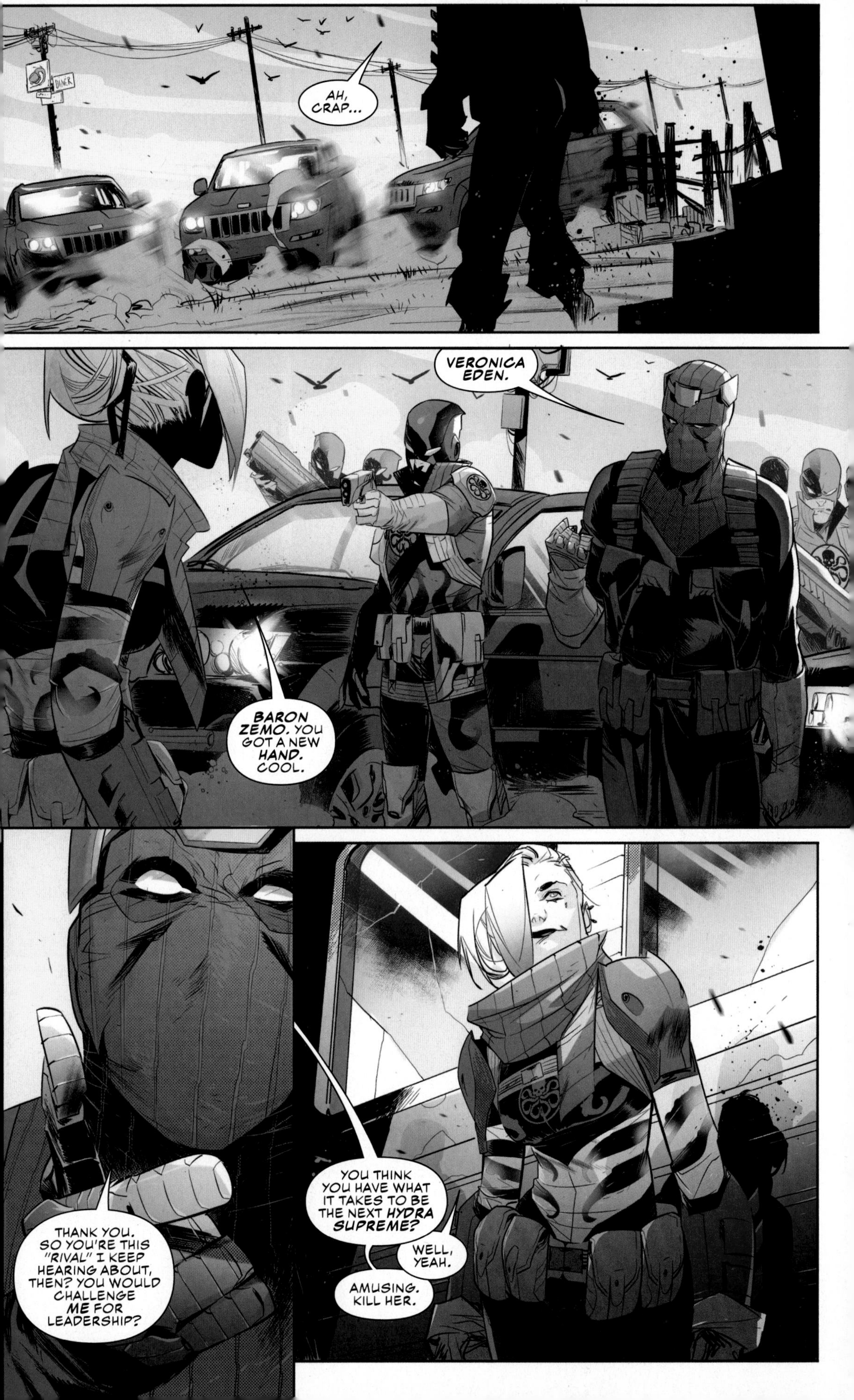
DINER
AH, CRAP...
VERONICA EDEN.
BARON ZEMO. YOU GOT A NEW HAND. COOL.
THANK YOU. SO YOU'RE THIS "RIVAL" I KEEP HEARING ABOUT, THEN? YOU WOULD CHALLENGE ME FOR LEADERSHIP?
YOU THINK YOU HAVE WHAT IT TAKES TO BE THE NEXT HYDRA SUPREME?
WELL, YEAH.
AMUSING. KILL HER.

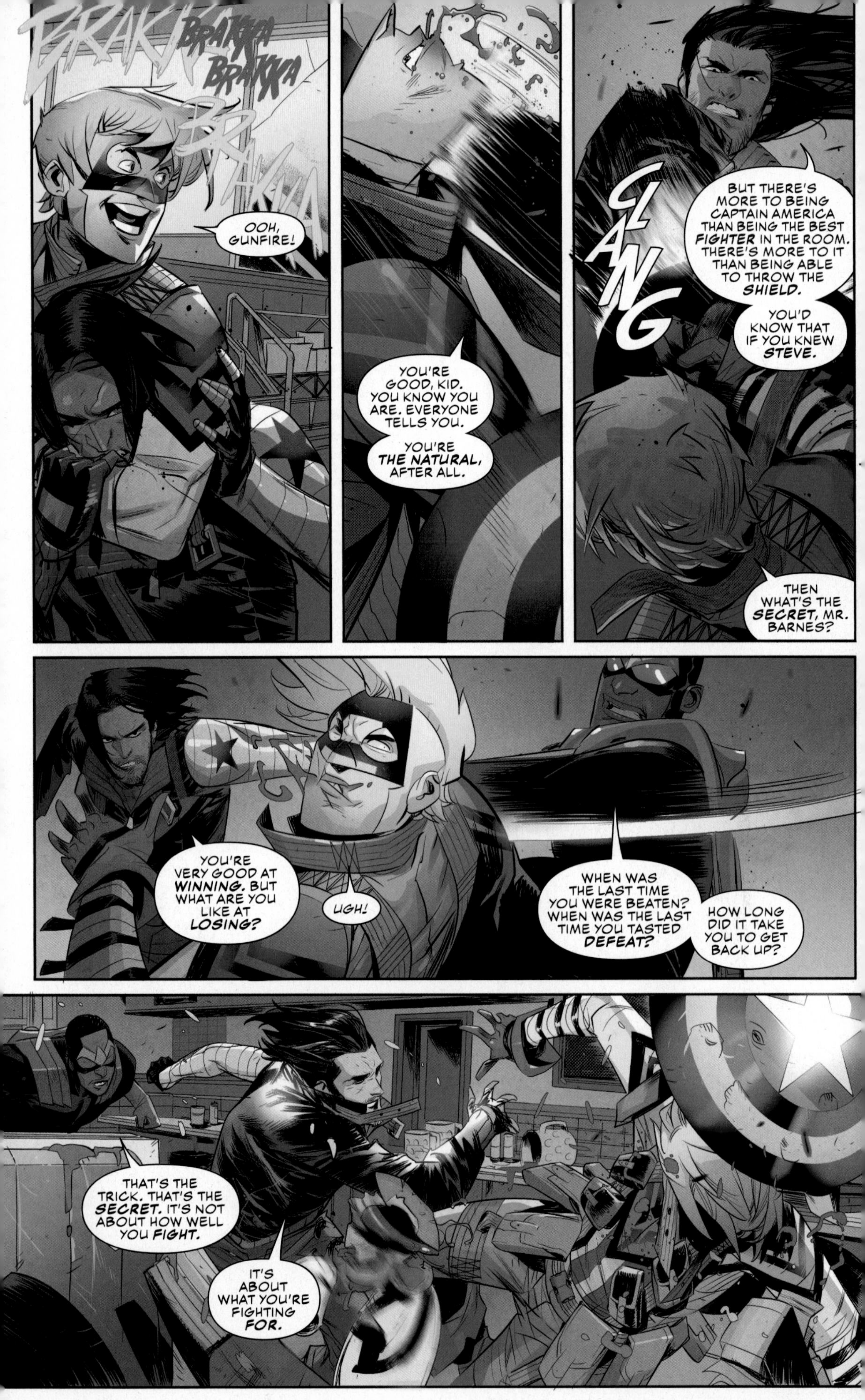
BRAKKA BRAKKA BRAKKA BRAKKA
OOH, GUNFIRE!
YOU'RE GOOD, KID. YOU KNOW YOU ARE. EVERYONE TELLS YOU.
YOU'RE THE NATURAL, AFTER ALL.
CLANG
BUT THERE'S MORE TO BEING CAPTAIN AMERICA THAN BEING THE BEST FIGHTER IN THE ROOM. THERE'S MORE TO IT THAN BEING ABLE TO THROW THE SHIELD.
YOU'D KNOW THAT IF YOU KNEW STEVE.
THEN WHAT'S THE SECRET, MR. BARNES?
YOU'RE VERY GOOD AT WINNING. BUT WHAT ARE YOU LIKE AT LOSING?
UGH!
WHEN WAS THE LAST TIME YOU WERE BEATEN? WHEN WAS THE LAST TIME YOU TASTED DEFEAT?
HOW LONG DID IT TAKE YOU TO GET BACK UP?
THAT'S THE TRICK. THAT'S THE SECRET. IT'S NOT ABOUT HOW WELL YOU FIGHT.
IT'S ABOUT WHAT YOU'RE FIGHTING FOR.

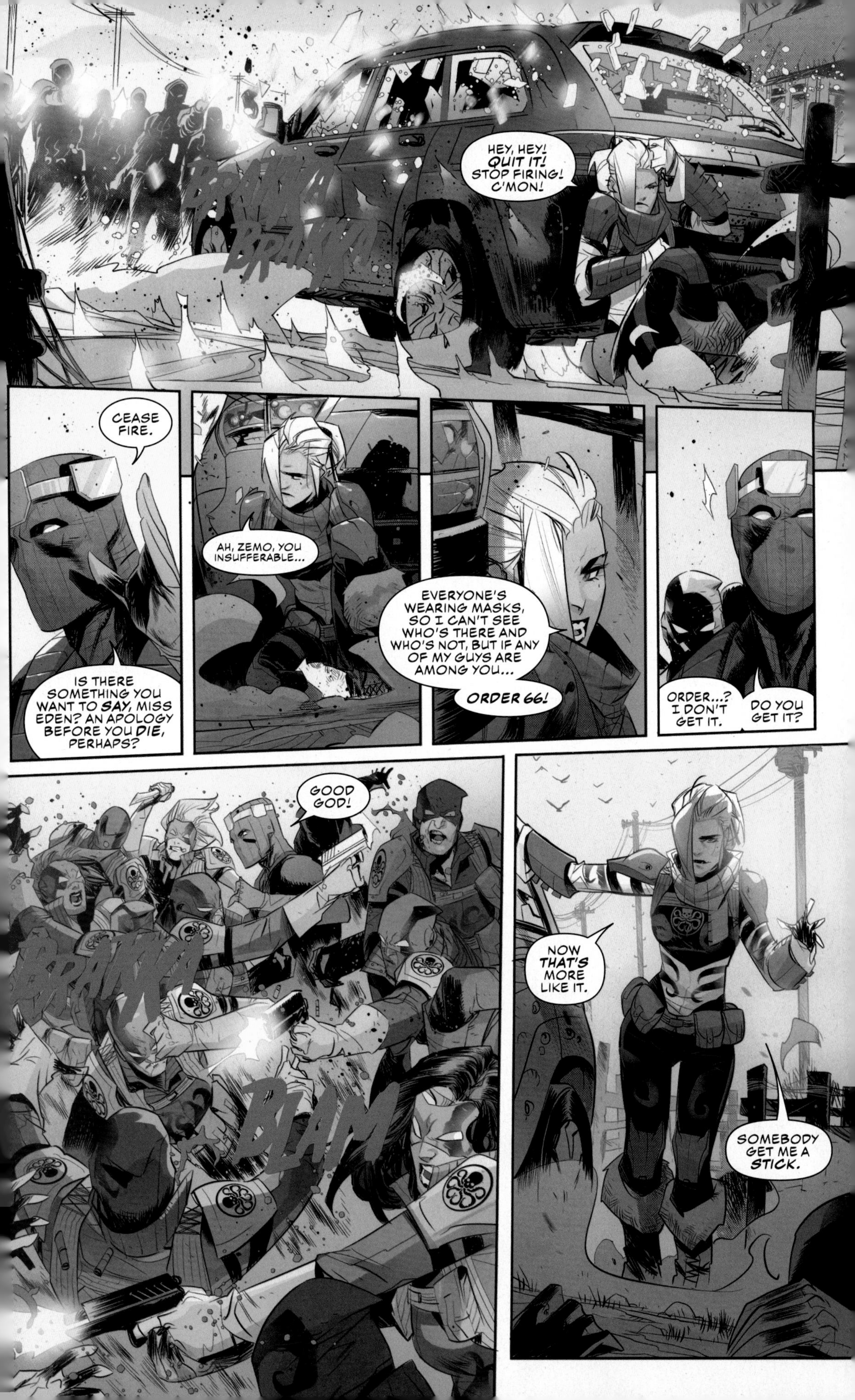
BRAKKA BRAKKA
HEY, HEY! QUIT IT! STOP FIRING! C'MON!
CEASE FIRE.
IS THERE SOMETHING YOU WANT TO SAY, MISS EDEN? AN APOLOGY BEFORE YOU DIE, PERHAPS?
AH, ZEMO, YOU INSUFFERABLE...
EVERYONE'S WEARING MASKS, SO I CAN'T SEE WHO'S THERE AND WHO'S NOT, BUT IF ANY OF MY GUYS ARE AMONG YOU...
ORDER 66!
ORDER...? I DON'T GET IT.
DO YOU GET IT?
GOOD GOD!
BRAKKA
BLAM
NOW THAT'S MORE LIKE IT.
SOMEBODY GET ME A STICK.

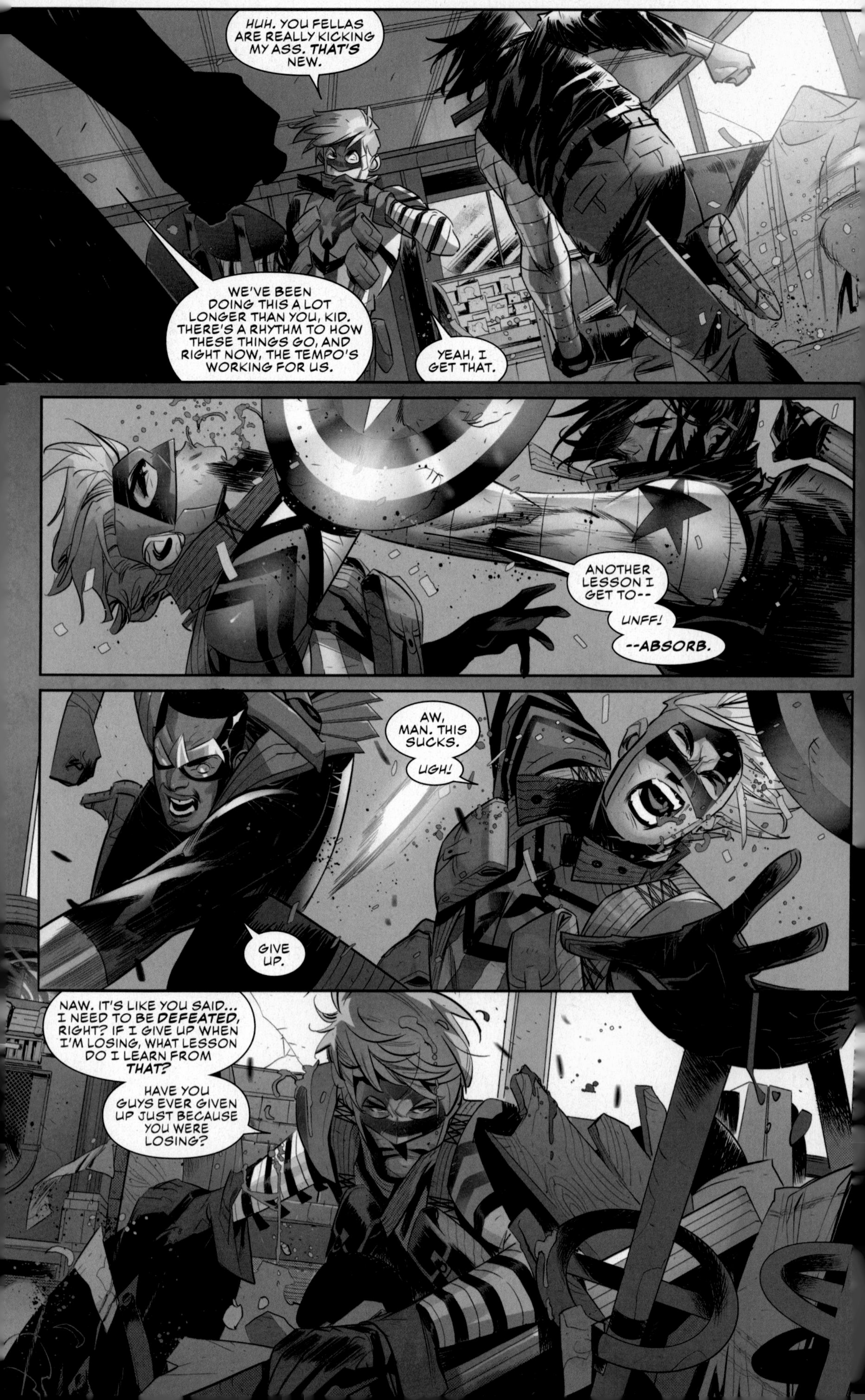
HUH. YOU FELLAS ARE REALLY KICKING MY ASS. THAT'S NEW.
WE'VE BEEN DOING THIS A LOT LONGER THAN YOU, KID. THERE'S A RHYTHM TO HOW THESE THINGS GO, AND RIGHT NOW, THE TEMPO'S WORKING FOR US.
YEAH, I GET THAT.
ANOTHER LESSON I GET TO--
UNFF!
--ABSORB.
AW, MAN. THIS SUCKS.
UGH!
GIVE UP.
NAW. IT'S LIKE YOU SAID... I NEED TO BE DEFEATED, RIGHT? IF I GIVE UP WHEN I'M LOSING, WHAT LESSON DO I LEARN FROM THAT?
HAVE YOU GUYS EVER GIVEN UP JUST BECAUSE YOU WERE LOSING?

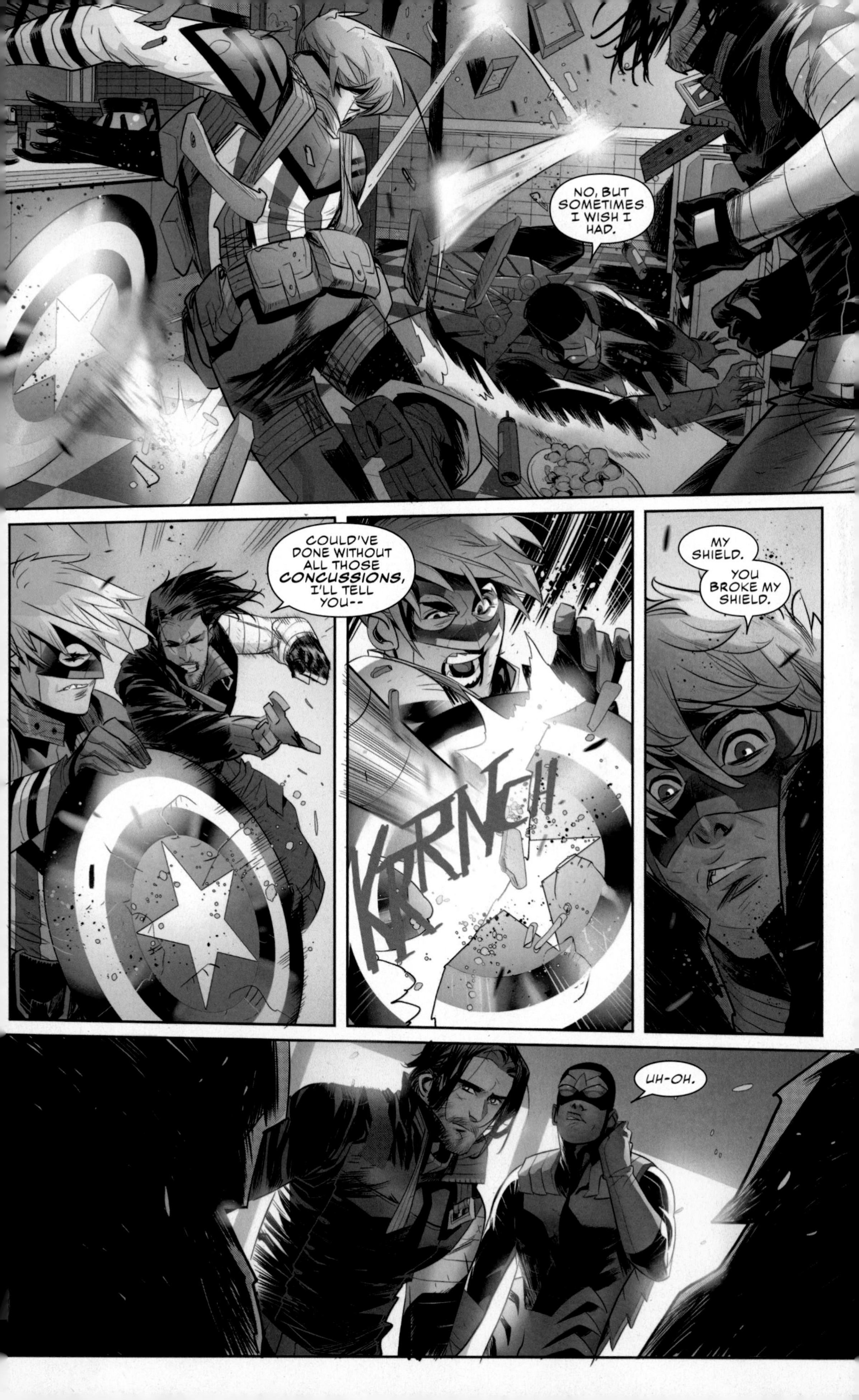

NO, BUT SOMETIMES I WISH I HAD.
COULD'VE DONE WITHOUT ALL THOSE **CONCUSSIONS**, I'LL TELL YOU--
KRRNCH!
MY SHIELD.
YOU BROKE MY SHIELD.
UH-OH.

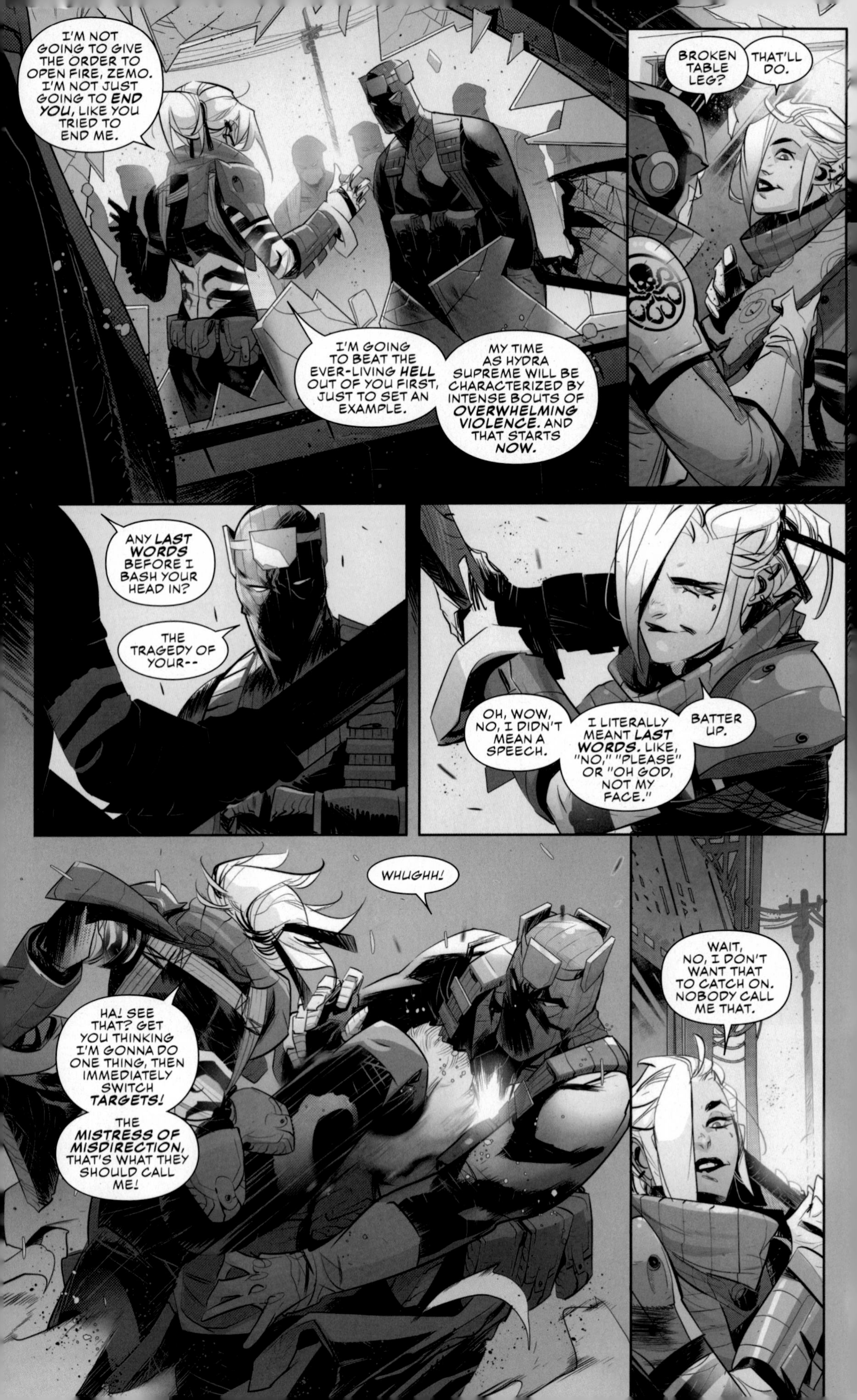
I'M NOT GOING TO GIVE THE ORDER TO OPEN FIRE, ZEMO. I'M NOT JUST GOING TO END YOU, LIKE YOU TRIED TO END ME.
I'M GOING TO BEAT THE EVER-LIVING HELL OUT OF YOU FIRST, JUST TO SET AN EXAMPLE.
MY TIME AS HYDRA SUPREME WILL BE CHARACTERIZED BY INTENSE BOUTS OF OVERWHELMING VIOLENCE. AND THAT STARTS NOW.
BROKEN TABLE LEG?
THAT'LL DO.
ANY LAST WORDS BEFORE I BASH YOUR HEAD IN?
THE TRAGEDY OF YOUR--
OH, WOW, NO, I DIDN'T MEAN A SPEECH.
I LITERALLY MEANT LAST WORDS. LIKE, "NO," "PLEASE" OR "OH GOD, NOT MY FACE."
BATTER UP.
WHUGHH!
HA! SEE THAT? GET YOU THINKING I'M GONNA DO ONE THING, THEN IMMEDIATELY SWITCH TARGETS!
THE MISTRESS OF MISDIRECTION, THAT'S WHAT THEY SHOULD CALL ME!
WAIT, NO, I DON'T WANT THAT TO CATCH ON. NOBODY CALL ME THAT.

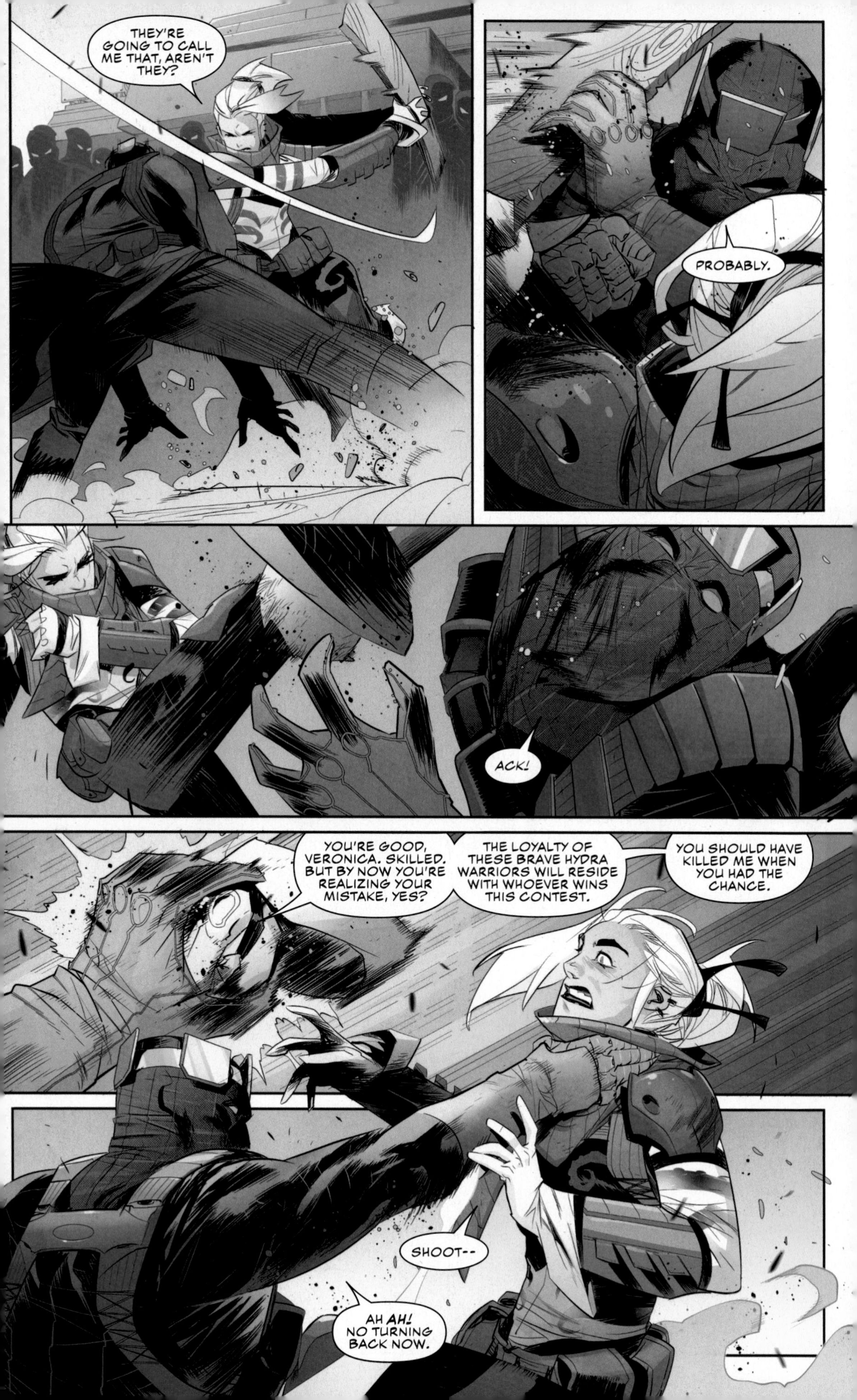
THEY'RE GOING TO CALL ME THAT, AREN'T THEY?
PROBABLY.
ACK!
YOU'RE GOOD, VERONICA. SKILLED. BUT BY NOW YOU'RE REALIZING YOUR MISTAKE, YES?
THE LOYALTY OF THESE BRAVE HYDRA WARRIORS WILL RESIDE WITH WHOEVER WINS THIS CONTEST.
YOU SHOULD HAVE KILLED ME WHEN YOU HAD THE CHANCE.
SHOOT--
AH *AH!* NO TURNING BACK NOW.

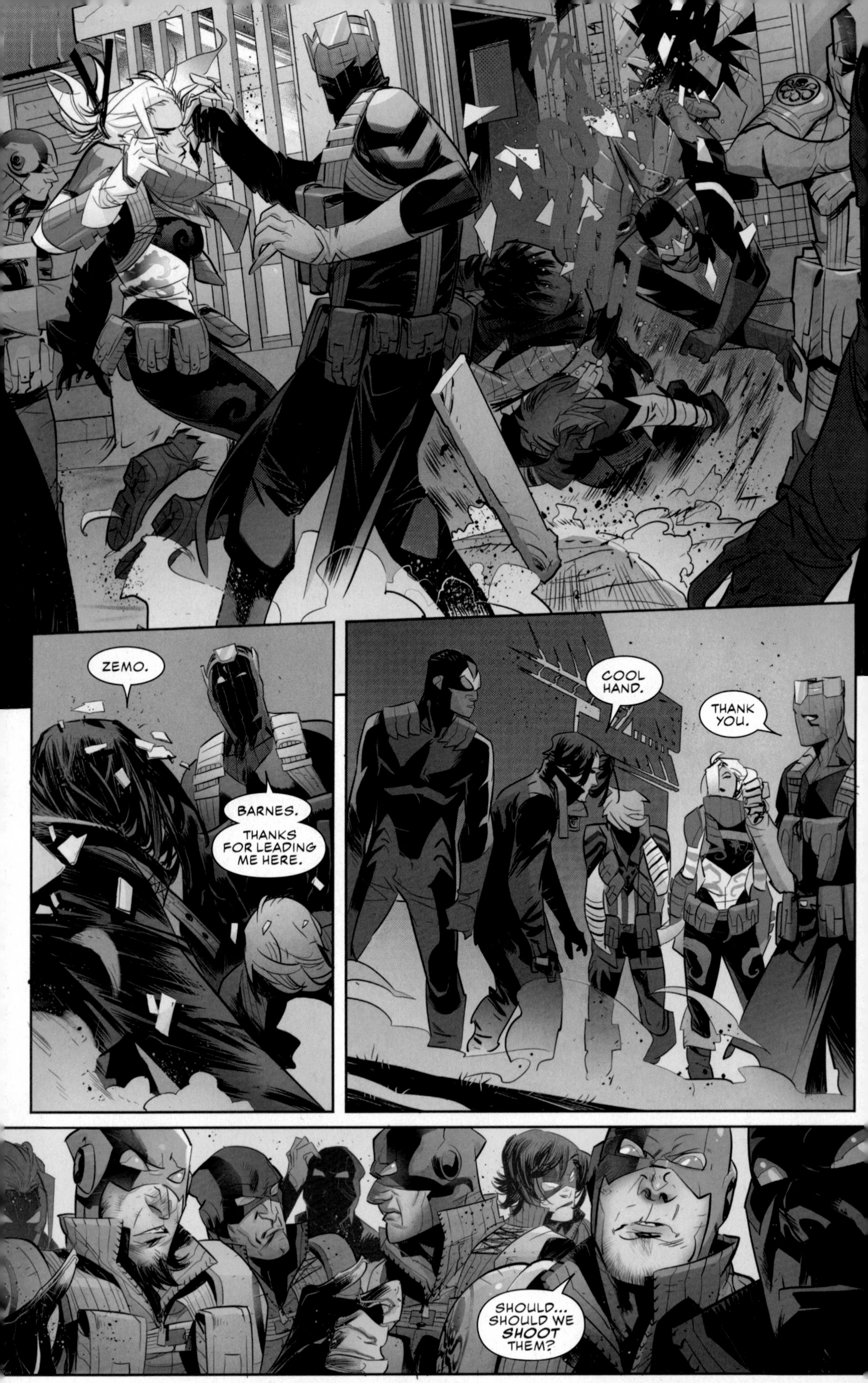
ZEMO.
BARNES.
THANKS FOR LEADING ME HERE.
COOL HAND.
THANK YOU.
SHOULD... SHOULD WE *SHOOT* THEM?

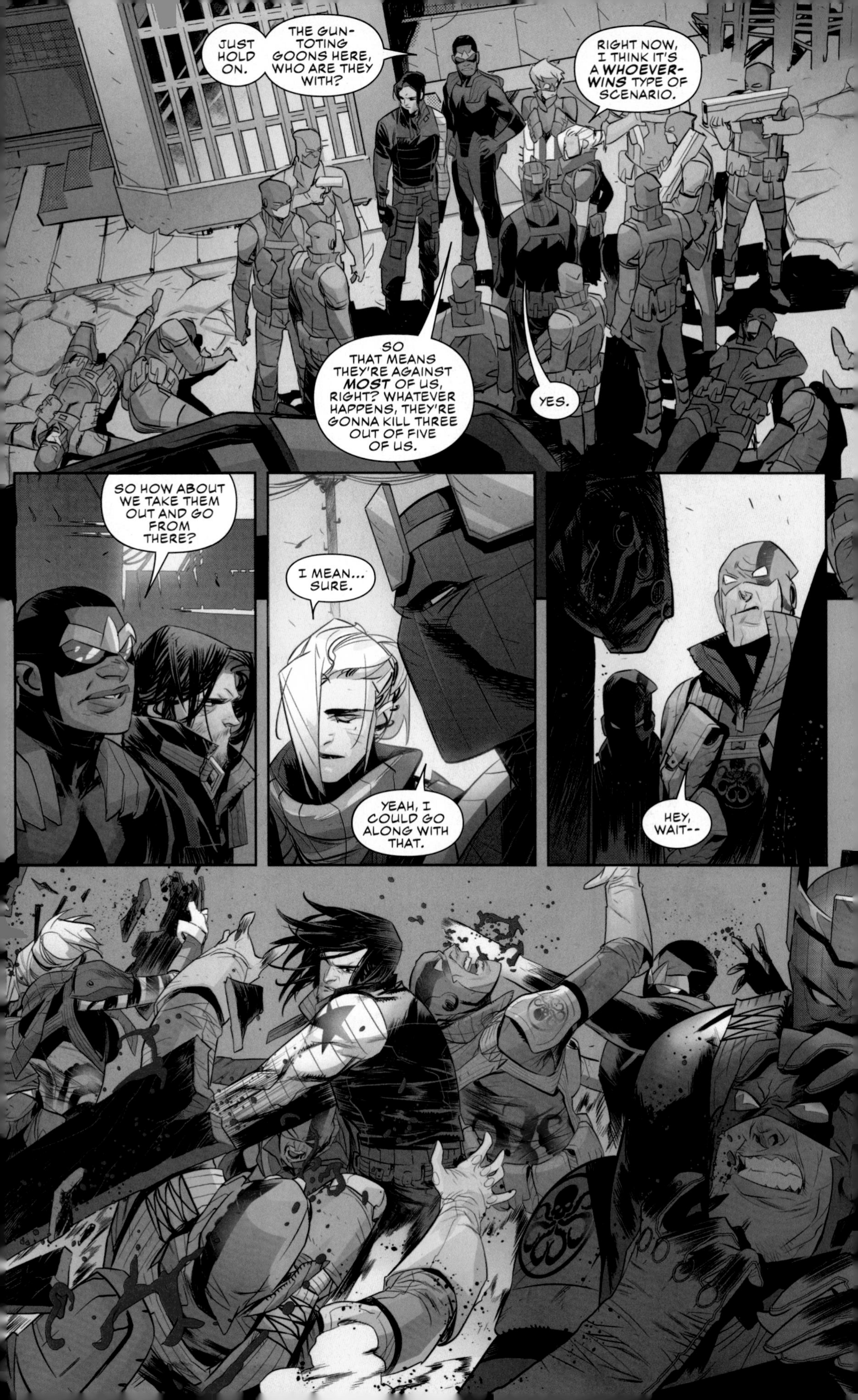
JUST HOLD ON.
THE GUN-TOTING GOONS HERE, WHO ARE THEY WITH?
RIGHT NOW, I THINK IT'S A **WHOEVER-WINS** TYPE OF SCENARIO.
SO THAT MEANS THEY'RE AGAINST ***MOST*** OF US, RIGHT? WHATEVER HAPPENS, THEY'RE GONNA KILL THREE OUT OF FIVE OF US.
YES.
SO HOW ABOUT WE TAKE THEM OUT AND GO FROM THERE?
I MEAN... SURE.
YEAH, I COULD GO ALONG WITH THAT.
HEY, WAIT--

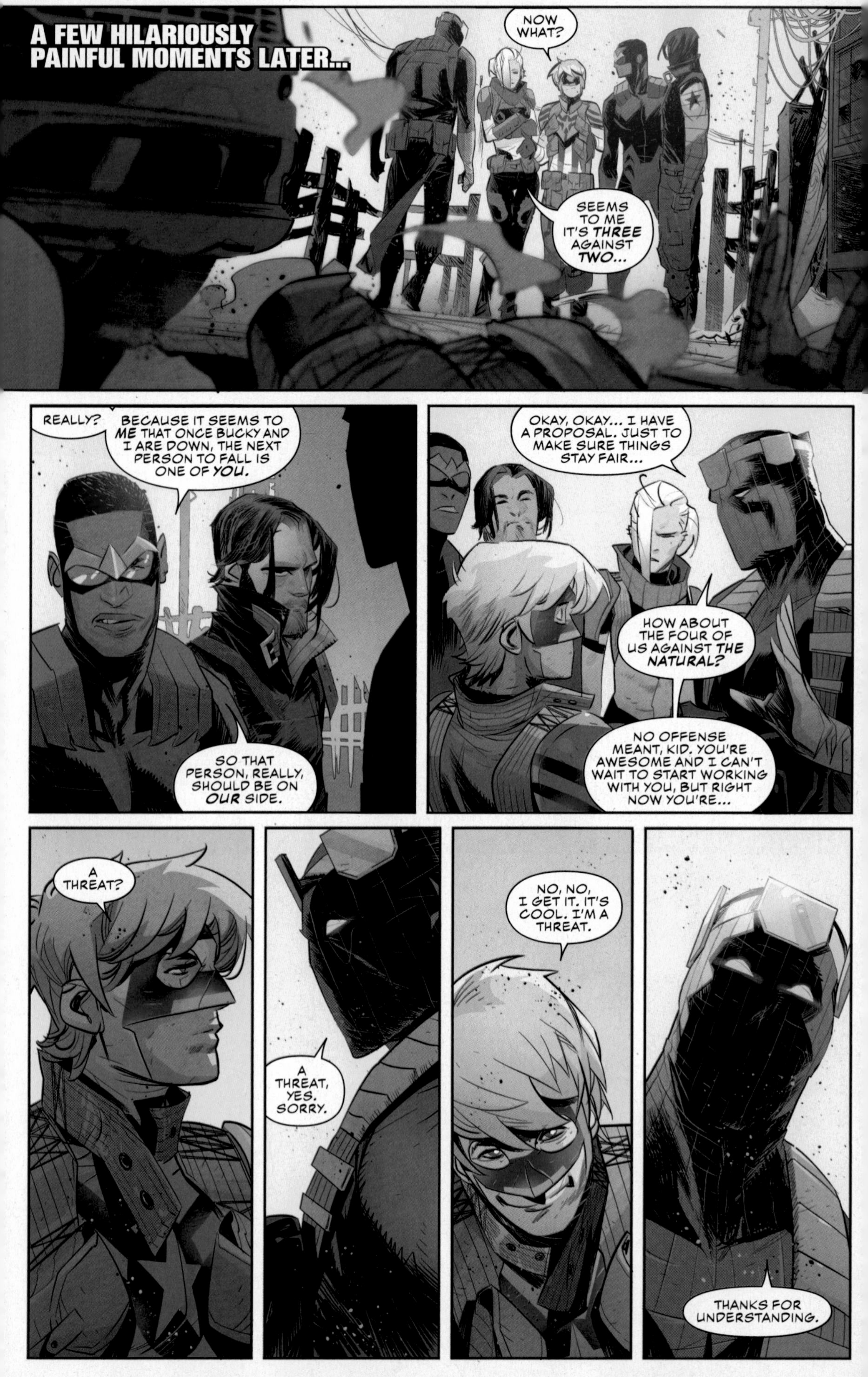
A FEW HILARIOUSLY PAINFUL MOMENTS LATER...
NOW WHAT?
SEEMS TO ME IT'S THREE AGAINST TWO...
REALLY?
BECAUSE IT SEEMS TO ME THAT ONCE BUCKY AND I ARE DOWN, THE NEXT PERSON TO FALL IS ONE OF YOU.
SO THAT PERSON, REALLY, SHOULD BE ON OUR SIDE.
OKAY, OKAY... I HAVE A PROPOSAL. JUST TO MAKE SURE THINGS STAY FAIR...
HOW ABOUT THE FOUR OF US AGAINST THE NATURAL?
NO OFFENSE MEANT, KID. YOU'RE AWESOME AND I CAN'T WAIT TO START WORKING WITH YOU, BUT RIGHT NOW YOU'RE...
A THREAT?
A THREAT, YES. SORRY.
NO, NO, I GET IT. IT'S COOL. I'M A THREAT.
THANKS FOR UNDERSTANDING.

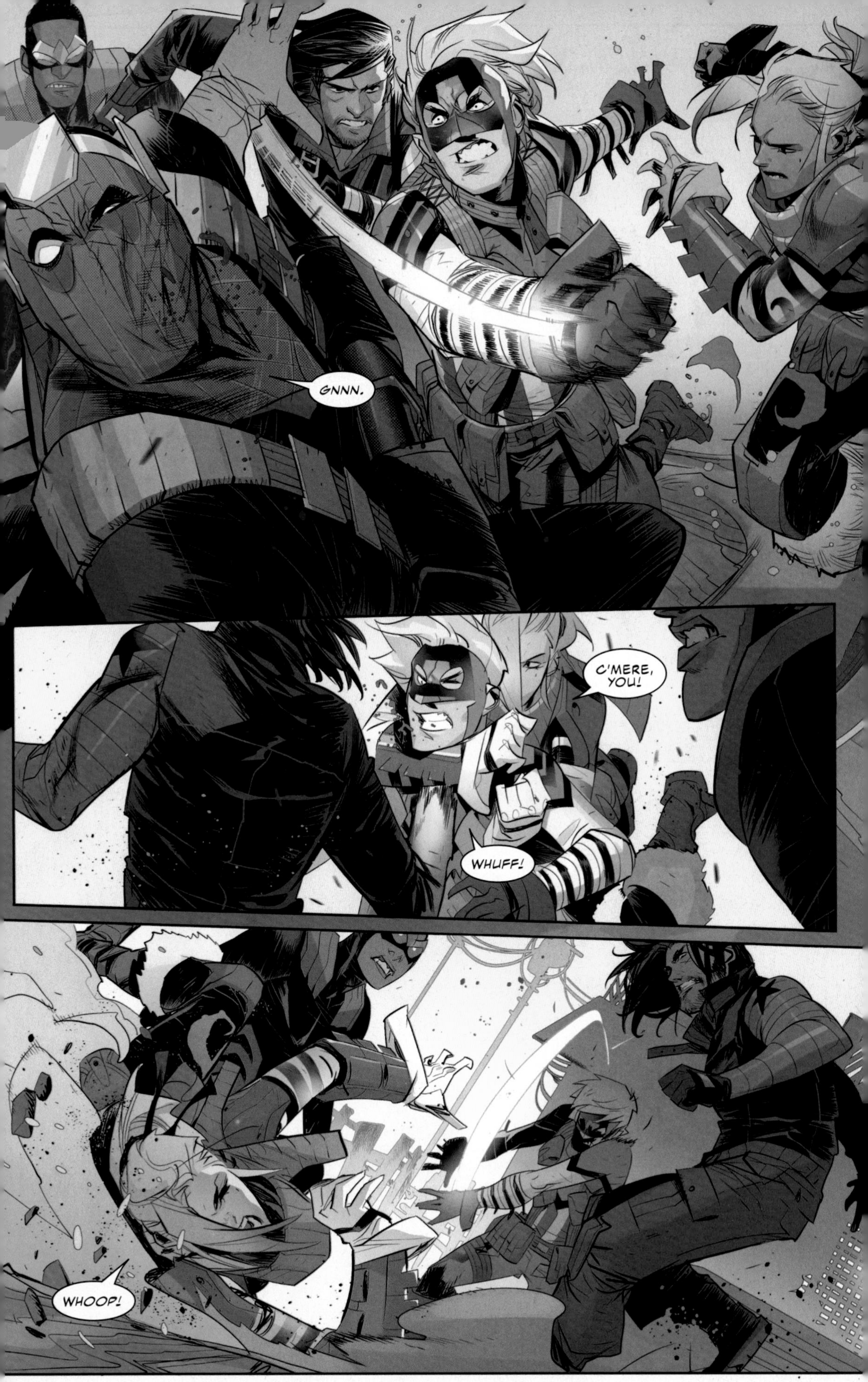
GNNN.
C'MERE, YOU!
WHUFF!
WHOOP!

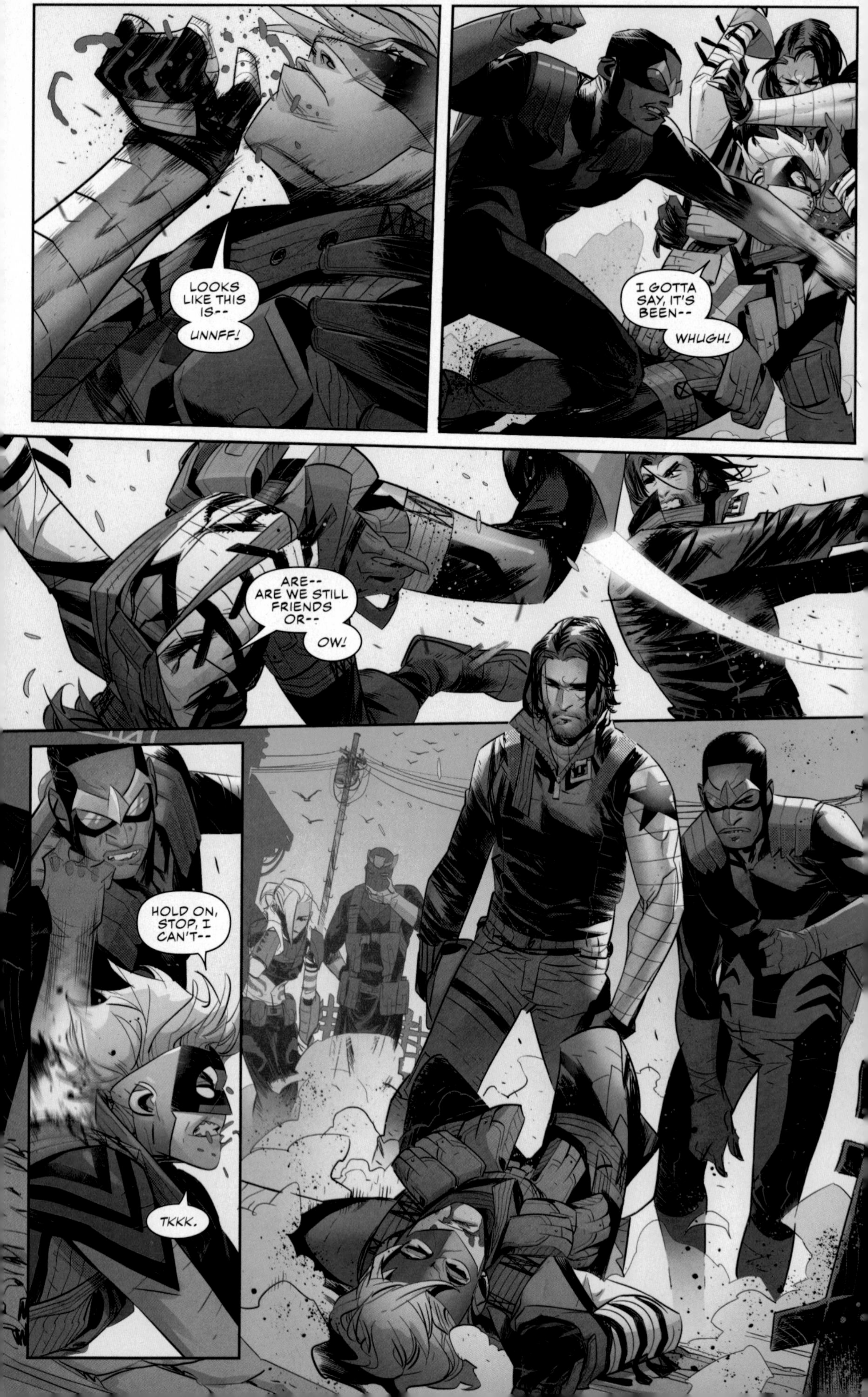
LOOKS LIKE THIS IS--
UNNFF!
I GOTTA SAY, IT'S BEEN--
WHUGH!
ARE-- ARE WE STILL FRIENDS OR--
OW!
HOLD ON, STOP, I CAN'T--
TKKK.

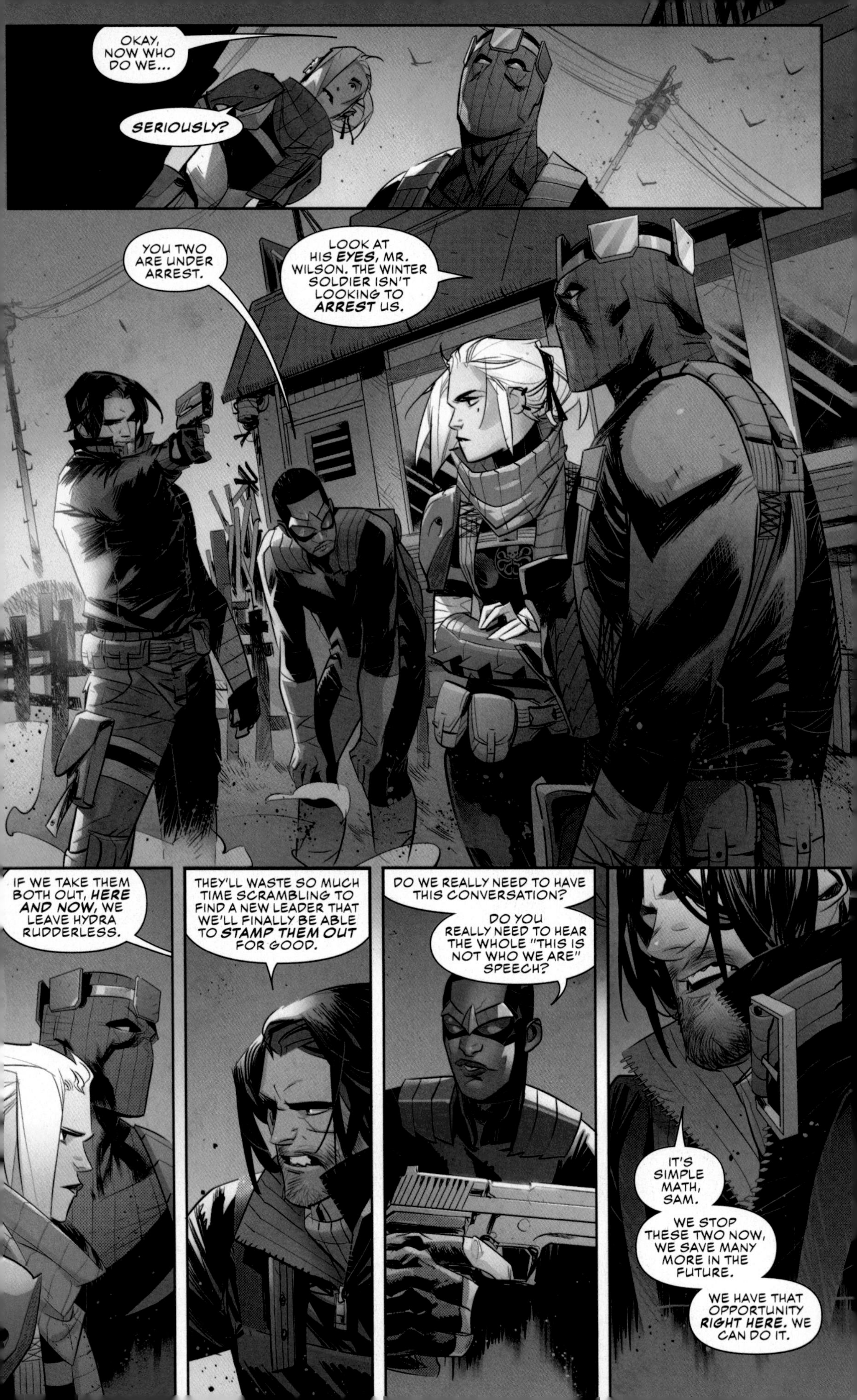
OKAY, NOW WHO DO WE...
SERIOUSLY?
YOU TWO ARE UNDER ARREST.
LOOK AT HIS EYES, MR. WILSON. THE WINTER SOLDIER ISN'T LOOKING TO ARREST US.
IF WE TAKE THEM BOTH OUT, HERE AND NOW, WE LEAVE HYDRA RUDDERLESS.
THEY'LL WASTE SO MUCH TIME SCRAMBLING TO FIND A NEW LEADER THAT WE'LL FINALLY BE ABLE TO STAMP THEM OUT FOR GOOD.
DO WE REALLY NEED TO HAVE THIS CONVERSATION?
DO YOU REALLY NEED TO HEAR THE WHOLE "THIS IS NOT WHO WE ARE" SPEECH?
IT'S SIMPLE MATH, SAM.
WE STOP THESE TWO NOW, WE SAVE MANY MORE IN THE FUTURE.
WE HAVE THAT OPPORTUNITY RIGHT HERE. WE CAN DO IT.

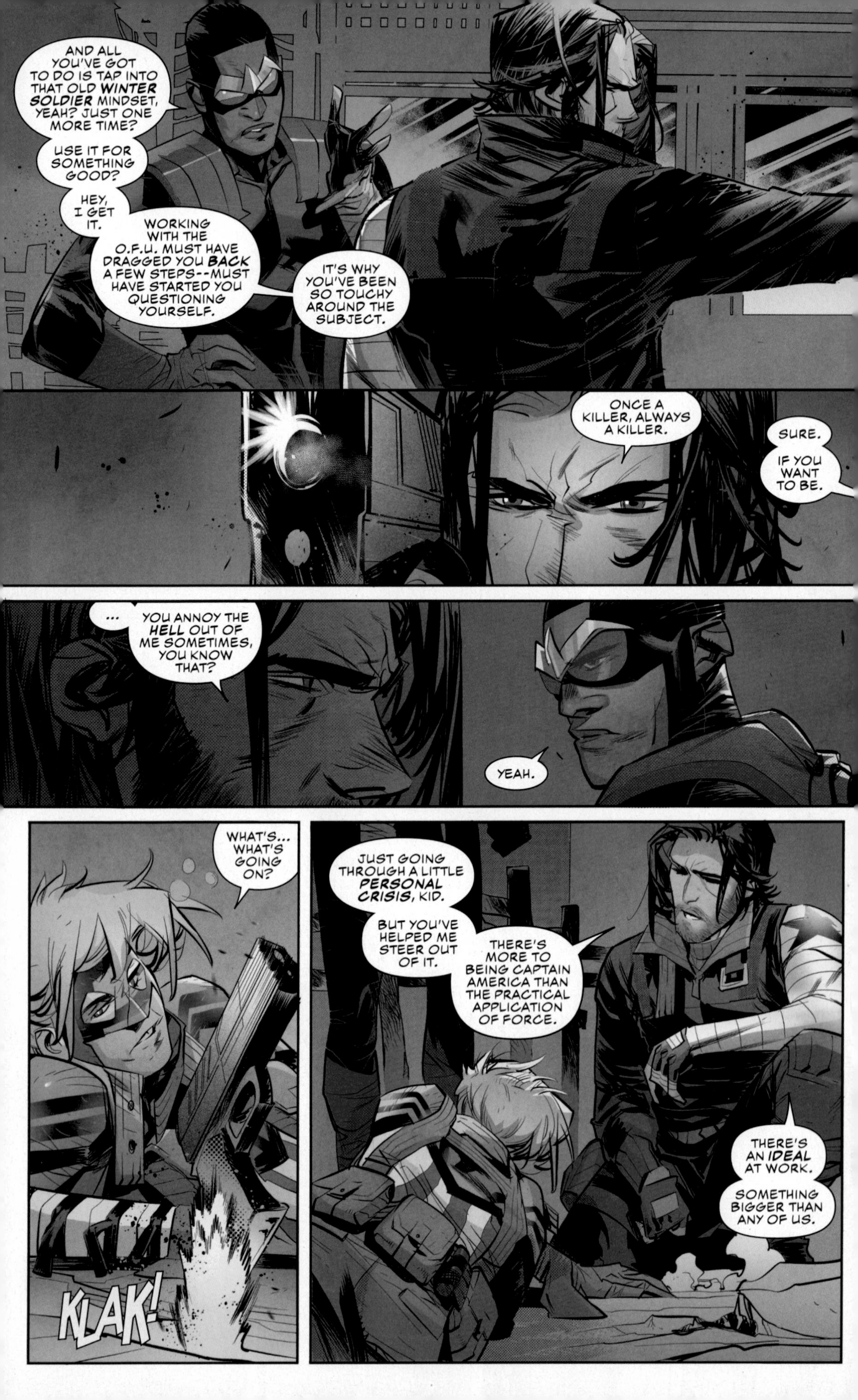
AND ALL YOU'VE GOT TO DO IS TAP INTO THAT OLD WINTER SOLDIER MINDSET, YEAH? JUST ONE MORE TIME?
USE IT FOR SOMETHING GOOD?
HEY, I GET IT.
WORKING WITH THE O.F.U. MUST HAVE DRAGGED YOU BACK A FEW STEPS--MUST HAVE STARTED YOU QUESTIONING YOURSELF.
IT'S WHY YOU'VE BEEN SO TOUCHY AROUND THE SUBJECT.
ONCE A KILLER, ALWAYS A KILLER.
SURE.
IF YOU WANT TO BE.
...
YOU ANNOY THE HELL OUT OF ME SOMETIMES, YOU KNOW THAT?
YEAH.
WHAT'S... WHAT'S GOING ON?
KLAK!
JUST GOING THROUGH A LITTLE PERSONAL CRISIS, KID.
BUT YOU'VE HELPED ME STEER OUT OF IT.
THERE'S MORE TO BEING CAPTAIN AMERICA THAN THE PRACTICAL APPLICATION OF FORCE.
THERE'S AN IDEAL AT WORK.
SOMETHING BIGGER THAN ANY OF US.

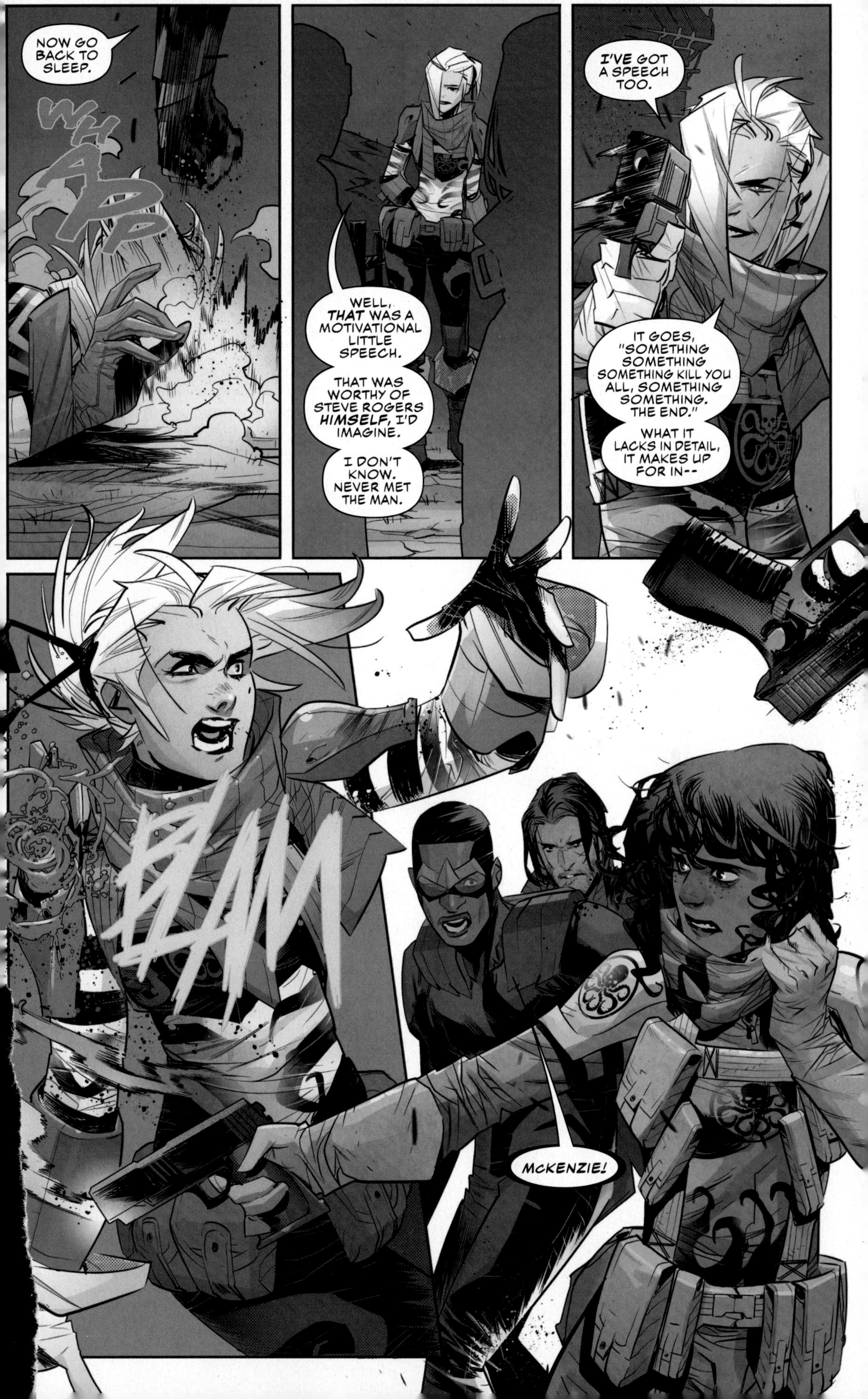
NOW GO BACK TO SLEEP.
WHAAPP
WELL, THAT WAS A MOTIVATIONAL LITTLE SPEECH.
THAT WAS WORTHY OF STEVE ROGERS HIMSELF, I'D IMAGINE.
I DON'T KNOW. NEVER MET THE MAN.
I'VE GOT A SPEECH TOO.
IT GOES, "SOMETHING SOMETHING SOMETHING KILL YOU ALL, SOMETHING SOMETHING. THE END."
WHAT IT LACKS IN DETAIL, IT MAKES UP FOR IN--
BLAM
MCKENZIE!

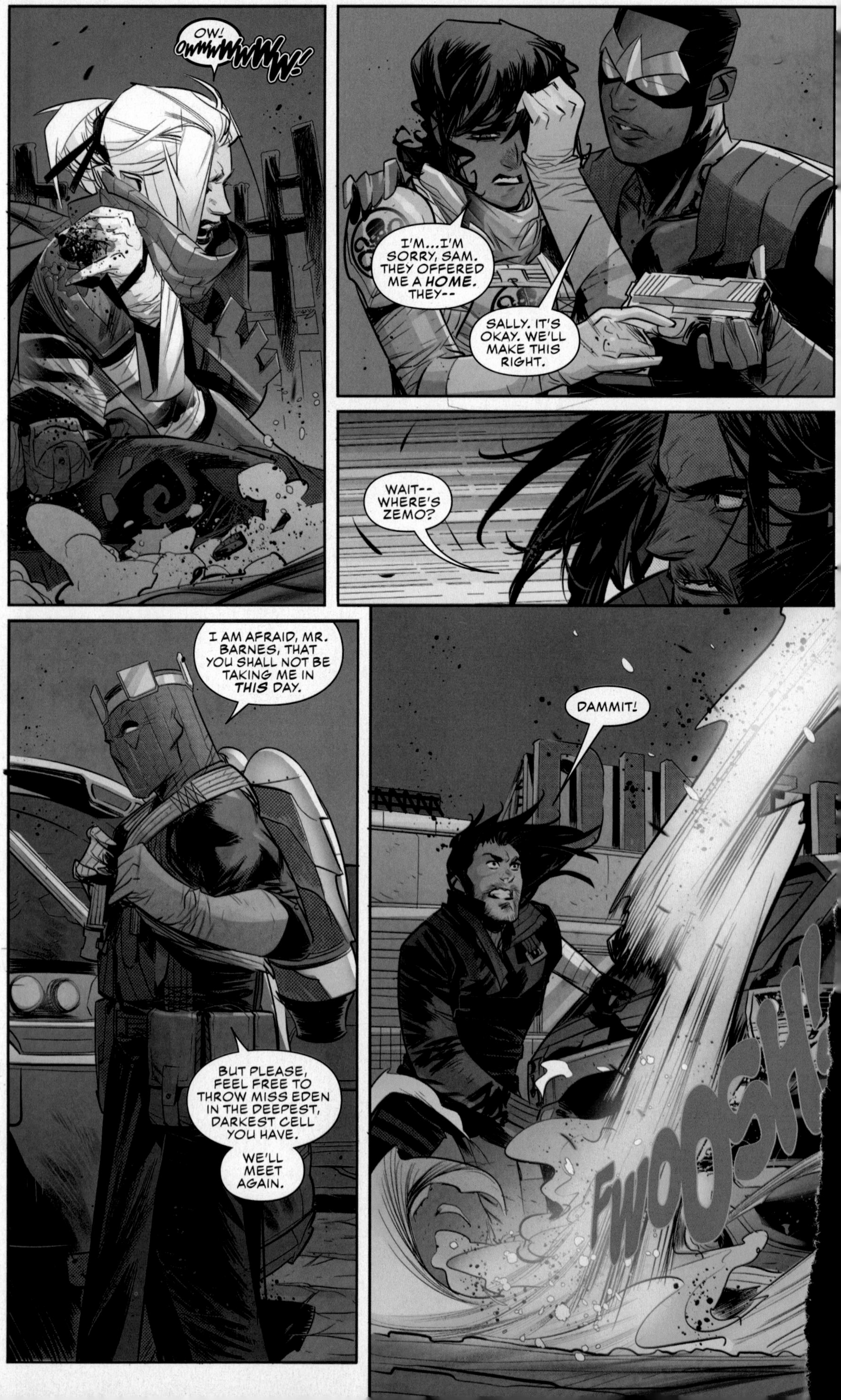
OW! OWWWWWWWW!
I'M...I'M SORRY, SAM. THEY OFFERED ME A HOME. THEY--
SALLY. IT'S OKAY. WE'LL MAKE THIS RIGHT.
WAIT-- WHERE'S ZEMO?
I AM AFRAID, MR. BARNES, THAT YOU SHALL NOT BE TAKING ME IN THIS DAY.
BUT PLEASE, FEEL FREE TO THROW MISS EDEN IN THE DEEPEST, DARKEST CELL YOU HAVE.
WE'LL MEET AGAIN.
DAMMIT!
FWOOSH!

NICE GOING, IDIOT.

WHAT?

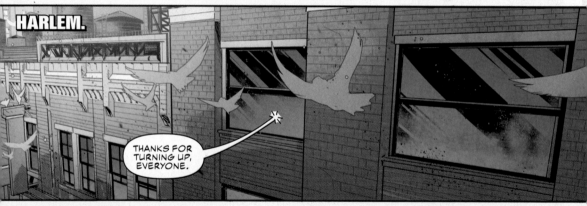

HARLEM.

THANKS FOR TURNING UP, EVERYONE.

I'M NOT OFFERING ANY MAGICAL SOLUTIONS HERE.

THIS IS JUST A PLACE TO TALK TO PEOPLE WHO'VE BEEN THERE. PEOPLE WHO MIGHT BE ABLE TO UNDERSTAND WHAT YOU'RE GOING THROUGH.

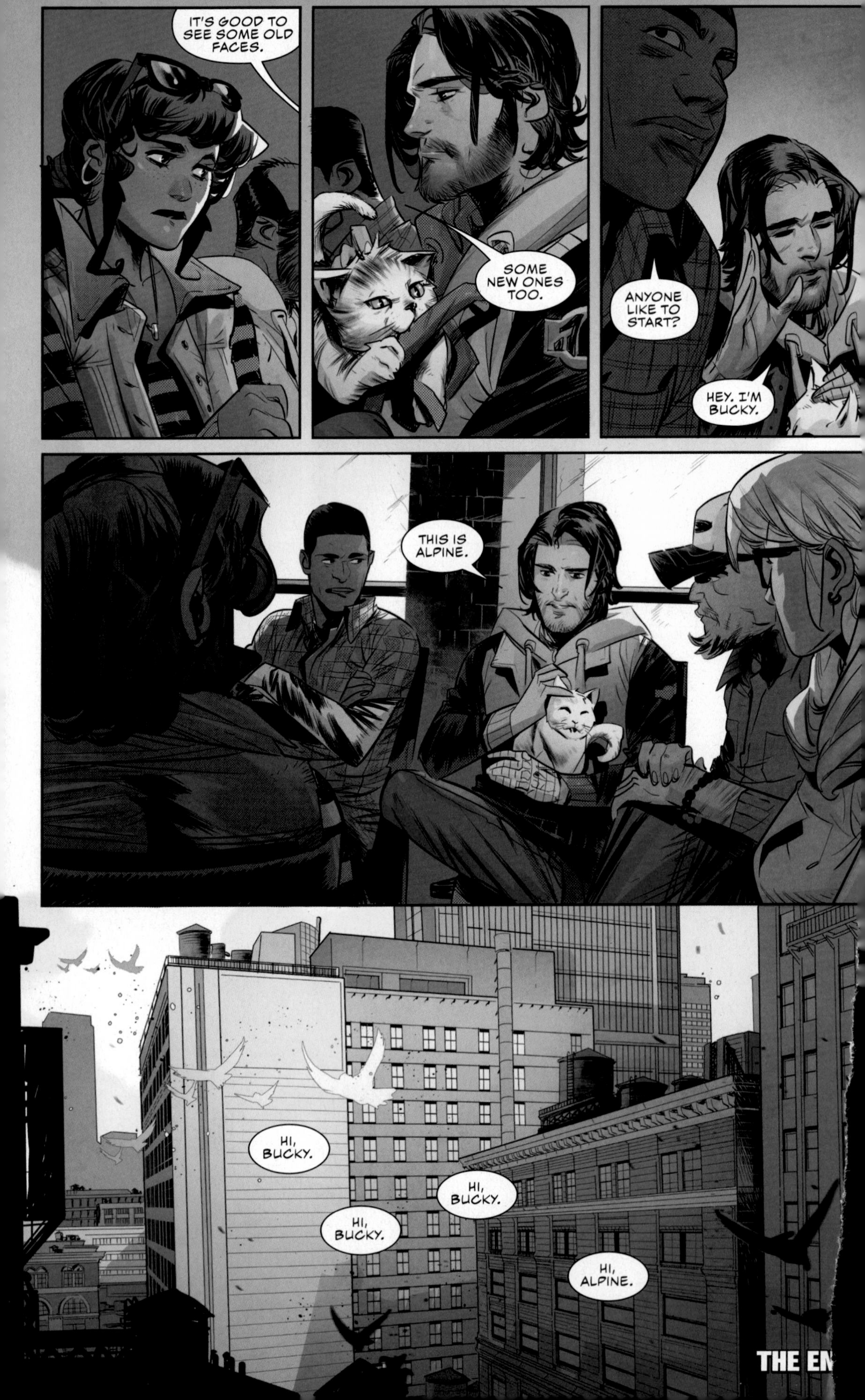
IT'S GOOD TO SEE SOME OLD FACES.
SOME NEW ONES TOO.
ANYONE LIKE TO START?
HEY. I'M BUCKY.
THIS IS ALPINE.
HI, BUCKY.
HI, BUCKY.
HI, BUCKY.
HI, ALPINE.
THE EN

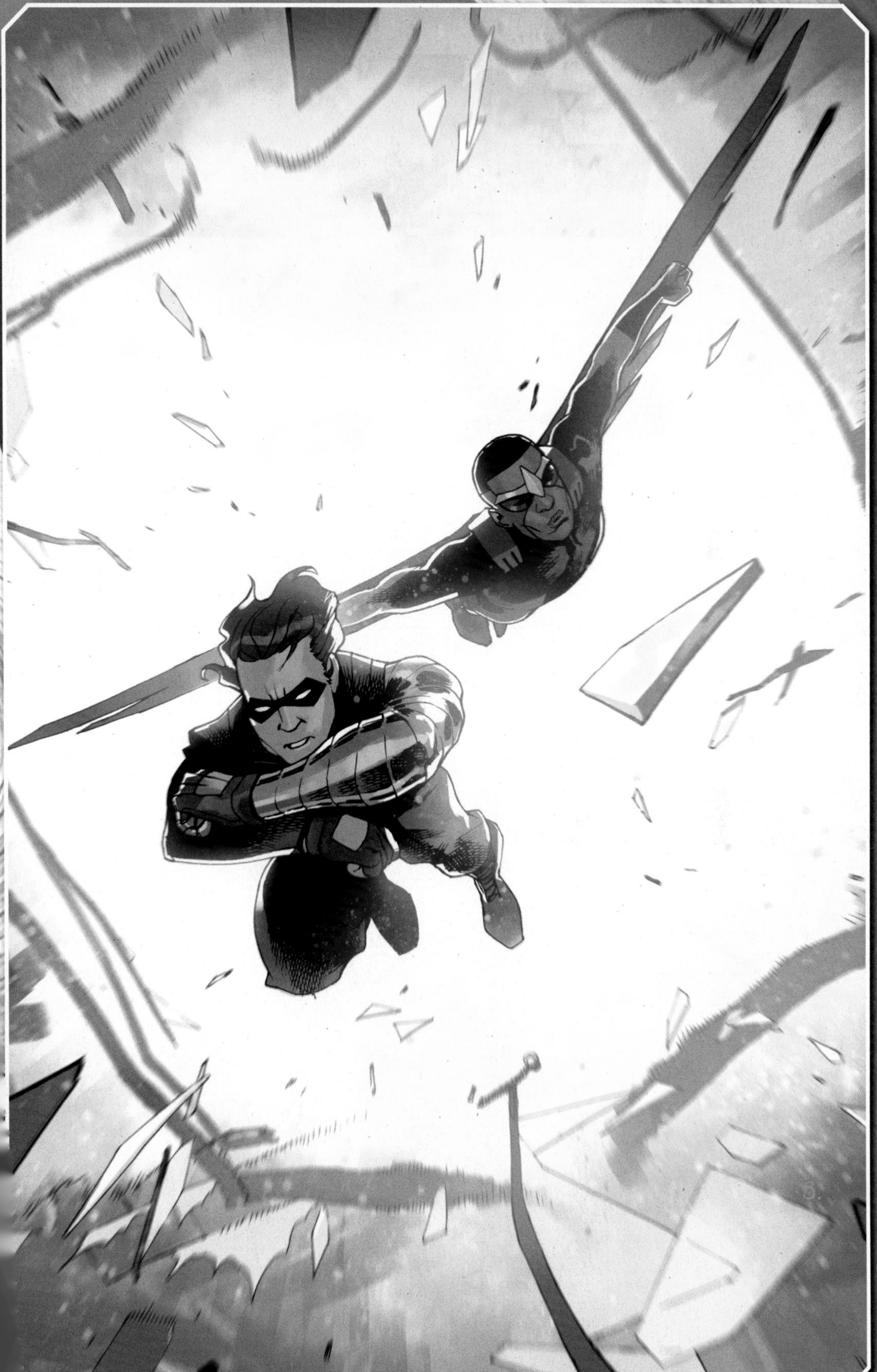

BENGAL
#1 VARIANT

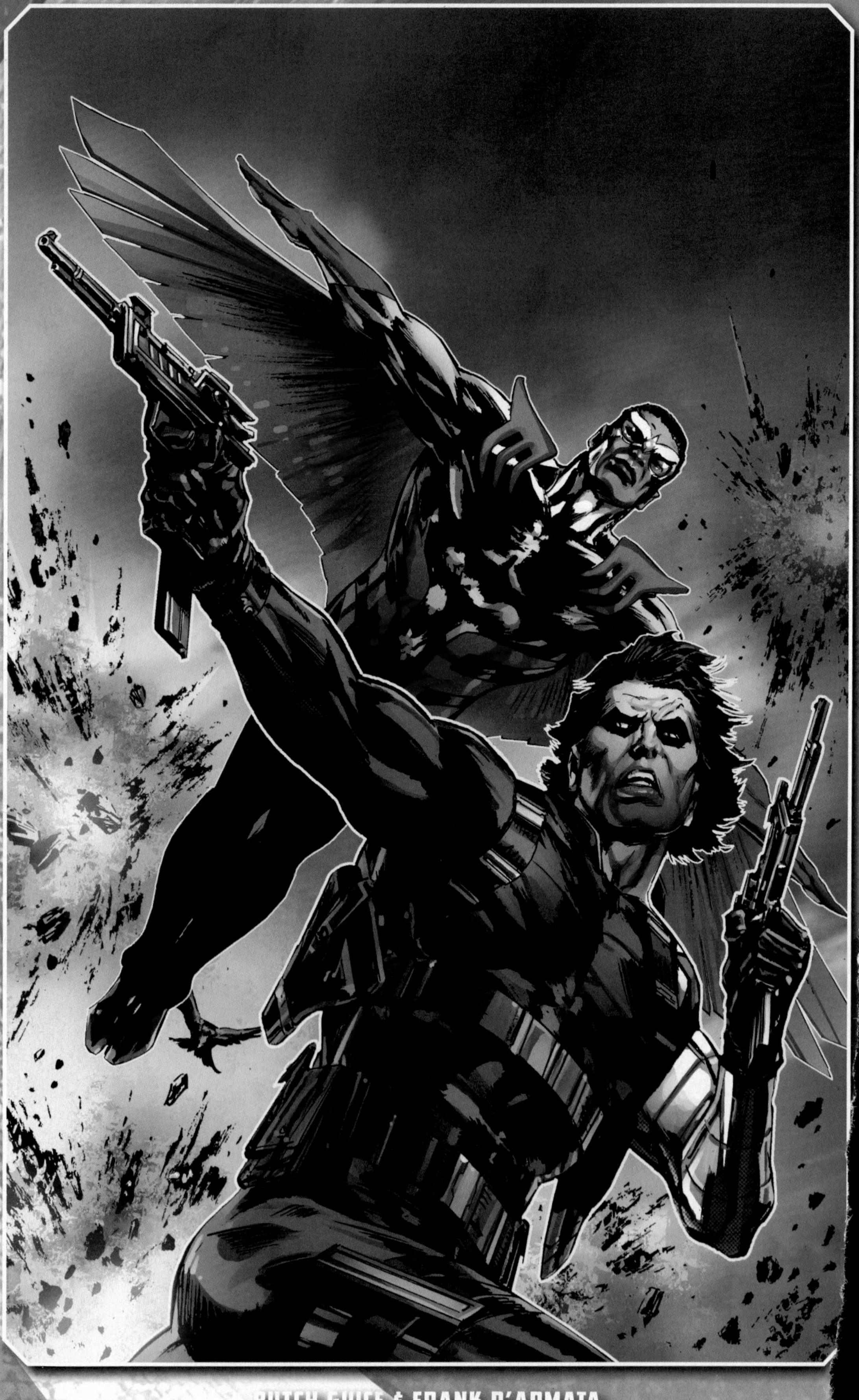

BUTCH GUICE & FRANK D'ARMATA
#1 VARIANT

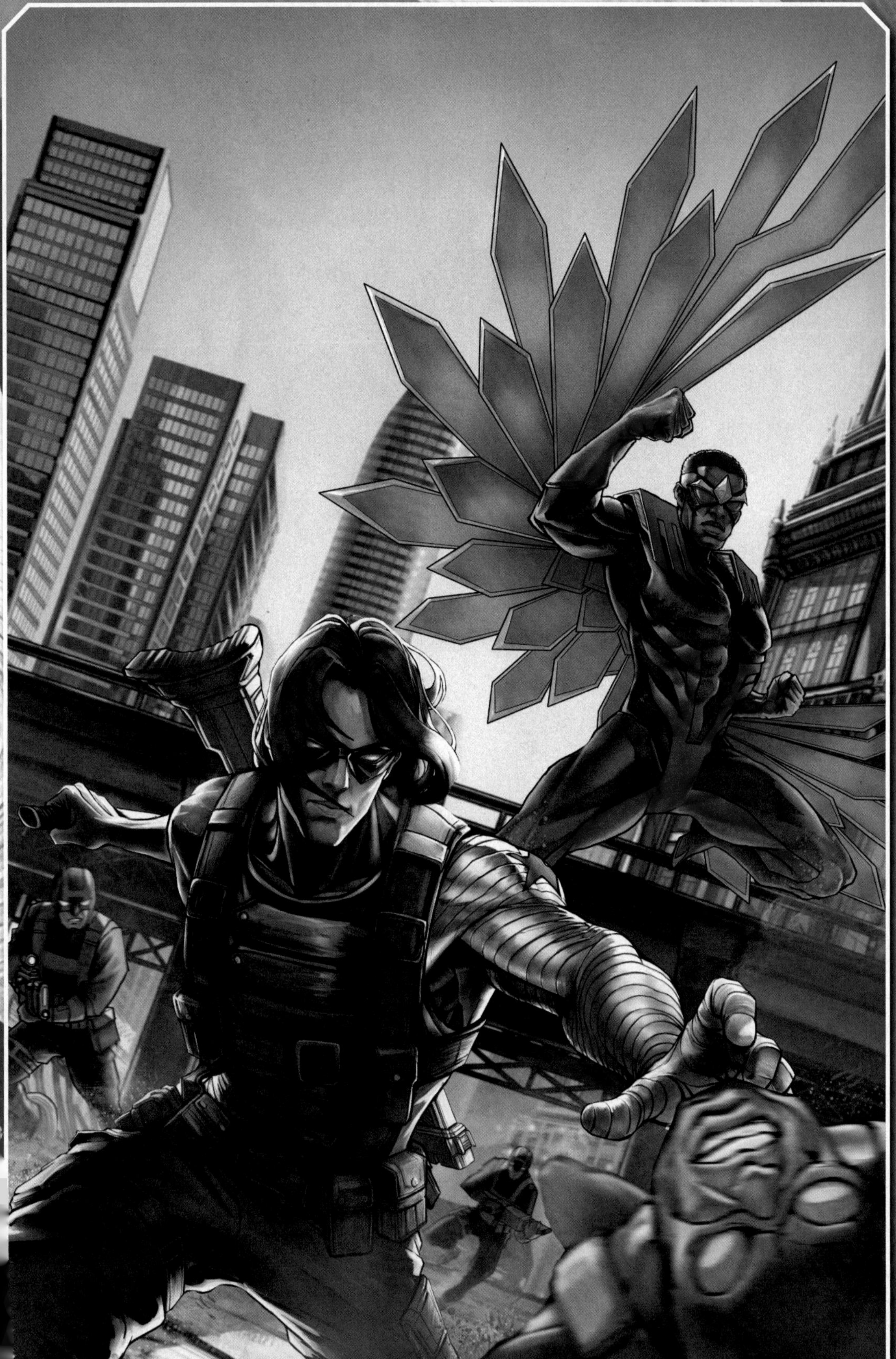

ZIYIAN LIU
#1 VARIANT

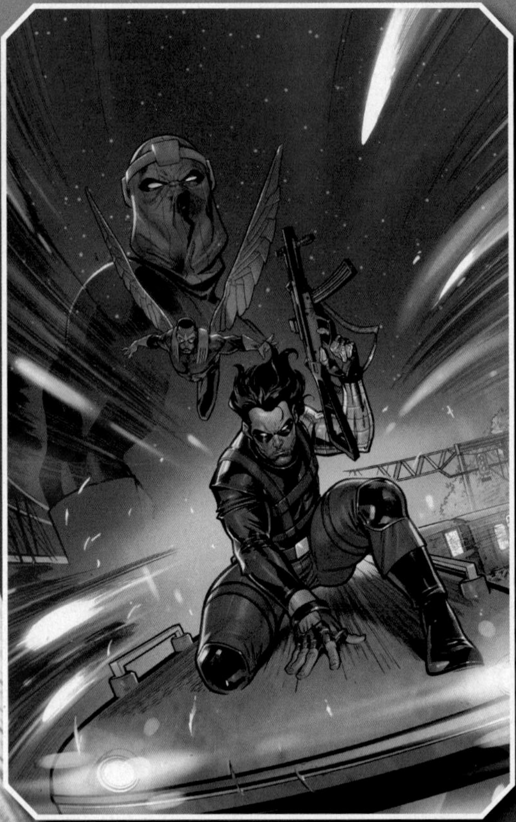

PACO MEDINA & JESUS ABURTOV
#2 VARIANT

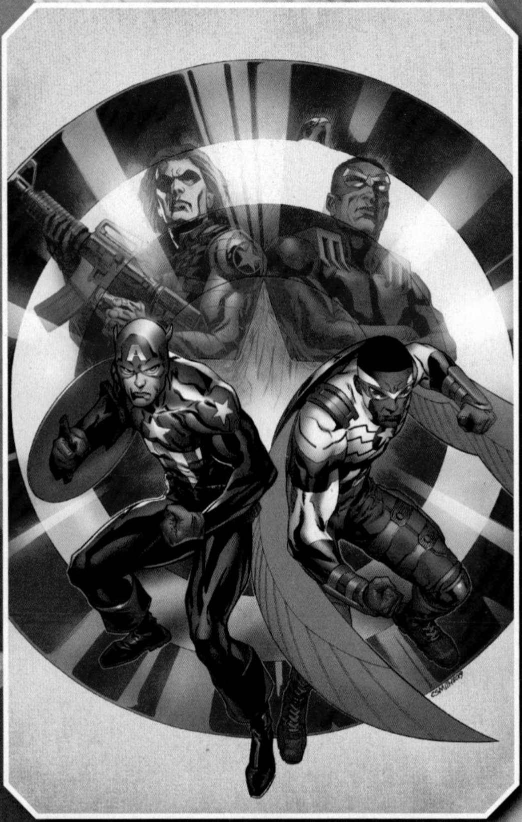

CORY SMITH & MATT MILLA
#3 VARIANT

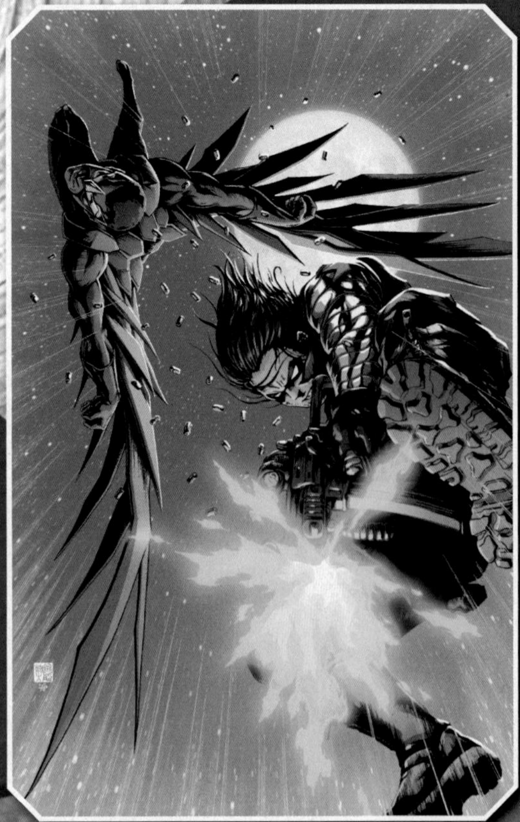

TAKASHI OKAZAKI & FELIPE SOBREIRO
#4 VARIANT

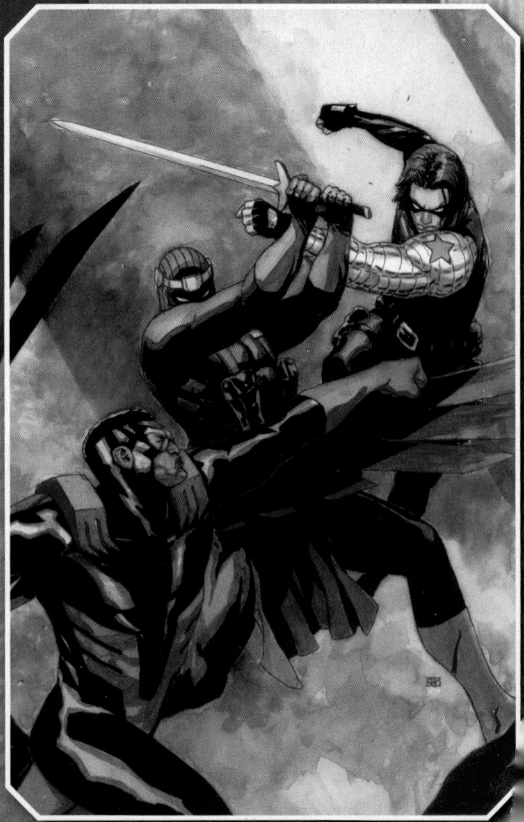

KHOI PHAM & MORRY HOLLOWELL
#5 VARIANT